MAONOMICS

MAONOMICS

Why Chinese Communists Make
Better Capitalists Than We Do

LORETTA
NAPOLEONI

Translated from the Italian by Stephen Twilley

7

SEVEN STORIES PRESS
NEW YORK

Seven Stories Press
140 Watts Street
New York, NY 10013
www.sevenstories.com

College professors may order examination copies of Seven Stories Press titles for a free six-month trial period. To order, visit www.sevenstories.com/textbook or send a fax on school letterhead to (212) 226-1411.

Book design by Jon Gilbert

Library of Congress Cataloging-in-Publication Data

Napoleoni, Loretta.
[Maonomics. English]
Maonomics : why Chinese communists make better capitalists than we do / Loretta Napoleoni ; translated from the Italian by Stephen Twilley. -- Seven Stories Press 1st ed.
    p. cm.
ISBN 978-1-60980-341-4 (hbk.)
 1. China--Economic conditions--2000- 2. China--Economic conditions--1976-2000--Congresses. 3. Globalization--Economic aspects--China. 4. China--Foreign economic relations. I. Twilley, Stephen. II. Title.
HC427.95.N3713 2010
330.951--dc23

                                        2011027285

Printed in the USA.

9 8 7 6 5 4 3 2 1

CONTENTS

PART FOUR: IMAGES OF THE FUTURE

PREFACE

Can the extraordinary events that took place in North Africa and the Middle East in 2011 provide the framework for a much-needed critical evaluation of the Western economic and political system? And can this analysis be conducted using the Asian model of development not as an alternative to the traditional Western socioeconomic paradigm, but as something different, new, unique? From the outset of globalization this new formula has proven successful in all the emerging countries that have embraced it.

This unusual exercise could help us to understand our mistakes and find reasonable answers as to why our economic model suddenly seems out of sync with the world we live in. And perhaps it could also shed some light on the murky complexity of a globalized economy. As we sail toward a multipolar world, it becomes apparent that no ideal development model exists, no single economic or political system fits every country. Complexity breeds uniqueness.

Thus, a comparison between the economic performance of two distinct models of development, the Western and the Chinese, is a much needed exercise, one that opens a window upon the new world because it offers a sneak preview of the future. Indeed, while the West struggles to recover economically and the Middle East is on fire—an explosion caused by social and economic injustice—Asia is booming. For the first time in generations wealth is empowering people: economic growth brings better living standards and new business opportunities, and breeds a higher degree of independence.

However, only a few of us seem conscious of the slow-motion movement toward political participation that the Asian economic growth propels; even fewer people are aware of the fundamental shift in the socioeconomic paradigm known as "capitalism and democracy" that is taking place in Asia, a political earthquake not caused by a revolution, but by maintaining a centralized form of government, which many still define as communism.

As the freedom bug infects North African countries ruled by fake democracies and dictatorial regimes, as the masses attempt to depose oligarchic leaders whom the democratic West has backed for decades, the formula of Eastern authoritarianism, coupled with economic freedom that we in the West have for so long criticized and misunderstood, becomes an appealing alternative to an obsolete Western socioeconomic model of development. Ask yourself a fundamental question: if I were an Egyptian today, which economic system would I want to emulate, the Western or the Asian? Would I trust Western leaders and corporations, which for decades have been doing business with the oligarchic elite that oppressed and robbed me? Or would I look to politicians and firms from emerging countries, people who until a few decades ago were as poor and dispossessed as I am today?

The propaganda machine that blinds the world would like us to believe that the Middle East ordeal has nothing to do with our political and economic model and that we have not fostered repressive and dictatorial regimes disguised in the cloth of economic freedom and democracy. In 2010 the European Union sold almost €400 million worth of arms and armaments to Libya's Gaddafi alone—weapons that in 2011 he used against his own people. The price of our democracy could well be the defense of undemocratic regimes in far away countries such as Saudi Arabia, a repressive kingdom where women have fewer rights than men. Imagine the economic consequences of the fall of the House of Saud, the second-largest oil producer in the world after Russia, and the biggest exporter to the West. Our comforts could vanish in the blink of an eye.

The credit crunch and the recession have outlined the endemic instability of our economy, exposing its idiosyncrasies and contradictions; the Arab uprising may well reveal the fragility of our democracies when deprived of endless cheap energy supplied by oligarchs and dictators who also keep our defense industry afloat. In a society truly ruled by democracy, an ideal world, who would buy our arms and political protection?

The world is changing fast, too fast for those who desperately cling to a past long gone. Once again, in the space of a decade, the West has been taken by surprise by perfectly predictable events. And we feel once again deeply exposed. As stories of the atrocities that modern Arab dictators inflicted on their population reach our living rooms, as the media unveils the true nature of North African democracies and Gaddafi morphs back into a bloodthirsty madman, Westerners watch their certainties vanish. Egypt is a democracy and yet it was ruled by a dictator; China is a communist country and yet it champions capitalism.

The propaganda machine hid the gathering political storm in North Africa and the Middle East. Constantly focusing on China's atrocities and lack of democracy, our leaders and media ignored the abysmal human rights record of Mubarak in Egypt, the ruthless repression of opposition by Gaddafi, Ben Ali's theft of Tunisia's wealth, and so much more. The propaganda machine also hid from us both the true nature of the Chinese economic miracle and the difficulties of our own model.

The world is changing fast and we must open our eyes if we want to avoid ending up crushed under its wheels. Demography is reshaping the Middle East. Over the last three decades, a population boom has taken place in this deeply volatile region. A youth explosion coupled with economic pressures—

not Islamist terrorism—has brought down ruthless dictatorial regimes. There were no swords brandished against the West in Tunisia or Egypt, no bearded man preaching the Sharia, but young people armed with iPhones and Blackberries. They defied the traditional media propaganda thanks to Facebook, YouTube and Myspace, forcing us Westerners to confront a new, deeply uncomfortable reality.

In Asia a different revolution is taking place and we are totally unaware of its nature and objectives. Billions of Asian people are catching up with our standards, and soon they will be the driving force of major economic and financial changes that will impact our everyday lives. We may never see Chinese youth challenging the status quo; those images may never reach our screens, but our destiny is deeply intertwined with theirs. And to understand what awaits us around the corner, we must rise above the propaganda and look at China and Asia with humility and hope, not with arrogance and bigotry.

INTRODUCTION

Nearly a quarter century after the end of the Cold War, Western democracies are struggling to cope with the first real economic crisis of globalization. Communist China, meanwhile, has not only managed to limit the impact of the crisis, but is taking advantage of shrinking world demand to set in motion revolutionary social and economic reforms. Among them are greater security for workers and the drafting of a new international monetary system, potentially pegged to the Chinese currency.[1]

Economic stability's "true north" is relocating to China thanks to a series of financial cataclysms that are reshaping the macroeconomic structure of the planet. The latest, the credit crunch and the recession, has catapulted China into the ranks of the most powerful nations in the world. Today no one can deny that the Chinese "New Deal" has provided an anchor of salvation in this perfect storm of a recession and prevented the world from plunging into a new Great Depression. Many are convinced that the changes now underway will precipitate the end of the United States' economic supremacy.

The transformations in China are not, however, limited to the reshaping of the economy according to the principles of free trade. Gross domestic product (GDP) growth goes hand in hand with social and political reforms unthinkable under Maoism, an odd couple in a still-communist country. From the defense of human rights to the development of renewable energy, going so far as to include respect for the rules of the

1

World Trade Organization (WTO) and aspirations to participatory democracy, this nation seems fully committed to producing a new model of society. Even if for the moment Western-style democracy does not appear to figure among China's aims, it is nonetheless true that for at least a decade the nation has distanced itself from its postwar totalitarianism and looks solely to a bright economic future. Can we speak of a capitalist-communism, or capi-communism? A political and economic hybrid that could very well become the model for the twenty-first century?

A visit to a city like Shanghai or Beijing offers a preview of the metropolises of tomorrow and a sense of what China's new modernity means. The dynamism of these cities is a drug intoxicating for everyone, especially foreigners. Thousands of young Westerners choose to live in Shanghai because there they feel on the very edge of a new world. Those who have lived in China for some time are well aware of the imminence of the future and know they are participating in its creation; for them, China represents a breeding ground for socioeconomic transformations as well as political ideas.

Western metropolises, still mired in postmodernism, project an entirely different image. A sense of decadence permeates their institutions; the political machine is rusty with age and the effects of deregulation. We're old, say the faces of commuters, each day boarding ever more crowded and inefficient transport systems. We're old, say our young people destined for precarious work or unemployment. We're old, and the future wealth of Europe could be reduced to the historical and cultural patrimony of the continent, transformed into the world's largest museum.

Our economy too is old, and even our democracy shows signs of dementia. The young Westerners who do find work draw salaries too low compared to the cost of living; their parents, the golden generation of the baby boomers, continue to support them. Discrimination against immigrants performing the most menial tasks is the order of the day; they have become the scapegoats for the mismanagement of our political class, an elite no longer the expression of the popular will but a caste working exclusively to remain in power. And the press seem incapable of exercising the liberty that inspired so many struggles and cost so many lives in the past.

Looking closely, it becomes clear that the origins of Western senility coincide with those of China's socioeconomic rebirth: the fall of the Berlin Wall.

Who really did win the Cold War?

THE PYRRHIC VICTORY OF THE WEST

Let's go back to that fateful year, 1989, marked by two ostensibly opposing events: the violent repression of the Tiananmen Square protests and the fall of the Berlin Wall. Both set the process of globalization in motion and influenced the planet's future economic policies. The Western Left imploded and neoliberalism became the triumphant socioeconomic and political model for the entire planet. In the euphoria of that neoliberal victory, few suspected that globalization represented the end of Western economic supremacy. Twenty years on, as the epochal reforms and readjustments produced by these two events redraw the geopolitical map in favor of communist China, it's easy to regard the victory as a Pyrrhic one. But twenty years ago expectations and the official interpretation of such traumatic changes were quite different.

To this day, the West sees in Beijing's armed response in Tiananmen Square the violent repression of Western-style democracy, and in the pulling down of the Berlin Wall its triumph over the communist world. And the West maintains that the Cold War ended with a clear victory for the democratic system, considers the former Soviets who embraced democracy the lucky ones, and the still-communist Chinese the unlucky. In this scenario China replaces the Soviet enemy:

a dictatorial regime without respect for human rights, a hypocritical country that falsifies economic data and wickedly exploits its workers, a nation far from being able to aspire to the role of the globalized world's first superpower. All of this, naturally, is attributed to the absence of democracy, without which there is no well-being or progress.

Too bad that this line of reasoning rests on several errors, if not out-and-out myths.

In terms of economic objectives achieved in the last twenty years, China has handled the process of globalization much better than Western democracies. Since that distant 1989, China's average standard of living has radically improved, while in Eastern Europe and in the territories of the former Soviet Union, where Western-style democracy has taken root, poverty and illiteracy are again on the rise. Not to mention Iraq and Afghanistan, where the exportation of democracy by force of arms has lead to civil war.

One of the powers that supposedly emerged "defeated" from the Cold War in that distant 1989 today declares its candidacy for leader of the globalized economy. A paradox? No. An error of interpretation, rather, born from the political shortsightedness and arrogance of the West, accustomed to seeing in every manifestation of dissent coming from the communist world—a system perceived as antithetical to the West—the desire to replicate its own model of society. An error that, twenty years later, stands in need of correction.

THE DIVERSE MEANINGS OF DEMOCRACY

With the cry for "democracy" in Tiananmen, as in Berlin, the people were not calling for a government identical to our own. They were demanding, rather, access to our living standards. In 1989 neither the Chinese nor those trapped behind the Iron Curtain knew much at all about Western democracy, possessing only a romanticized vision distorted by both Western and communist propaganda. What they wanted was a distinct improvement in economic conditions, which, given the visible wealth of the democratic West, they confused with a change in political paradigm. The idea that to become rich one needed to embrace democracy was very widespread.

"It's not elections the people are dreaming of, but economic freedom," the chief of the national bank of Hungary often used to repeat when I worked for him in 1981. "On the scale of communist desires, private property is worth more than the right to vote." And in the name of these economic conquests people were willing to do anything.

What went missing in the communist bloc was not so much ballot boxes as the profit motive, the very thing Karl Marx described as the fulcrum of the entire capitalist system and that, as we all know, has worked well under democratic governments. With the exception of China, no communist country has understood the force and the importance of this economic need.

One of the startling truths to emerge from reexaminations of the past twenty years is that the Berlin Wall didn't fall because the West's favorite form of government won the Cold War, but because so-called real socialism didn't understand Marxist theory. The Soviets' error was to remove profit from the economic equation, thinking such an amputation was enough to give life to the dictatorship of the proletariat—the only part of Marxist analysis based not on the observation of facts but on a series of hypotheses. This error in interpretation is paradoxical because the best analysis of capitalist profit is precisely the one produced by Marx. Anyone who studies it closely knows that Marx would never have dreamed of removing the fulcrum of the production system; on the contrary, his objective was to have the working class take possession of it and benefit in proportion to its own contribution, i.e., according to the surplus value produced.

Marxist theory is fundamentally an economic doctrine, not

a form of government, but first the Soviets and then, soon after, the Americans transformed it into the antithesis of democracy. Distorted by Leninist political ideology, then turned into a repressive dictatorship by Stalin, and finally deprived of a sense of proportion by Cold War rivalries, Marxism in the USSR became something else: a totalitarian regime. In turn, that regime became a synonym for communism as the antithesis of capitalism. Is it any wonder, then, if that part of the world where it was applied, where the loss of the profit motive also removed any incentive for growth, was reduced to an economic desert?

Even if, twenty years later, we continue to celebrate the victory of the democratic West over the totalitarian East, the truth is that the Soviet economic adventure fell apart on its own. As we will see, the ideological rhetoric of Reagan and Thatcher, along with the foundations of neoliberalism and the democratic framework that the West built around it, have absolutely nothing to do with the fall of the Berlin Wall. Western propaganda manufactured what is still today the prevailing opinion: the equation that links the disintegration of the USSR to the triumph of democracy.

This certainty is an inexhaustible source of political security for us all, leading us to believe that "our democracy" is superior not only to Marxism as synonymous with Soviet totalitarianism, but also, and above all, to the current version of Chinese communism. However, China's success confirms that Marx is not the one whom history has proven wrong. Unlike the Soviets, the Chinese have managed to create a form of communism that works economically, that evolves, one that guarantees progress and well-being more than other systems as confirmed by startling economic data: from 2009 to 2010 the average Chinese per capita income increased in real terms, and the GDP rose by 9 percent during a period of high unemployment and zero growth in Western democracies.

Critics challenge this data with an ideological objection:

China is a corrupt dictatorship without respect for human rights. Even this criticism is rusty and old because it refers to a different nation than contemporary China, and, therefore, is only partly accurate. In the matter of human rights, for example, China has taken giant steps toward an ever-greater respect for the individual. We are still far the from the finishing line, but no one, from the United Nations (UN) to the World Bank to the most respected nongovernmental organizations (NGOs), denies that the Chinese are on the right track.

The West, on the contrary, appears to be moving in the opposite direction, along a path paved with hypocrisy. We are the incorruptible champions of international justice, even as we export our ideas with B-52s and cut deals daily with organized crime. How can we explain the armed intervention in Iraq on the basis of false information? Or the use of torture, the "extraordinary renditions" approved by the Bush administration and employed by the English as well, the Guantánamo Bay detention camp? These are institutions in clear contravention of the Declaration of Human Rights and the Geneva Conventions.

Sadly, examples of how the West violates human rights are countless, everyday occurrences. And the same goes for the corruption and fraud that can be found everywhere: from Madoff on Wall Street; to the Central Intelligence Agency (CIA) in Afghanistan paying Karzai's brother in order to maintain contact with the warlords; to Blackstone, the US company of contract mercenaries implicated in corrupt dealings in Iraq; to the daily scandals of the Berlusconi government; to the appropriation of government funds by British members of parliament; to Sarkozy's links to donations from the heiress of L'Oréal. Like old people affected by dementia, we are going backwards, along the way losing memories of our loved ones—of the values that we have won for ourselves over centuries of social struggle.

China, on the contrary, is moving forward, improving day by day. But, according to our criteria, these conquests are meaningless because China is not democratic. And here we arrive at the heart of the problem: this estimate of the Chinese population's lack of political freedom is once again the fruit of a conceptual misunderstanding. For the Chinese who occupied Tiananmen Square in 1989, beneath the giant poster of Mao, democracy was synonymous with economic equality, and thus equal opportunity for growth, something that in the last twenty years a large segment of the Chinese population has obtained.

Unlike their Soviet comrades, for the Chinese, "democracy" was not a new word, or an "imported" political concept like elections. In his speeches, Mao had used the word democracy hundreds of thousands of times to explain that the government exists to promote the interests of the people, deliberately opposing himself to "other" leaders who oppress the people, as the Western colonizers did prior to the Chinese Revolution of 1949. Now, the idea that the state "serves the people" is still profoundly rooted in Chinese society. Can we say the same of our own democracies, rocked almost daily by political scandals?

There is yet another key element: for the Chinese, the origin of democracy is revolutionary, not elective. Zhou Youguang, who at 103 years old has lived through a sizable slice of China's turbulent history, reminds us of how Zhou Enlai always maintained that the Chinese Communist Party (CCP; also known as the Communist Party of China, or CPC) was a democratic party.[2] There is nothing more democratic, in their collective imaginary, than a revolution that ousts those who govern badly. And the criteria by which they assess the negligence of governments are nearly all economic. Dynasty after dynasty, for five thousand years, China has lived according to these principles.

Today, just as twenty years ago, democracy comes within

the purview of the Party; it does not exist outside it and it certainly does not exist in opposition to it. In the book *Out of Mao's Shadow*,[3] which reexamines the events of Tiananmen in 1989, the lawyer Pu Ziquiang, one of the participants in the protests, described the students' motivations in the following manner: "We wanted to help the government and the Party to correct the mistakes they had made." Not overthrow it or substitute it with another political system. The Chinese students and workers in that square were calling for an opening of the entire system, one that would offer an improvement in living standards. "Democracy" was simply the name of this liberalization, an instrument for guaranteeing the opportunities that belonged by right to the Chinese population.

Could it be that the significance of the fall of the Berlin Wall and of the events of Tiananmen were entirely lost in the political translation? Nothing could be simpler. The Soviets and the Chinese, in fact, knew little to nothing about our form of government; at the same time the West was completely in the dark about the different interpretations of communism. Democracy for us is a political animal that feeds on regular changes in government, and if we were obliged to choose a term to define it, we would opt for "universal suffrage." The Chinese, for their part, would choose "capitalism."

Here it is necessary to take a step back and remember that, in Western political culture, economics and well-being have nothing to do with a system of government. Born in a society where slaves oversaw the economy, Athenian democracy belonged to free men, who built it upon the basis of free discussion of political and philosophical values, far, far away from the demands of commerce and agriculture. When economic expansion became a necessity justifying military aggression, Athenians turned to ideology, as they did in presenting the colonization of Magna Graecia as an expression of generosity, the export of Athens's model of liberty and justice. This is a rhetorical move that modern democracies still employ today, just as the invasion of Iraq became a generous gift of Western democracy presented in military gift wrapping.

Prosperity and democracy are so disconnected in our world that in a system rocked by ruinous crises nobody dreams of overthrowing the ruling class, or even of admitting it is part of the problem. Everyone knows that standards of living in the West in the last twenty years have deteriorated, but rather than turn to the government with demands for concrete policies we ask them to excel in the art of persuasion. Historically, in Europe, as in America, it was free trade that brought wealth, not government by elected representatives. The Founding Fathers themselves were devoted free traders, preaching free markets and the noninterference of the state in commerce.

In Europe the connection between prosperity and democracy was forged in the aftermath of World War II, as the continent was rebuilt according to the democratic model with funds from the Marshall Plan, the cocktail that created the economic miracle. Once again free trade and reconstruction gave birth to prosperity, but the Cold War narrative developed by Western propaganda lead us to believe that democracy generated economic growth.

Words such as "democracy" and "prosperity" lose their meaning in the political translation between two opposite ends of the earth: in the West "democracy" is synonymous with good governance, even when history indicates otherwise, whereas in the East democracy and prosperity become two aspects of the same phenomenon.

HAPPY AND UNHAPPY COUPLES

In the global village the marriage of democracy and prosperity is therefore an unhappy one. Here, then, is the greatest limit of what Churchill called "the worst form of government, except for all those other forms that have been tried." And this maxim, which might have been true in a Europe preyed upon by dictatorial regimes, torn apart by World War II and then by the Cold War, today sounds out of place in the context of a globalized economy and the rise of China. In a system in which the financial elite decide the fate of the world and divide up among themselves the majority of the wealth produced, while the politicians line up behind them, what does the word democracy mean?

Europe's abundant corruption, and the scandals that involve our politicians, are all attributable precisely to this: the anachronism of our form of government today. In the last twenty years democracy has not managed to evolve, instead maintaining that safe distance from the economy, so dear to the Athenians, that Plato severely criticizes in *The Republic*. Since the fall of the Berlin Wall the neoliberal theory, whose mantra says the market regulates the economy better than governments do, has kept politics and economics at bay. It is no wonder that globalization has turned out to be a winning proposition for China, a country in which the state still guides economic transformation, and a losing one for us in the West, where guidance of the economy is instead delegated to the market, so often a source of corruption. Global capitalism's latest crisis seems to tell us that, at least in this phase of evolution, there is a need for the presence of a strong state. The Chinese experience demonstrates that the economy functions better if guidance remains in the hands of those who represent, to the greatest degree possible, the interests of the people and not those of the elite. The word "communist" is not a synonym for politburo but for the vigilant presence of the state in the economy as a guarantor of the interests of the population.

The capitalist-communist pair or capi-communism, for us an absurdity, is for the Chinese a fact of life. And it is a happy coupling, blessed by Karl Marx. Why? Because the Chinese leaders read Marx's *Das Capital* and understood it to be an analysis, not the destruction, of capitalism. Marx never wrote about bringing down the system of production in order to replace it with another one; didn't exhort people to burn factories and return to an agricultural economy; didn't talk about protectionism or the end of international trade. Rather, he described the replacement of capitalism's leadership with the dictatorship of the proletariat as the natural evolution of this system toward its highest point: the classless society. And this is the direction in which the Chinese are moving.

In 1989 Deng Xiaoping knew that the real motivations behind the protests in Tiananmen Square could be traced to the population's confusion about the true meaning of capitalism and democracy. His response, therefore, was to open up the country economically, to make the profit motive available to the people and encourage production. "Get rich" became the mantra, one that echoed across a China still shaken by bloody repression. As we will see, farmers who had barely managed to survive were granted mobility and the right to sell what they produce; others who lived in the countryside were given the possibility of becoming migrant workers and to earn enough in a few years to return home and start their own businesses. These revolutionary political and social changes had begun to take shape already in the late 1970s, just a few years after Mao's death. Thus 1989 constituted an interruption that lasted until 1992, when Deng won the battle within the party, and the experiment took off again, soon gaining greater momentum and producing success.

History tells us that capitalism naturally evolves toward globalization, because the engine of growth is the progressive exploitation of new resources. Democracy, too, tends toward globalization. But the numerous economic disasters of the last few centuries are there to remind us that the capitalism-democracy pairing is dysfunctional during this stage of globalization, whereas capi-communism could be better equipped to exploit both the ascending and descending phases of the globalized economy.

Behind the credit crunch and the recession, therefore, looms a profound revolution that is breaking down the assumptions of the past, including the social, economic, and political preeminence of the Western democracy as the ideal form of government—an epochal upheaval that above all redefines the concept of modernity.

Could it be that Marx won the Cold War?

What is certain is that in order to understand the changes underway there is a need to reread Marxist theory in the context of Beijing. So far, the Chinese model could provide the right lens through which to analyze the decadence of Western society and the decline of our capitalism, a lens that could help us to correct the mistakes of the last twenty years.

DEPRESSIONS IN PROGRESS

The specter of depression stalks the planet—but not everywhere. From Beijing to Cape Town, from Singapore to Rio de Janeiro, it's not the entire world that is on Prozac. In the East and below the equator, people are happier, or at least more content: they spend less, save, and enjoy life. The depressives live in the West. Here the uncertainty of tomorrow torments and corrodes the capitalist democracies and the economic crisis transforms entire continents into sanitariums for the anxious. Afflicted with this psychosis are primarily those between the ages of eighteen and thirty-five, whose future prospects appear darkened by a series of discouraging realities.

In China, on the other hand, people are living with a higher rate of not only growth, but of happiness as well.

Why is it that East and West react differently to the problems of globalization? At the root of this psychological and economic disparity are expectations for the future and the influence of the past.

We in the West are too easily overwhelmed, crippled by memories and stupefied by dreams, to the point of being unable to live in the present. And according to psychiatrists, the way in which we most successfully avoid facing up to daily life is to consume—shopping as therapy.

Those living in the global South have no need of such assistance to make it through the day and instead live under the banner of carpe diem. Their magic words are "today" and "now." Not only are the less rich happier than us, but the economies of the countries where they live are growing while our own show no signs of ceasing to contract.

Recession and depression, then, travel in tandem. It doesn't take much to fall into the abyss. What the statistics are saying is clear: the number of suicides is once again on the rise in Western countries, the first increase since the beginning of the 1980s, during the last recession. And yet it wouldn't take much to reassure us, some stable point of reference, a sliver of hope, one simple fact—the end of the crisis, for example.

The psyche and the market, globalization and anxiety, would appear to be connected. And psychoanalytic theorists such as Zygmunt Bauman describe the complete absence of stable points of reference in which the globalized individual is obliged to live as "liquid modernity," a limbo whose horizon is pure survival, and which presupposes the adaptation to the practices of the group and the disappearance of the individual into the multitude. No wonder we're afraid to face up to everyday reality.

As chance would have it, "liquid modernity" is also one of the central aspects of consumerism, a by-product of the mass market, fertile ground for the advertising campaigns with which the multinationals ceaselessly bombard us. The most successful, once again, are the perfect union of psyche and economics. They push the right buttons, the ones that control crowd behavior, that make us automatically stretch out our arms to grab a specific product from the supermarket shelf and not the one next to it.

Many psychoanalysts identify consumerism as the primary cause of the malaise gripping the wealthier areas of the planet: the individual struggles to deal with daily consumption, which turns out to be an inexhaustible source of stress. In short, a dog biting its own tail. Trapped in a vicious cycle, we consume to escape the stress of everyday reality, and this very activity is a source of constant stress. The solution? Prozac.

Since 1988, the year Eli Lilly launched Prozac, more than

forty million people have taken it as an antidepressant. The results? Meager. A 2008 study published in the *Journal of the Public Library of Science* by Professor Irving Kirsch of the department of psychology at the University of Hull, along with other American and Canadian psychologists, finds that patients who swallow Prozac are no happier than those who are administered a placebo.[1] And where Prozac fails, so do Paxil and Zoloft. The source of the malaise afflicting the West isn't the kind that antidepressants can treat, but rather our style of life.

According to the World Health Organization (WHO), since the beginning of the 1990s the number of depressives has increased precisely in the countries in which indebtedness has assumed biblical proportions—the rich nations—and roughly in proportion to the average increase in individual debt load. Depression and defaults, therefore, are multiplying where wealth and democracy reign, starting with the United States, the richest and most democratic country in the world, and spilling over into the stock markets of the global village, while we obsessively ask the economists when and how GDP and employment will start growing again. But neither psychoanalysis nor economics is an exact science; they lack the instruments to give us this type of certainty.

Falling into this crisis we have learned the hard way that unbridled consumption, far from being the engine of growth, is the cause of the recession, causing individuals—and with them the banks—to go into debt in order to live beyond their means. In other words, we live in a mirage in which lines of credit have been mistaken for wealth. And the mantra that in the Roaring Nineties resounded throughout American business schools—"I'm worth as much as I can borrow"—has become the anthem of globalization. The code of conduct to which we have conformed is absurd, one that ends up falsifying the assessments of financial risk.

And yet our governments urge us to use our credit cards

with the same abandon as before the crisis. Consumer spending is our economy's lifeblood, without it we'll never get back
on track—this is the substance of the message. Is it possible
that those who should be helping us back up the slope are in
fact the ones pushing us further down? A paradox of the contemporary economy? It would seem so.

There is, however, a significant difference between economics and psychology. Whereas the latter seeks to treat and avert
psychic disturbances, identifying their causes, the former
seems incapable of preventing the financial disasters that have
occurred with ever-greater frequency in the last twenty years.
Indeed, globalization seems to go hand in hand with financial
crisis. Why?

As opposed to the discipline of economics, the study of the
human mind keeps pace with the times, and has thus taken
on a great deal of modernity. In the past fifty years, psychoanalysis has fiercely criticized classical Freudian theory. No
longer does anyone outside of Woody Allen films lie down on
the couch to talk over traumas and childhood sexual fan-
tasies. Today the discipline embraces a full spectrum of
approaches and Prozac is combined with not only classic psy-
chotherapy but also yoga and, if necessary, even video games.

Whereas psychoanalysts, thanks above all to the contribution of Carl Gustav Jung, succeeded in escaping the cage of
Freud's theory of the unconscious, economists are still today
shackled to Adam Smith, the father of classical economics.
And yet the model he describes is based on a reality that no
longer exists. Few today believe that the selfish behaviors of
the multitude produce the wealth of nations. It is difficult to
find a link between the billion dollar bonuses of high finance
and the growth of GDP; indeed, the opposite is true. And yet
from 1989 up through the onset of the crisis, every Western
democracy, along with a great many of the new democratic
regimes, has applied—has embraced in toto—the ideology of
the market. None have cast doubt upon the extraordinary

powers of its "invisible hand," even when it created profound disparities in income, social injustice, abuses, and even colossal fraud.

Today the majority of politicians encourage us to spend money we don't have because, when it comes to getting the economy moving, none of them can call on an alternative to the now-obsolete consumerist model. Since the fall of the Berlin Wall the economy has become monothematic. And as the West confronts the greatest economic revolution since the days of Adam Smith, the globalization process, it remains constricted by neoliberalism.

Rather than rendering it more flexible and suitable to the demands of a present in constant movement, financial deregulation has made the capitalist economy more susceptible to abuse. For twenty years no one concerned themselves with studying or creating a new model and no one criticized the current one. How did the euphoria of the victory over communism blind the West to the point of convincing us that our flawed economic system was already perfect? Because neoliberalism won the Cold War, everyone imagined the "solution" was valid forever. Instead, just at that moment, to use Fukuyama's terms, the discipline of economics came to the end of the line and abuses soared.[2]

And so we have remained stuck with an economic theory born out of the Industrial Revolution, prisoners of a dream, of a trick of the unconscious, of psychological repression. The Western economy, like the psyche, is trapped within the vise of our expectations of the future and dogmas of the past. For twenty years the deflationist policy of the Federal Reserve has acted as financial Prozac, allowing the West to ignore the economic crisis by suppressing its symptoms. Both recession and depression have been kept under control by antidepressants, which act on the signs without removing and treating the sources of the problem. Now, however, they've stopped working.

But what is the alternative? Has there ever existed a Jung of the economy capable of overturning the dogmas of Adam Smith's classical liberalism and freeing this discipline from its cage?

Yes, in fact, and his name was Karl Marx.

Marxism, like Jung's theory, is born of empirical observation. Its object of study is the production system, the behavior of the labor force, and the concentration of capital in the hands of the elites, a deterioration that imperils civil society. Marx, like Jung, distanced himself from the prevailing interpretation of his time, and the formulation of his critical approach is so similar to that of the Swiss psychiatrist that we can indeed call him the "Jung of economics." His analyses, going completely countercurrent, offer a different way to read economics, breaking with traditional methods; but at the same time they speak to the best possibility for capitalism's development, not to its destruction.

Now, the modernity of psychoanalysis derives precisely from the dichotomy between its two founding fathers, Freud and Jung, a tension that has not diminished with time. In economics, on the other hand, this dialectic underwent a historic shift. Marx, like Smith, is one of the founding fathers, but Marxist theory, considered a radical alternative rather than a constructive criticism of the liberal capitalist model, ceased to influence Western economic thought.

For this reason the world today no longer has at its disposal an economist like John Maynard Keynes, whose thought was formed within a vibrant and constructive dialectic. His exchanges with the Marxists at Cambridge were fundamental to the formulation of *The General Theory of Employment, Interest, and Money*, his masterpiece. Thus the Bretton Woods Agreements and the economic and financial system that framed the postwar economic miracle owe as much to Marx and the critique of capitalism as to the "invisible hand" of Adam Smith. But after the fall of the Berlin

Wall, Marx was swept away along with the Soviet regime and real socialism, and his books have ended up collecting dust in libraries. The dynamic relationship that existed between classical liberalism and Marxism deteriorated and with it the economy's modernity. This explains why in the West economics has become monothematic, celebrating a single model.

But not in the East.

After 1989, it was only in China that Marxism continued to be studied, along with all the other economic theories. This work led to the creation of a new, modern model, stamped with the most severe pragmatism. Like psychoanalysis, "Made in China" capitalism uses everything that works (from private enterprise to capital controls) and is therefore more flexible and up to date than the Western version. The Chinese model is capable of adapting the economy to sudden, epochal changes such as the globalization process, and this flexibility helped China become the global village's superpower and redefine the parameters of modernity.

How it could have happened that, from the theoretical scrap heap of Western capitalism, the Chinese miracle was born? At the heart of the story is the prodigious rise of a country that, whether out of pure ignorance or outdated ideology, we continue to misunderstand, a country that frightens us because it's different. At the same time, this book warns of the equally prodigious collapse awaiting our system if we continue to insist on celebrating an exhausted economic and political model. However, a cure does exist, and it could be effective against the economic and psychological depression afflicting the West. Call it Chinese capitalism or Chinese medicine; all that's required is that we find the will to adapt it to the physiology of our democracies.

PART ONE

GLOBALIZATION AND COMMUNISM

CHAPTER 1

EXPLOITATION FACTORIES

CHARLES DICKENS IN SHENZHEN

The workers' charred corpses are everywhere: pressed up against the four emergency exits, all bolted shut; atop metal ladders, melted in the blaze; along the assembly line; and even in the second-floor bathroom, where a few desperate individuals, to no avail, sought refuge. In just a few minutes, flames transformed the factory into a furnace.[1] On that afternoon of November 19, 1993, most of the 135 workers rushing to fulfill Christmas orders died inside, burned alive.

The fire destroyed everything, from machines to materials, stacked up against the emergency exits because the plant doesn't have warehouses. This is where the flames started, a short circuit set fire to a pile of raw materials, which exploded, launching burning fragments more or less everywhere. In just a few minutes, the entire assembly line was swallowed up by the fire. Anyone who found themselves on the ground floor ran for the only exit, but for the others, those who work on the second floor, there was no way out, and they died in the blaze.

Only the metal window bars survive intact, above the piled bodies of the unfortunates who tried in vain to force them open.

WESTERN CAPITALISM ENCOUNTERS CHINESE SOCIALISM

Let's begin our journey, then, with a tragedy from the 1990s in Shenzhen, the most important Special Economic Zone (SEZ) in China. Not far from Hong Kong, in Guangdong, the area has been called "Communist China's capitalist laboratory," a definition that sums up its experimental character well. The 1990s are an exceptional period in China, when the "open door" policy, the opening to capitalism promoted by Deng Xiaoping, begins to bear fruit and to shape a new nation. These are, then, years of radical change, of great sacrifices and incredible economic growth, during which the country patiently weaves the fabric of its future modernity.

But let's return to the fire at the industrial facility, a toy factory called Zhili, belonging to a Hong Kong industrialist. An apocalyptic spectacle awaits the inspectors and Chinese journalists who arrive a few hours later. Everyone has the sense they're confronting a tragedy that could have been avoided. The management, also from Hong Kong, has in fact violated every security measure imposed by Chinese law: from the elevator without fire doors, which could have saved the lives of dozens of workers trapped on the second floor by the flames, to the single entrance, an extremely narrow corridor, a channel eight meters long and just eighty centimeters wide that the workers were forced to pass through one at a time. Not to mention the iron bars on the windows and the lack of an evacuation plan in the event of a fire. The managers, located in a separate building from the assembly line, did not even rush to help the poor people as they burned alive, instead watching from a safe distance.

Inspectors and journalists well know that Zhili is not the only foreign factory in Shenzhen to economize on the backs of its workers. The practice is sadly widespread in the region. Just months before this fire, a group of inspectors had denounced fully eighty-five industrial facilities, including Zhili, and fourteen companies located in the same district. The report stated that they were all at risk of fire because they did not observe the security measures required by Chinese labor regulations.[2]

In the 1990s, such citations are the order of the day. Security measures cost money, and the first foreign industrialists to try their luck in China don't want to invest money to protect the local labor force, as they would have been obliged to do in their own countries. They are here precisely in order to cut labor costs. Although the local press periodically launches campaigns against their abuses, denouncing also the corruption of local officials, and Chinese public opinion is shocked by the news, resistance is minimal. Foreign capital is untouchable. The reason? China's desperate need for foreign investment.

"Profit is more important than the workers who produce it": an adage that resonates with the unscrupulousness of the English factory "bosses" during the Industrial Revolution, which in the 1980s and '90s became the mantra of industrial pioneers in China. But we're not in the English Midlands of the end of the eighteenth century any more. We don't have before us a situation like that described by Marx in *Das Capital*, in which the proletariat, devoid of class consciousness, is unaware of its own strength. And we certainly can't compare the Chinese Communist Party (CCP) to the eighteenth-century English Parliament, which had only a vague idea of what was happening in the factories, and an even hazier one of the consequences of the Industrial Revolution.

The Chinese workers know as well as the politicians that the foreign industrialists are exploiting the local labor force, but they know, too, that above all it's a step both necessary and inevitable if China is to *modernize*. And to achieve this result they are ready to do anything, even to risk their lives in factories.

Even if, more than a century since the Industrial Revolution, identical conditions of exploitation appear to be emerging in China, it's important to underline some fundamental differences. As we will see, it is these differences that make the Chinese modernization process unique.

DENG'S SPINNING JENNY

Notwithstanding the fact that twenty years of Maoism in China produced an annual growth rate of 4.4 percent and quadrupled GDP,[3] at the end of the 1970s the Chinese economy is in chaos. State-owned enterprises are failing to absorb the millions and millions of young people entering the job market every year, and the agricultural sector struggles to feed the population.[4] This is Mao's paradoxical legacy: socialism threatens to burst under the pressure of poverty and hunger because there are so many Chinese, perhaps too many. The economy's growth is insufficient. If the Marxist economic model is to survive, it needs to modernize.

In the Eastern Bloc as well, real socialism struggles. And both systems look to the West, where the postwar economic miracle has brought peace and prosperity. But Chinese communism will offer evidence of an intrinsic dynamism that Russian communism never knew.

Deng Xiaoping, the man who must preside over the post-Mao period, is an astute and pragmatic politician. He senses that foreign capital represents the only hope for the survival of Chinese socialism, and that in order to attract it, it will be necessary to make use of cheap local labor. Deng is convinced, therefore, that the Marxist model will be modernized by none other than its archenemy—Western capitalism.

"The economic reforms served to consolidate the single-party system," confirms Zhao Ziyang, general secretary of the CCP from 1987 to 1989, describing the aims of the "open door" policy.[5] On paper the strategy seems absurd: to create in China the conditions for the exploitation of workers on the part of industrialists from beyond its borders, and to do so in order to save the socialist system. But economic history is full of paradoxes—and it works.

Deng's plan comes to fruition thanks to delocalization. Moving foreign factories to China knocks down labor costs and thus also manufacturing costs. Profits rise in consequence. There's no better formula for attracting foreign capital. Thus begins the race to the East.

Delocalization is to globalization what the invention of the spinning jenny was to the Industrial Revolution. This machine, producing cotton in industrial quantities at prices accessible to everyone, revolutionized the world textile market, making England its new capital. In next to no time, in fact, the masses had access to cotton, a material both easy to work with and comfortable to wear. Similarly, in the 1990s, delocalization transformed China's languishing socialist economy into the global village's assembly line, on which all kinds of goods could be produced at rock-bottom prices. Thus, the West makes products "Made in China," until then too expensive for a mass market, accessible to every inhabitant of the global village.

The biggest winner in all this is foreign capital. From 1995 to 2003, Chinese exports increase from $121 billion to $365 billion, of which more than 65 percent is derived from the Chinese subsidiaries of foreign companies. The tremendous growth of "Made in China" is therefore attributable to these businesses using local labor; the profits end up swelling the GDP of wealthy countries.[6]

The establishment of a new balance of trade in the eighteenth and nineteenth centuries was due to a combination of factors—not just the spinning jenny but the invention of the steam engine and the issuing of the Inclosure Acts, which forced thousands of farmers to abandon their fields and seek work in the factories. An analogous cocktail of extraordinary events comes to revolutionize the global manufacturing system at the end of the twentieth century. The ingredients are the crisis of the Chinese agrarian economy, which convinces the government to introduce internal labor mobility in the country and gives rise to large-scale migration; deregulation, which after the fall of the Berlin Wall leads to the opening of world markets; and the low cost of oil, which during the 1990s knocks down the cost of transporting goods. It is the first of these phenomena that interests us here.

As with the Inclosure Acts, large-scale Chinese migration is the unexpected consequence of reforms having nothing to do with future changes in the global manufacturing system.

"In 1958, the Chinese government establishes a registry in which citizens are divided into urban and rural residents. This status is permanent; that is, it is forbidden for workers to move between countryside and city or vice versa," explains Liu Kaiming, director of the Shenzhen Institute of Contemporary Observation.[7] It is a division that reflects the Communist economic order. In the country, production is centered on the collective farms; in the city, on state-owned industry. Built along Marxist-Leninist lines, the paradigm aims to lift China from the poverty into which it plunged during the colonization of the preceding century. "What Westerners don't realize is that before the Revolution this was an extremely poor country," explains Maurice Ohana, head of Ohanasia, a company exporting clothing to France.[8]

We would do well here to take a moment to consider Ohana's point. Mao comes to power following a century of profound negative growth. In 1820, Chinese GDP per capita was equivalent to $600; in 1870, it had dropped to $530; in 1950, a year after the Chinese Revolution, it was $439, barely 70 percent of the 1820 figure. It's no surprise then that the Chinese refer to the preceding 120 years as the "century of humiliation."[9] Although Maoist economic policy curbs the fall of GDP, communism lacks the incentives necessary to make the great leap and lift the country back out of the subsistence economy in which it has plunged. By the end of the 1970s, agricultural and industrial production only barely manage to sustain the economy.

THE REVOLUTION OF MOBILE LABOR

With Mao's death, Deng devises reforms aimed at overcoming this impasse through the introduction of a series of incentives for growth. First to be modernized is the system of collective farms. The farmers can sell part of their crops rather than send everything into government warehouses, a reform representing a timid step in the direction of private property. The experiment pays off; agricultural production increases and becomes available in the public markets. It is at this point that the mobility of labor enters the scene. Farmers are permitted to travel among the smaller cities to sell what they have grown. Soon it is also possible to work outside of one's own village. For anyone unfortunate enough to be born in the countryside, a new series of opportunities opens up, such as becoming a *mangliu*, or migrant worker. As one migrant worker explains:

> Why would I want to hang around in Jianli? We've become floating workers because of all the inequalities. I didn't ask to be born in the countryside, but I could choose to leave.[10]

The migrations change China's future, just as centuries ago the Inclosures radically transformed England's, and restore to the country an ancient tradition. The migrant worker continues:

> All the founding emperors of China's dynasties started out as part of the floating population of migrant workers. Chairman Mao was a big *mangliu* himself. When he first came to Beijing from Hunan, Chen Duxiu [founding leader of the CCP]'s and Yang Kaihui [Mao's future wife]'s fathers were well-known professors. They made hundreds of yuan a month, but

Mao couldn't even find a decent job. He ended up earning eight yuan a month working at the Peking University library. Everyone treated him like a country bumpkin and laughed at him for his accent. But later Mao was chairman.[11]

In 1978 Deng creates the first Special Economic Zone in Shenzhen to attract foreign investors. Here the rules of production imposed by Chinese communism, and therefore also state-owned enterprise, melt away to leave space for a capitalist-style industrial system, with considerable incentives for outside entrepreneurs.

"In Shenzhen the government lets the market prosper. And market forces guide development. It's the economy that creates the miracle," explains Patrick Chovanec, who teaches economics at Tsinghua University in Beijing.[12] And the labor force to sustain the market comes from the Chinese rural reality. This is how the first migrations begin, profound changes that nevertheless do not create economic imbalances because they are introduced gradually. The entire "open door" policy is begun gradually. Deng is convinced that any form of shock therapy would be harmful to the system. And he's right.

In the initial phase, the migrations from the countryside to the cities are tightly regulated. In the early 1980s, anyone wishing to try their luck in the Special Economic Zones has to apply for a permit in their own village and specify the destination. "It is only with these passes, which in China are called temporary identity cards, that one manages to enter the SEZs, which are for all intents and purposes gated districts," Liu Kaiming explains.

It is only in the second half of the 1980s that the situation changes, making it easier and easier to obtain authorizations and move. Thus a new season begins: in 1990, there are already six million Chinese migrants; in 2003, when the government abolishes the temporary identity cards, the numbers grow further; in 2008, it is a question of fully two hundred million laborers. It is the largest migration in human history.[13]

And who benefits the most here? The foreign entrepreneurs, of course.

THE CHINESE DIASPORA RETURNS HOME

It's not easy, at the end of the 1970s, for the China of Deng Xiaoping to attract foreign capital. Mao still casts a shadow over every sector of the economy and the wounds of the Cultural Revolution remain open. What's more, China is a mystery for the West, unsure of where or how to locate it in terms of the bipolarity of the Cold War. Nixon and Kissinger's 1972 diplomatic opening notwithstanding, the country is a source of fear, and no one feels up to doing business with the Maoists.

Thus the first investors to venture into the Special Economic Zones come from Taiwan, from Hong Kong, from South Korea. They're Chinese and foreign at the same time. They belong to the country's diaspora, but their story is very different from that of the laborers they use. They are not communists, they know the capitalist system and what kind of products the Western market prefers. For them the role that China will play in international commerce is that of producing, at rock-bottom prices, the goods that Western consumers buy on a daily basis. And to their eyes, the army of Chinese laborers that they "employ" have neither name nor identity; they are, rather, only one of the means of production, a slightly revised and updated version of the proletariat described by Marx. And the workers know this too.

At the beginning of the 1990s, a worker in a Meteor[14] factory explained the situation in the following manner to the Sinologist Pun Ngai, who had succeeded in passing herself off as a migrant worker:

We're not treated as people, can't you understand that? We're like dogs, we never quit. When a supervisor asks you to do something you have to do it, it doesn't matter where you are or what you're doing . . . Who cares about us? We're nobody, we're only merchandise.[15]

Many industrialists from the Chinese diaspora consider Deng's opening to capitalism the sign of communism's defeat, and assume an arrogant attitude toward local authorities as well as the workers. "The communists destroyed the country's economy and now they turn to us; this time it would be better if they listen to what we have to say." This was how a Taiwanese entrepreneur commented on his presence in Shenzhen at the beginning of the 1990s.[16] Hence the brazenness with which they violate the rules of labor legislation is born also and above all from the conviction that Chinese communism won't last, undermined as it is by an incapacity to manage the economy. And no wonder: this is a period when the communism-capitalism coupling seems nothing short of laughable.

Naturally, these entrepreneurs preach and practice a coarse brand of capitalism, forbidden in their own countries, hearkening back to the cruelties of the Industrial Revolution. Visiting Shenzhen during the 1980s and '90s is like traveling back in time, an economic déjà vu. A canopy of smog covers the Pearl River delta, the tropical region of Guangdong, where the factories spew poison into the air day and night. Hundreds of millions of farmers, like their English ancestors, are effectively swallowed up by the foreign-owned factory dormitories. They live here in what are often disastrous hygienic conditions, working an average of twelve hours a day.

"The workers sleep twelve to a room, in bunk beds right next to the bathrooms; the rooms are filthy and smelly." Thus Liu Qaingmin, a factory worker, describes the plant where she works and lives in Shenzhen in the early 1990s, Carrin Electronics, a Hong Kong company producing alarm clocks, calculators, and electronic calendars that display the time in different cities of the world.[17] She continues: "The working day goes from eight in the morning to midnight, thirteen hours of work with two breaks for meals, seven days a week." Nearly two centuries ago, in England, the Children's Employment Commission had gathered a similar testimony: "The young woman . . . has worked in the fashion industry for several years . . . In the winter months, the work day goes from eight in the morning to eleven at night and from six or six-thirty until midnight in the summer months."[18]

The power of the boss is absolute, and the workers are equally subject to it during working hours and in their moments of free time. In the 1990s at Carrin it is necessary to request written permission to go to the bathroom, and the time allowed is ten minutes. Anyone caught talking is fined ¥5, a large sum for workers who only earn ¥300 a month. It goes without saying that humiliation is the order of the day. In March 1995, the Chinese press report on a collective form of humiliation at the South Korean–owned Zhuhai Ruijin Electrical Goods Company. The manager, South Korean obviously, forces the 120 workers to kneel on the ground because, during the ten-minute break conceded to them, they failed to leave the workplace in groups of four, as prescribed by the rules.[19]

Delocalization ensures that the barbaric practices in use in the factories of South Korea, Hong Kong, and Taiwan in the 1960s and '70s, since abolished by labor legislation in those countries, would in the next two decades be transplanted to China. We find them again, in the following decade, in Vietnam or in Indonesia, wherever the industrial production of globalized capitalism has delocalized in the meantime, pursuing lower and lower wages and more permissive legislation.

ENVIRONMENTAL DEGRADATION

In 1997, two journalists from the *Yangcheng Evening News*, one of the most important Guangzhou newspapers, got themselves hired as workers in the Yixin shoe factory, owned by an industrialist from Taiwan. Here they witnessed the brutal treatment meted out to the workers by the managers, also originally from Taiwan. A worker who attempted to rebel was beaten bloody by a foreman with a rubber truncheon in front of everyone, to the shouts of "I'll whip you till you don't have the strength to get up anymore."[20] Not only, then, does delocalization allow foreigners to exploit native labor, it also offers them the opportunity to do so in barbaric ways, ways forbidden in their own countries as criminal—including those that poison the environment.

An emblematic case is that of Putian, in the Shenzhen SEZ, where the entire footwear manufacturing sector of Taiwan, the biggest producer of footwear in the world, is relocated to in the 1980s. It is a massive investment: in just a few years the factories multiply across the zone, and by the end of the 1980s there are more than 150. Annual production is phenomenal, reaching one hundred million pairs of shoes. Earnings too are astronomical: ¥3.5 billion, more than $850 million, with a 50 percent return on capital investments. It's a land of plenty for any entrepreneur with access to a foreign market in which to sell footwear and leather goods, including those bearing international brand names. Of course, the wages of the zone's seventy thousand young workers are derisory, ¥300–¥400 a month for a minimum of ten hours a day, less than the price of a pair of Nikes or Adidas in a fashionable store in New York or Milan.

But there's another problem: every worker in Putian is constantly breathing a poisonous cocktail composed of benzene, toluene, and xylene. In the West, the employment of these chemical agents requires the use of special purifiers that reduce the harmful effects on workers. Similar legislation exists in China, but in the 1990s no one obeys it. It would in fact be enough to invest 1 percent of profits in order to install the purifiers in the factories and avoid having 2,500 tons of carbon monoxide end up in the lungs of the workers and residents of the zone. No one, however, wants to spend that money, even as the impacts on health are irreparable: permanent damage to blood cell production and the central nervous system.

Workers are nevertheless so abundant that replacing them does not represent a problem: for every poisoned worker forced to leave, there are at least ten younger ones ready to take their place. Thus, notwithstanding the repeated accusations in the national press and pressure from the unions, by the beginning of the 1990s, only four factories in the Putian zone have installed purification systems.

To function, delocalization must cancel out all the concessions won by Western workers since the Industrial Revolution and reproduce the conditions of exploitation of two centuries earlier. Only in this way can the truly lucrative union between foreign capital and Chinese communism be consummated, with the Western brand names acting as maids of honor.

A year after the Zhili tragedy, six managers and members of the local government are convicted for the fire at the plant. The owner from Hong Kong is given a two-year jail sentence but is out after a few months, returning home while still on parole. Zhili is ordered to pay $5,000 to the families of each of the victims, including the critically injured—the price of a life in a China on the threshold of capitalism. But the money never arrives. Some of the survivors turn to a Hong Kong NGO specializing in labor lawsuits, which launches a campaign aimed not only at Zhili, but also at the multi-nationals that Zhili produces toys for, among them the Italian company Artsana S.p.A/Chicco.[21]

Anita Chan, in her book *China's Workers under Assault*,

relates how in 1997 Chicco agreed to pay $180,000 in compensation to the victims, roughly $1,000 a head, a pittance even according to Chinese standards. In 1999, it is discovered that this money never arrived at its destination. Apparently sent to Caritas Hong Kong, the charitable organization charged with the distribution of the sums to the victims, it mysteriously turned up in the coffers of other Chinese philanthropic organizations.

CHAPTER 2

THE RACE TO THE BOTTOM

In the twentieth century, China was invaded by foreign businessmen very similar to those that, one hundred years earlier, Marx described as capitalists. That explains why, in 1994, when Beijing approved a law obliging businesses to draw up individual and collective contracts, very few foreign industrialists respected it. The fourteen suicides that took place in 2010 at the Taiwanese Foxconn factory, which produces for Dell, Apple, Cisco, and Intel, shocked the world. The youngest worker was just seventeen years old and the oldest one twenty-eight. What drove these people to end a life that had just started? According to several people, conditions in the factories resembled those of a labor camp.

It is nevertheless true that the local Chinese authorities, intent on attracting as much foreign capital as possible, took precious little action against those who broke their laws on a daily basis.

A few months before the Zhili tragedy, another Hong Kong–owned company, a clothing manufacturer in Guangzhou, caught fire and seventy-two people lost their lives. At the same time as investigations into the Zhili fire were ongoing, sixty workers burned at a Taiwanese company site in Fuzhou. And the authorities? They didn't bat an eye. A combination of corruption, ignorance, and laissez-faire policies served to keep foreign industrialists above the law, and during the 1990s workplace fires became tragically frequent.

Meanwhile the corruption of public officials continued to spread. A few months before the Zhili fire, the mayor of Kuichong had defended the owners from criticisms by the Shen-zhen inspectors. In a letter the mayor reminded the inspectors of the importance of Hong Kong capital to the zone's develop-ment, and assured them that safety measures would be improved in time for the next inspection. Worthless promises, naturally. The same day the letter was sent, Zhili managers agreed to increase the daily subsidy to the inspectors, all municipal employees. This is how a Chinese journalist, in an article denouncing the Zhili tragedy, described the deal: "A business transaction made on the backs of the workers and concluded in the name of national economic development."[1]

The journalist doesn't use the word "corruption," even if that's what it looks like to our eyes, and not merely for the sake of caution: the terminology employed sums up perfectly the reciprocal relationship that, at the dawn of China's new economic reality, connects the communist system to foreign capital. The exploitation of the labor force, at times barbaric, is the price that Chinese society has accepted to pay for eco-nomic growth, and that politicians have welcomed as a way to save socialism.

CHINESE CLASS CONSCIOUSNESS

More than a decade after the Zhili fire, in 2006, a report from the Economist Intelligence Unit reveals that 40 percent of the workers employed in the construction industry work without a contract. While factory conditions have improved, job secu-rity remains elusive. At the national level, the study estimates that in 2006, 60 percent of work contracts were still fixed-term and without any guarantees.[2] As we will see, major changes in job security took place at the end of 2007 when Beijing introduced new labor legislation, and in 2009 with the launch of an extremely ambitious program of industrial energy conversion.

In the 1990s and during much of the first decade of the

twenty-first century, China is globalized capital's promised land. But its great attraction is less the ease with which nearly two centuries of labor struggles fought in the West are wiped out, and more that the cost of labor is kept so consistently low. The phenomenon is connected to the great migrations, as a virtually unlimited standing supply of labor prevents wages from increasing. Thus in 2004 the *New York Times* reports that Chinese workers earn the same as they did in 1993.[3]

The consequences of this race-to-the-bottom wage competition, as economists have defined it, are disastrous for factory workers throughout the global village, as delocalization transforms the minimum wage earned in any part of the globe into a kind of international yardstick. Stephen Roach, an economist with Morgan Stanley, has christened this phenomenon "global labor arbitrage," whereby companies move production from one country to another according to the cost of labor.[4]

Thus in the 2000s many businesses moved from China to Vietnam and Laos, where the wages were more competitive. Nevertheless, since the Chinese possess a professionalism and work ethic that is rare, and which foreign entrepreneurs did not want to give up, attempts were made to take advantage of this even after further delocalization. In the second half of the first decade of the twenty-first century, China becomes the center of the global assembly line, the pieces produced at lower cost in neighboring countries and put together in Chinese factories.[5] Many foreign industrialists even export Chinese professionalism into Asian markets. A gem-setter from Panyu, in the Shenzhen zone, where twenty years ago the Indian jewel industry relocated from Hong Kong, tells of how he trained several Indians in the craft at the request of his employer. These men then returned to their native country to work for the company of this same entrepreneur who in 2009 closed the Chinese operation because it was too costly.[6]

Once again, Stephen Roach explains how race-to-the-bottom wage competition makes it so workers and communities located on opposite sides of the earth are competing against each other without realizing it.[7] What's missing is what Marx would have called a "global class consciousness."

Delocalization also acts as a powerful depressive agent in the creation of new jobs in rich countries such as the United States. If it costs less to produce in China or Vietnam, why do it in Arizona? This is the logic of the modern industrialist. At its base is a perverse mechanism that since the fall of the Berlin Wall has led the globalized economy to structure itself according to an absurd international division of labor: Western companies produce at knockdown prices in the East what is consumed by Western markets.[8]

Race-to-the-bottom wage competition, the absence of labor safety, and the absence of guarantees are an aberration to us in the West, but not to the Chinese. For the hundreds of millions of workers who move from the countryside to factories in Shenzhen, it's instead a unique opportunity to make money and return home with better future prospects.

Chinese workers are conscious of being exploited, and this is indeed a basic difference between two so apparently similar worlds—Marx's England and Deng's China.

Naturally, no one wants to reflect on the risks being taken, on the possibility that the dream of a comfortable old age could turn into a nightmare. The Chinese worker today, like the eighteenth-century English worker, cannot afford this luxury. And this is true to an even greater extent for the women, in China historically subordinate to men, for whom factory work is often an obligatory step toward emancipation.

The majority of the eighty-seven killed in the Zhili fire were in fact women, for the most part very young, young enough to play with the toys they produced.

In the 1980s and '90s, women represented 70 percent of

the labor force in Shenzhen.[9] Migrant workers all, *dagonzei* is the Chinese term coined for those women who left the countryside to seek their fortune in the factories of the SEZ. The youngest, women under twenty-five, primarily work in light manufacturing, like the Zhili toy factory, the first foreign industry to relocate to China. It suits investors to turn to female workers because they work hard and know little about their rights. Before long, young female workers came to represent 90 percent of the light industry labor force.[10]

THE BAD CONSCIENCE OF THE WEST

The Chinese economic miracle, therefore, begins in Guangdong and is directed by foreign capital. It's not the first time foreigners have upset the economy of the Pearl River Delta. In the nineteenth century, opium smuggling by English merchants devastated the region. In the summer of 1839, Lin Zexu, the imperial commissioner of the Qing Dynasty, a special position created specifically to resolve once and for all the problem of the opium trade in the country, orders the destruction of twenty opium dens near the bay of Humen, a town within Dongguan, not far from where Shenzhen is today. The decision unleashes the First Opium War between China and England. The dispute is centered in the Guangdong province, which the British Navy do not hesitate to carpet bomb.

With the Treaty of Nanking of August 29, 1842, which puts an end to the conflict, China is forced to cede the bay of Hong Kong to His Majesty and open its own ports to English ships and international commerce. This is the beginning of foreign domination, a period of great humiliation which leads to the collapse of the Qing dynasty, civil war, and invasion by Japan, and will only conclude with the victory of the communists in 1949.

The Chinese "century of humiliation" is characterized by emigration. Leaving behind villages in flame in the Pearl River

Delta, an army of laborers sets off for the American West. They are absorbed for the most part by a railroad industry engaged in the colossal project of connecting the two coasts by rail. The Chinese are the ones to build it, one of the least known aspects of the myth of the Far West. The level of exploitation is inhuman and death very common. In the most arduous stretches, in the Rocky Mountains, it's said that every mile cost the lives of one hundred Chinese. Beside the single track, the survivors write the names of the fallen on pieces of white paper, so that they are not consigned to oblivion. For these people, who worship their ancestors, to be buried in a foreign land, thousands of miles away from home, is a source of great distress, because they are afraid of being forgotten.

Chinese labor was already very much in demand. After all, the people who built the Great Wall had a perfect résumé—there weren't better workers on the planet. The American railroad companies even sent emissaries to China to recruit laborers. For barely a dollar a day, former farmers and fishermen crossed the ocean in the ships' holds, as if they were merchandise. Once they finished building the railroad in the United States they moved to Canada, starting in Vancouver and working their way east.[11]

The present resembles this past a great deal, especially if we consider the inhuman exploitation of Chinese laborers that we find in Old Europe. We know little or nothing about it because they are clandestine immigrants, virtually invisible. "If a Chinese worker is illegal you'll never see him. He lives in the shadows and stays in the shadows," says Fausto Zuccarelli, District Attorney in the Public Prosecutor's office in Naples, Italy, and Deputy Director of the National Antimafia Office.[12]

In 2009 in Milan, Italy, a bunker-style hotel was discovered in the basement of a building frequented by illegal Chinese workers, accessible by way of manholes. It was run by an Italian woman, who had in the narrow space found room for sixty mattresses, two bathrooms, and a tiny kitchen with four liquid gas cylinders. Exposed electrical wires and wretched sanitary conditions—these are the characteristics of invisible workers. "At the first spark," one agent recounted, "there would have been a massacre."[13]

The exploitation of Eastern labor by Westerners is a constant across the planet. And yet, global public opinion expresses precisely the opposite conviction, namely, that the exploiters come from the East. In the Western collective imagination, China is a communist country whose people are slaves to a cruel dictatorial regime taking advantage of its own people. Few people distinguish, for example, between the Chinese and the North Korean systems; communism continues to have a single face and it's not pleasant to look at.

During the Cold War, to promote this mythology—because this is what we're talking about here—was the task of that segment of the Western press and political class with interest in keeping alive the dichotomy between good and evil, an image that celebrates Western democracy and denigrates everything else. Thus the exploiters are the Chinese communist industrialists, and not our fellow countrymen.

Now the Cold War has been over for twenty years but, in the general ignorance about this remote part of the world, this simplistic vision still enjoys a large following.

"In the West on one side there are those who still see the Chinese as people who put on a uniform and wave Little Red Books around, on the other as a nation of super-rich exploiters," sums up Arthur Kroeber, managing director of the economic research firm Dragonomics in Beijing.[14]

The generation of politicians who came to power in the West after the fall of the Berlin Wall does nothing to contradict this comic book vision of China, and indeed contributes to the creation of new myths shoring it up. Upon his nomination by the Obama administration, the United States Secretary of the Treasury Timothy Geithner denounced China for not revaluating their national currency, a policy, according to him, aimed at ensuring the high competitiveness of the "Made in China" label. And this propaganda diverts the public's attention from the credit crisis and from the recession created by Wall Street, the principal agents of which are now advisors to the American president. We should ask ourselves who in recent years has earned the most if Chinese products have dominated the international marketplace: the foreign businesses that produced them in China, and certainly not the Chinese assembly line workers.

A VERY INCONVENIENT TRUTH

For us Westerners the truth is extremely difficult to swallow. In order to modernize China, it's true that Deng laid the foundations of a system to exploit its labor force, but the ones to recreate the inhuman conditions of the Industrial Revolution in the country were entrepreneurs from Western democracies. And we find confirmation of this in our own backyard, in European factories, for example in the high-fashion sector where, according to the International Labour Organization (ILO), illegal Chinese workers toil day and night for starvation wages.[15]

The truth is also dangerous, because it would have us reflect on the role that large Western corporations play in the global village, and on the role reserved for us as consumers. A boycott of products sold by those responsible for such suffering is not so improbable a scenario. But do we have the courage to do it? The establishment thinks so; that's why newspapers are unwilling to publish articles denouncing companies that, among other things, pay large sums for advertising in their pages.

The truth is also very complex. The exploitation of Chinese labor is cruel, but does bring wealth to China. It's true that, in the 1980s and '90s, it was foreign industrialists who enjoyed the greatest advantages of delocalization, but it's also true that thanks to this the living standards of the Chinese people have improved significantly in the last thirty years.

Father Mario Marazzi, a missionary who spent forty years in Canton, agrees that China has finally escaped the grips of poverty, an assertion confirmed by the latest report of the International Monetary Fund (IMF) published in December 2009. Since 1950, when per capita income was at its lowest, the Chinese economy has made enormous progress, and in 2009 was equal to 13 percent of the world economy. The aim established by Deng at the end of the 1970s—the modernization of the country—is every day closer to being achieved. It is perhaps the greatest obstacle for us Westerners: to admit that a communist regime has done in China what capitalism did in England two centuries earlier; that two parallel worlds, those of Marx and of Deng, have in just two centuries converged; and that the "bad guys" are once again our own industrialists. But is this really what happened?

The Industrial Revolution had its own mythology too, rooted in the ideological battles of those years, which still today leads us to look at this phenomenon—from a social perspective—as an aberration rather than a necessary step in human progress. From this mythology is born the idea of the good and the bad in economics. Writers like Charles Dickens contributed to the creation of these myths in describing a world divided between good and evil. Their concern was with telling their readers about the great transformations of those years, and this Manichean vision of the world is among the best basic plots for a novel.

Dickens was not a reporter or an analyst, but a narrator—one could venture to describe his books as nineteenth-century pulp fiction. Against the backdrop of the great changes taking place, in as simple and compelling a manner as possible, he gave the readers what they wanted to read. His formula was a well-proven one: in the plots, women and children are exploited by a society in the process of industrialization. They are immortal stories, which had the merit of giving form to the specters looming over the period, but they do not necessarily cover reality in all its facets. Thus in *Hard Times*, the work that best describes the terrible consequences of the Industrial Revolution, the author never stops to look at the changing world with the eyes of the ex-farmer and now factory worker, concentrating rather on judging the capitalist exploiter.

But it is a fact that in England the division of labor and technological innovations produced by the Industrial Revolution improved the living conditions of the poor.

W. H. Hutt, in his 1925 essay "The Factory System of the Early Nineteenth Century," wrote:

> Compared to the factory workers, the agricultural laborers lived in abject poverty, and the work to which country children were put was far more exhausting than factory labor.[16]

A study by T. S. Ashton that Hutt cites in his essay shows how in 1831 the cost of the standard diet of the English poor was identical to that of 1791. But working in the factories and earning a wage, they could afford to eat more. The same can be said with regard to Chinese industrialization: in the 1950s and '60s, farmers were starving to death; from the time they became migrant workers their stomachs were doubtless less empty.

In comparison with the serfs and slaves of previous centuries, the workers described by Dickens in *Hard Times* are fortunate. And the Chinese who work in our countries today have better prospects than their grandparents and great-grandparents who were subjugated by Western colonialism. A forty-year-old Chinese man working illegally as a welder in a city in Tuscany, Italy, gives us a good picture of this

unknown aspect of capitalist exploitation.[17] He earns between
€700 and €800 a month. A pittance, by our standards. But all
the factories he worked in provided room and board and thus
he managed to send home €600 every month. Since his arrival
in Italy he has repaid the money he borrowed for the trip and
bought himself a house in China. His dream is to return to his
native country with ¥200,000 or ¥300,000 (approximately
€20,000 to €30,000), enough to buy his two sons a house and
live out his old age in peace. It is a feasible goal, which his
parents could never have even dreamed of. What made it
accessible to his generation was Deng Xiaoping's "open door"
policy and globalization.

Dickens wasn't the only one not to see any positive aspects
to the Industrial Revolution for those whom it exploited.
According to economist Thomas Malthus's renowned phrase:
"The increase in the wealth of nations had contributed little
or nothing to an improvement in the living conditions of the
poor." On the other side of the ideological barricade we find
Adam Smith who, as previously mentioned, sees in the egoism of nascent capitalism the divine power of the economy in
the form of the market's "invisible hand." And at an equal
distance from both positions? That's exactly where we find
Marx.

Karl Marx condemns the modes of production but does not
reject the process in toto. He's aware that industrialization,
whose troubles he knows well, is part of progress and a necessary phase of historical materialism. He maintains that the
exploitation of labor is an indispensable stage en route to the
dictatorship of the proletariat. It's an entirely similar argument to the one that led Deng Xiaoping to launch the "open
door" policy. Deng modernized Marx in order to apply him
to late twentieth-century China.

Outside mythologies past and present, the Industrial Revolution is simultaneously the triumph and the shame of the
Western bourgeoisie. Many people suffered but, for the first

time in history, control of the economy had nothing to do with birthright. And this is a great achievement. In the same way, Chinese capitalism is the triumph and the shame of Marxism. Its shame may have been widespread injustice, lack of personal freedom, and for many years a low standard of living. Its greatest achievement is to have made wealth accessible to all, without destroying socialism.

CHAPTER 3

CHINESE NOUVELLE CUISINE

MARXISM IN A NEOLIBERAL SAUCE

"Democracy in the West is a buffet where the customers select the cook, but not the dishes he serves. In China, on the contrary, it's always the same person doing the cooking and the customers choose what to eat from a rich menu." With these words the well-known Chinese political expert Fang Ning explains the difference that exists between our two worlds. The most famous Chinese chef, of course, is Deng Xiaoping, an ingenious cook who figured out how to transform the recipes of Marxism into an appetizing à la carte menu.

The death of Mao in 1976 closed an important and controversial chapter in China's history. The Cultural Revolution, to which even Deng fell victim, is a process that used violence to remove all traces of the West from historical memory and to reconnect the nation to its luminous imperial past.[1] Post-Maoist China appears on the world scene with a solid national identity, whose roots are in a culture belonging to the distant past, to the golden age of ancient dynasties. To become one of the protagonists of the future while remaining communist, this large nation needs to catch up with the times. That means adapting Marxism to the process of globalization; in other words, the cook will keep his position only if he learns how to cook new dishes.

51

INCREMENTAL DEMOCRACY

If today Shanghai is the new New York, an energetic and energizing metropolis, it is so thanks to Deng's "open door" policy. In contemporary China, as in few other nations in the world, one has the impression of being part of history, even if only in the capacity of spectator. Deng's dream, or, as he defined it, "socialist modernization," is thus taking shape.[2] But how many of us are aware of this? The media and our politicians' rhetoric continue to paint China as a nation oppressed by dictatorship, emphasizing its social inequalities—which certainly do exist—and remaining silent about its progress and modernizing thrust. And yet it is this socialist modernization that the Chinese celebrate today. According to Arthur Kroeber, freelance journalist and resident in China since 1987:

> The great achievement is that the Chinese government and the population have managed to creatively overcome the great historical challenges of the last thirty years. They have dismantled the majority of the socialist economy without creating social, political, or economic distortions. At least this is what happened to state-owned enterprises. They got started at the end of the 1990s, and in 2005 the workers in this sector only numbered 50 million, a process that lead to the breaking of some very old social promises. People lost pensions and health care guaranteed by the socialist system. But the government directed the transition well. In exchange for these certainties the population received the right to property, for example to the house in which they lived, but also the opportunity to become their own bosses. Thus the dismantling of the socialist economy assumed human connotations.[3]

Let's review some aspects of this metamorphosis in order to understand the passage from Maoism to the capitalism of today, but also to question some stereotypes.

At the end of the 1970s, the formula employed by Deng is that of the four modernizations: agriculture, industry, defense, and science. The first two, in particular, are significant because they open the economy up to the foreign market.

As we have already noted, between 1979 and 1981 the Party dismantled the collective farms, the old warhorse of Maoist Marxism. Farmers are permitted to raise pigs and poultry privately. It's the first step toward the institution of private property. Immediately afterward, the farmers start to rent small plots of land and to cultivate what they want to sell at the markets.[4] These changes are enough to shatter the collective farms, one of the cornerstones of Maoism, in only two years. And no one bends down to gather the shards; even the ultraconservative wing of the Party is happy about the results obtained. According to Zhao Ziyang in *Prisoner of the State*:

> Abandoning collectivization resolves a series of agricultural problems that beset the leadership, starting with the meager returns and productivity of the land, owing to the use of inappropriate crops.[5]

That's just what happened in the northwest of Shandong province.

Until 1983, the collective farms in this area had produced grain because the country experienced chronic shortages and Mao was obsessed with alimentary self-sufficiency.[6] During the Long March he had seen the poverty of the countryside first hand and resolved to put an end to it with collectivization. The northwest region of Shandong, however, where the soil had a high alkali salt content, was more suitable to the production of cotton. This too was in short supply in the country, but national agricultural programming gave precedence to food crops over all others—so Beijing forced the Shandong farmers to cultivate grain with mediocre results. Deng and Zhao revolutionized the system, introducing one of the basic concepts of the free market: trade with the outside world.

Thanks to imports, Shandong could trade cotton for grain crops.

"The farmers would sell cotton to the state (at the time, the state was importing large quantities of cotton), and in return the state would provide them with grain supplies," recalls Zhao in his memoirs.[7] Behind this reasoning we find David Ricardo's theory of comparative advantage. Why plant grain with meager results when you can successfully produce cotton and exchange it for imported grain?

The experiment pays off, such that in the course of two years Shandong is producing a surplus of cotton and cotton seeds as a by-product, which are used as fertilizer.

The dismantling of the collectives brings with it important changes for the federal and local governments of the villages; it is now the inhabitants who elect representatives to the village councils. By 1994 more than half of the villages are going to the polls and by 1998 they all are. No one in the West receives the update; the bombshell comes and goes completely unobserved.

What we have here is the most timid of first steps toward a system of popular participation. The candidates are in fact chosen from within the local branch of the Communist Party, but it is nevertheless a democratic achievement. It's important to remember that China likes to walk steady, not run pell-mell, to get where the nation is going.

"As we cross the river we touch one by one the boulders in the riverbed, stone after stone, only thus is it that the current will not carry us away," Deng used to repeat. And in 1998 in Buyun, a small town in Sichuan province, participative democracy takes another step toward the other bank of the river: anyone can stand for office, no party membership card necessary.

In an interview, Yu Keping, deputy director of the Compilation and Translation Bureau in Beijing, an organization of the foreign ministry born in the 1930s to instruct the Chinese in communism, called these changes "the stages of an incremental democratic process."[8] The meaning of this is explained for us by a university professor in Beijing who prefers to remain anonymous:

> Incremental democracy is slow democracy, a very pragmatic concept that is not very different from the political vision of Deng Xiaoping. It's a process of democratization, not a revolution. In the past there have been various attempts to create a democratic mechanism, between the parties and experiments at the village level. The real obstacle to democratic reforms in China is represented by the tension that exists between the traditional procedures of the CCP and democratic ideas.[9]

The supporters of incremental democracy reject shock therapy as it was imposed on the former Soviet bloc the day after the fall of Berlin Wall—the transition from communism to capitalism in the blink of an eye. Rather, democratic principles must spread out like a cascade that splashes water more or less everywhere. It's thus a matter of encouraging civil society to create isolated experiments, like the one in Buyun, which, if successful, can be replicated in other communities.[10] In the Chinese waterfall, it's a good idea to direct the water's path, rather than let it merely fall according to the laws of gravity with no other guidance. The democratic experiments in fact begin at the base of the social pyramid, in the agricultural villages. They start in the 800,000 villages and then move to the 38,000 small towns, the 2,500 counties, the 330 prefectures, the 34 provinces, and only then will they arrive at the central government.

In reality, our own democracies and our own bourgeoisie are also born at the base of the pyramid, as Patrick Chovanec points out:

> When we talk about China we always have to remember that in the last thirty years there have been incredible changes, like the development of a real middle class that is educated and owns property. We should reread Tocqueville's *Democracy in America*. It's essential to recognize that democracy's roots are first and foremost social. And this happens when people make themselves heard because they know they have to do it. Without well-being and personal freedom, all this would be impossible.[11]

SUPER DEMOCRACY: THE REALITY OF THE GLOBAL VILLAGE

Super Girl is one of the most popular television shows in China. It's a Chinese version of *American Idol*, an amateur singing contest. Every week, television viewers vote for who stays in the competition and who has to go home. Like all reality shows, the program has very little in the way of cultural aspirations. During the last season, in 2006, it received eight hundred million text messages. Many have attributed *Super Girl*'s popularity to the fact that viewers can exercise their right to vote. It's possible, but this explanation fails to take into account the fact that the Chinese, as inhabitants of the global village, are voyeurs. Indeed, as in all reality shows, the victory never goes to the singer with the most talent, but to the one with whom the majority of the viewers identify.

In the West, we enjoy instead a political reality show that we might call "Super Democracy." The characters are the politicians of the former Soviet bloc countries. Here as well we cheer on contestants with little talent for democracy simply because they mimic the behavioral models exemplified by our own equally untalented politicians. Just look at democratic Russia, where the people brought to power by the fall of the Berlin Wall have managed to recreate the poverty, inequality, corruption, and widespread organized crime characteristic of the darkest years of czarism. Russia's current "czars" are among the best friends of many Western governments, starting with Italy.

In the program's Afghan version, Hamid Karzai is reelected despite evidence that corruption and criminality have increased under his direction. We watch as our leaders celebrate his victory, even as only days before the European Union and the United States had denounced the many instances of electoral fraud. Karzai wins the "Super Democracy" reality show because he's the candidate we Westerners identify with the most—he speaks our language, has studied and lived in the West for years, and knows how to flatter our politicians. He also wins because for us, who only vote, who no longer take to the streets or frequent the local branch of some party, politics has become completely voyeuristic.

In China, the people still interact, especially when it's a question of matters that affect them. In the neighborhoods, when something's not right, people get together; we've all seen the battles fought by those unwilling to abandon their houses to make way for new skyscrapers. Victory is irrelevant; what matters is that politics is part of daily life and doesn't degenerate into a reality television show, as has unfortunately happened in many formerly communist countries.

The democracy + well-being pair whose praises were sung by those living in the Soviet bloc was in fact reduced to rubble along with the bricks of the Berlin Wall. The Chinese took note of this, and while they import our music and television formats, they haven't bought the political reality show. Why?

In China, Western-style democracy is often associated with

three great political upheavals: the disintegration of the Soviet bloc following Gorbachev's opening up to the west (Perestroika); the popular democracy of the Chinese Cultural Revolution, persecuted by Mao in the purges; and the independence of Taiwan after the escape of Chiang Kai-shek.[12] Thus, democracy is a synonym for chaos, for a lack of control. And the Communist Party of China contributed to this "apocalyptical" vision when, after the events of Tiananmen and the fall of the Berlin Wall, it emphasized the equation "Western democracy = chaos."

Since 2001, it has become more and more difficult to combat this vision, ever since, that is, the images of "democratic" Iraq in flames, the explosion in the production of opium in Afghanistan, and the accusations of fraud in the Afghan elections have filled television newscasts the world over.

The Chinese have no interest in importing our democracy because it is unsuitable to the Chinese reality. Beijing is perfectly aware that universal suffrage can be introduced with relative ease in a country in transition—just call for elections. Rather less simple is the prospect of accompanying them with a respect for the rule of law. In the "Super Democracy" reality show, it's easy to vote for the candidate we identify with the most, but it's virtually impossible to evaluate if he or she really holds the values that we, and not our politicians, consider indispensable. Will he really be as honest as he says? Will she allow herself to be corrupted? Questions that, at home on the couch, we are unable to answer.

Seen from Beijing, it's of little importance that they're voting in Iraq or Afghanistan, nations in the grip of wars which have destroyed the very fabric of civil society, countries where hundreds of thousands of people have been killed and even greater numbers displaced. In these democracies there is no respect for the law, the sole instrument that limits the power bestowed by the people on those who represent them.

Democracy creates the rules, the law ensures that they are

respected; this is the principle of good government. Without the law, rules remain just words. But whereas democracy as a "technique" can be exported, the spirit of respect for the law is a cultural acquisition, impossible to impose on a people. And the key question those in Asia have been asking themselves for the last twenty years is the following: which of the two achievements, universal suffrage or rule of law, is more important for an emerging country? Is it better to rely on the law (as the Asian Tigers Singapore and Hong Kong did) or on the ballot box (as did so many developing nations, from the ex-Yugoslavia to Rwanda)?

Those who after the fall of the Berlin Wall chose the second option did so for economic reasons, because the democracy package proposed progress, well-being, and wealth. It's time we realized that it was on the economic rather than the ideological front that the Cold War was fought. In the collective imaginary of communist bloc inhabitants, the West's victory was to have cemented the equation "democracy = American consumerism, well-being, and modernity." And this is true for all those countries in transition that have embraced the Western democratic model. On the home stretch of the race to the ballot box one could make out not "Universal Suffrage" but "Riches," and the vote became the doping that would allow for winning the race and with it the purse.

EN ROUTE TO MODERNITY

China is taking part in the same marathon but with different stimulants. Upending the concept of Western democracy that the Chinese consider synonymous with disorder, the Party has concentrated on the rule of law. Even the Chinese intellectual Left, the so-called New Left, agrees on the fact that "the Chinese model rests on the rule of law and on the direct participation of citizens rather than on elections."[13]

It is undeniable that in the last twenty years China has

taken giant steps toward the empowerment of its juridical institutions, for example in the business field—even the Americans admit it. In an editorial published on November 11, 2009, in the *International Herald Tribune*, John Watkins, president of the American Chamber of Commerce in China, affirmed precisely this: "China is enacting a series of laws in defense of the environment and against corruption and has respected the legal framework of the WTO."[14]

Watkins is also convinced that Beijing has demonstrated great juridical maturity with respect to the tariffs on imports imposed by Washington, DC, at the end of 2009, remaining unmoved in the face of American protectionism during 2010 and 2011 as well.

It is also the case that in the last twenty years China has invented forms of alternative participation, obviously guided by the state, that involve the population in the political decision-making process, such as public consultations, meetings with experts, social research, and experiments at the level of civil society. As we will see below, the press plays an important role in the continuous dialogue that is established between the public and politicians.

Wang Shaoguang, leader of the New Left, terms this model "deliberative democracy." The days when the great helmsman keeps the ship under control are over.

"Every new Chinese leader has less power than his predecessor."[15] Thus Jing Huang describes the changes at the summit of the Party. He is echoed by Wang Dong, a political expert at the Brookings Institution in Washington, DC, when he claims that the majority of the policies are the fruit of deliberation and therefore that Hu Jintao cannot dictate law to the politburo.

In the future, Chinese politics will revolve around the concept of deliberative democracy and the elections in which civil society will participate will play a supplementary role for the central government.

Today many foreigners cannot manage to understand how it is possible that China is growing economically without a form of government similar to Western democracy. The challenge for the government is how to ensure sustained growth while maintaining stability. This is a complex question. The country must solve the problem of corruption, reinforce the rule of law, and reduce economic imbalances (especially those between city and countryside). But many of these problems are interconnected.[16]

To return to the culinary analogy, civil society must figure out how to communicate to the chef what it wants to eat. But the chef must convince civil society that it is better if the composition of the main course, the side dish, and the presentation are left to him.

China thus draws inspiration from the success of other Asian countries, the so-called Tigers: Singapore, Hong Kong, Taiwan, and South Korea. These are not democratic countries, but societies in which the rule of law is strong. The Asian Tigers figured out how to create a new type of government, the development state,[17] in which legitimacy is not connected to democratic elections but to the ability of leaders to sustain uninterrupted economic growth.[18] Deng took them as examples when he became convinced that the CCP had to modernize the country if it wanted to survive. The first step became to bring profit back to the center of the economy.

At the end of the 1970s, Deng knew that the class struggle belonged to the past, to Maoism, which had used it as an instrument to redesign national identity. He didn't know what to make of this weapon; he needed different instruments, those of the market economy. Paradoxically, only then would he be able to complete the work begun by Mao—restoring the greatness of China—and, as we will see, that of Marx as well—overcoming the stage of the dictatorship of the proletariat to give life to a new and modern society. Here then is the recipe for Deng's nouvelle cuisine: Marxism in a capitalist sauce.

The hard-to-swallow ingredient on this menu is the economic inequalities that the new system necessarily creates, heresy in a communist society. In order to make it more palatable to the Chinese, Deng coined new mottos, diametrically opposed to the Maoist ones: "Let some people get rich first, so they can help others do the same."

The formula worked, and the Chinese abandoned the class struggle for that of the market, even at the risk of being discriminated against economically; thanks to the profit motive, everyone hoped to be among the first to enrich themselves.

And only Deng could attempt this experiment because he knew Western economic theories so well. He first started to analyze them in the 1970s when he fell out of favor and was forced to retire in disgrace from all of his positions. Unlike Mao, who never left China, Deng is part of the first generation of the revolutionary elite to have lived abroad. In 1924, at the age of twenty, he worked in a Renault factory in Billancourt, France. In 1926 he moved to Moscow where he studied Marxism-Leninism, and it is only in 1927 that he returned home with the idea of applying Marx's principles to China in innovative and pragmatic ways, distancing himself from the Soviet experiment.

Deng is a man who knew how to look beyond the Great Wall, and this curiosity led to his being purged from the Party three times and even to his being pilloried as a traitor to the nation, one of the "capitalist roaders." It was precisely beyond the Great Wall that he was looking when in 1979 he managed to take Mao's place. The goal he set for himself, to reconcile Marxist theory with Western neoliberalism, is an enterprise that many judge to be, not only impossible, but absurd.

"Planning and market forces are both ways of controlling

economic activity,"[19] Deng affirmed in the phrase that sums up his philosophy. But they are not opposing theories; socialism does not exclude the market economy because "whatever promotes the socialist economy is socialist."[20] Here is the motto that would allow the Communist Party of China to survive the disintegration of the ideology defeated with the collapse of the Berlin Wall.

Deng was right. Economic theory only provides instruments with which to guide the economy; the tools of Marxism do not exclude those of the free market and vice versa. The error of the USSR was precisely their dogmatic interpretations of Marxism-Leninism and Stalinism, a rigidity then exported everywhere under the banner of the hammer and sickle.

At this point, between the 1970s and '80s, Deng is no longer the only one making such reflections. All the communist leaders were perfectly aware of the error undermining their governments, but no one had the courage to confront it or knew how to resolve it. In 1979, the Soviet KGB went so far as to produce a series of documents predicting the collapse of communism in the Soviet Union in the course of a decade. The reasons were all linked to the inefficiency of the socialist economic system.[21]

Meanwhile, beyond the Iron Curtain in Western Europe and the United States, the standard of living continued to improve. The principles of the free market offered democratic politicians a series of instruments easily adaptable to the contingent needs of their respective nations. The response to the first oil crisis of 1973–1974 became a key example of the Western capitalist model's greater flexibility with respect to the Soviet model, emerging as it did from the Bretton Woods Agreements, which created institutions such as the IMF and the World Bank.

Thanks to the intervention of the IMF, the West avoided, in the short term, the worst of the energy crisis. The IMF became the guarantor for the recycling of petrodollars, channeling the larger deposits from the producing countries, linked to the increase in the price of crude oil, to the accounts of the big Western banks. The banks then used these deposits to reduce the trade deficit of the oil-importing countries. In effect, OPEC loaned money to its own customers, against whom it had launched an embargo on account of their support of Israel, and left the management of everything to their own bankers. Hypocrisy? Perhaps, but it worked, and it was this result that counted in Deng's eyes. Western governments had used the principles of capitalism to resolve an international political crisis. These are the strategies that Chinese Marxism would need in order to not end up as Russian communism did—in ruins.

Thus, when the new leader set to work, he did so in a pragmatic manner: putting an end to ideology, for starters. The trial of the Gang of Four was transmitted worldwide; Maoism's deterioration could be seen on the planet's television screens. The charge was having manipulated power. An analogous situation in the Soviet Union, with its politburo mummified by ideology, would have been unthinkable. The Chinese leadership itself thus admitted that communism can err, that it is not infallible; and what mattered was that the Party realized this and sought to do something constructive about it. To condemn communism in toto and seek its end would mean throwing out the baby with the bathwater.

In the end, the people had the impression that justice had triumphed. The person who benefited from this consensus was Deng, with whom many identified in a way they never had with Mao. No longer was it a case of a man presenting himself as the reincarnation of the emperor, an impersonal leader devoted to the cult of personality. The new helmsman reached people's hearts by using their language and interacting with them. In the reality show of Chinese politics, entirely unlike our own, Deng had talent to burn and displayed a modernity ahead of his time. His popularity undoubtedly aided the transition to capitalism.

The ideological cleansing renewed the pragmatic spirit innate in the Chinese people and prepared the country for the great leap. It demolished the existing relationship between ideology and state organization as shaped by Mao, in which the state's function is to manage economic affairs. *Coordination* and *consensus* became the government's magic words, concepts replacing the revolutionary and Maoist *contradiction* and *class struggle*. The return to pragmatism spurred private initiative and recognized the importance of market forces. But in all this, China remained a communist country—the cook is the same, he's just trying out new specialties.

CHAPTER 4

BEYOND THE GREAT WALL

In 1421 a fleet of eight hundred Chinese ships set off for the world. It was an exceptional event, because China had always been an isolationist and not very curious country. The inspiration for the expedition was the emperor Zhu Di. The fleet was tasked with gathering riches and completing a detailed map of the continents. But the real aim was another: to make the greatness of China known to the barbarians who lived in faraway lands, in order to assimilate them culturally and have them live according to Confucian principles of harmony. The aim bears a striking resemblance to modern globalization, with the difference that today's homogenizing element is Western culture.

The fleet set sail and arrived in America seventy years before Christopher Columbus, discovered Australia and New Zealand more than a century before European navigators, and circumnavigated the globe one hundred years before Magellan. During the voyage, the Chinese left behind on the various continents a trail of agricultural products from the mother country, plants and spices that in the centuries to come would feed and clothe the entire planet. According to this reconstruction, a substantial part of the products that the conquistadores brought back to Europe from the American continent originally hailed from China.

Upon its return, the Chinese fleet discovered a nation profoundly different from the one left behind two years earlier. The emperor had been deposed and the country had fallen prey to political and economic chaos, torn apart by fratricidal struggles. No one was interested in listening to the stories of the expedition and learning about its discoveries. The ships rotted in the ports, the onboard diaries were destroyed together with the maps of the continents visited; nothing of that historic voyage was saved, everything swallowed up in the oblivion of the civil war. Once peace had been restored, after years of instability, China again withdrew into strict isolation.

The story that Gavin Menzies tells in *1421*, a book that traces the Chinese fleet's voyage around the world in great detail, leads us to rewrite our history but not China's.[1] The desire to live behind the Great Wall is a constant that has characterized the country for five thousand years, to the point where disinterest in the world has often been mistaken for its great strength.

Every time that China attempted to open itself up to the world, something would happen to force it to retrace its steps. The last instance dates back to the first half of the twentieth century, during the regime of Chiang Kai-shek, when an unprecedented flood of Chinese students poured into Western universities.

European culture attracted the intellectuals, including members of the Communist Party. Mao was among the few to prove unsusceptible to such fascination and remain in the country. However, this exchange with the external world became a mere interlude, cut short by the civil war between the CCP and the Nationalists, the Long March, and the invasion by Japan. Following the Communist Party's victory, the Great Helmsman imposed a period of isolation both economic and cultural. Once again, China had burned its bridges with the world. As in 1423, what had been learned in the West was left to rot, a process of forgetting that the Cultural Revolution completed with surgical precision.

According to this reading of China's history, the Great Wall is first of all a state of mind, a protective barrier against everything that comes from the outside, which the Chinese have always perceived as dangerous. To look beyond China seemed unnatural, dangerous, and useless. But in the end, to save socialism, it would be necessary to do so. This is just what Deng decided in 1979. It wasn't enough to declare, as Deng often did, that Mao had been "right 70 percent of the time and wrong 30 percent," it was necessary to tear down centuries of isolationist culture, and make people forget the humiliation of colonization, the atrocities of the Japanese army, and the loss of Taiwan. It was an almost impossible operation.

MARKET MARXISM

The debate about the creation of the first Special Economic Zone in Shenzhen, which inaugurates the industrial sector's process of modernization, epitomizes the tension inside the CCP between futurists (Deng's supporters) and dogmatists (those who remained bound to Marxism-Leninism).

In 1979, the national Chinese and provincial Guangdong governments rechristened the small city of Bao'an, with just over 300,000 inhabitants, with the name Shenzhen. The proximity of Hong Kong, still an English colony, was fundamental because it was China's natural outlet to the world, a trade channel of great importance. Thus, Hong Kong played a key role in the development of the first Special Economic Zone, not only for reasons of geography but also due to political factors. Deng ably "negotiated" with the English for the colony's return. He proposed a new model: a single nation with two economic systems.[2] Hong Kong would remain capitalist even when it returned to communist China. Shenzhen became the bridge between these two realities, the communist mainland and neoliberal Hong Kong. More importantly, Shenzhen became the laboratory where China's new economic formula was tested.

Naturally, Shenzhen lacked the infrastructure needed to conduct this experiment in "market Marxism," but the state did not have the money to finance its construction. The alternative was to license the land to foreign industrialists and use these proceeds to begin the work. This was the first real obstacle Deng encountered within the Party.

The dogmatic wing was violently opposed to the idea, and justified their position using the example of Macao. Licensed to Portugal in the sixteenth century as a place for fishermen to dry out their nets, the island was transformed into a Portuguese colony. It's one thing to reduce one's labor force to a commodity, another to "mortgage" the land, even if only for a limited period—this was the opposition's message. It took Deng months to put down the revolts inside the CCP and defend himself against those who called for his resignation; the opposition was as intense from the traditionalist conservatives, as from the Marxist-Leninists.[3] In the end, as often happens in China, practical sense won out; given that the country lacked the economic and financial muscles to modernize on its own, there was no alternative but to make use of foreign capital. Thus the land was licensed to foreigners.[4]

Of course, the experiment remains strictly limited to the Special Economic Zones. In 1987, an American of Chinese origin, Ling Tung Yen, asked to rent for twenty or thirty years the uninhabited zone of Pudong in Shanghai, the current financial center of the city. The offer was extremely generous and the project ambitious, but the Party refused. In *Prisoner of the State*, Zhao makes the comment that if Ling Tung Yen had had his way, Pudong would have been developed fifteen years earlier. But China had no intention of rushing.

Despite the fierce opposition, Deng's policy ultimately changed the Party and restructured it according to new principles. An ideological earthquake was taking place in the minds of CCP members.

The ruling class, made up of men and women born during

the century of foreign humiliation, who had seen the country rise again after the shameful experience of colonialism thanks to Marxism and Maoism and who had survived the Cultural Revolution, reinvented themselves, this time based on certain principles of the market economy. Deng suggested that they study the example of the Asian Tigers, among them Taiwan, which had for more than thirty years been a real thorn in China's side.

This might not seem like much, but let's ask ourselves what Western democracy today would be disposed, for the good of the country, to so completely question itself, and what government would have the courage to distance itself politically to such an extent, not just from a precedent of the same political stripe, but from itself. When Deng proposed abolishing the collective farms, the cornerstone of Maosim, and renting out Chinese land to foreigners, this is precisely what he did.

What European head of state today would admit that the exportation of democracy to Iron Curtain countries was an error, that the transition should have been planned; what American president would publicly declare that the invasion of Iraq has been counterproductive for world peace? China, in putting the Gang of Four on trial, made just such a mea culpa. We tell ourselves that democracy also means the freedom to change one's mind; it would thus seem logical if our governments admitted to their own errors with greater serenity than a communist regime does under the same circumstances—and yet that's not the case.

Let's return to the culinary analogy from the last chapter. In the West, universal suffrage is the instrument employed to change the cook in the kitchen. As we will see in the third part of this book, today this type of change is not so easy; no politician or party believes any longer in alternating governments, and this is also true for those who have burned every dish, or who offer us the same menu day after day. No one has the courage to experiment with new specialties for fear of being fired—not by the customers, the people, who don't count, but by the older cooks. There are no substitutions and no innovation, apart from some sauce. The result is not very satisfying, the food at the democracy buffet is poor, and the customers are unhappy, but don't really know why.

Mark Leonard, in his book *What Does China Think?*, argues that "unlike the political parties in Western democracies, the CCP possesses a great capacity for self-criticism, in short it knows how to question itself."[25]

It's possible. Modernizing China required uncommon mental honesty and a good dose of courage because it bound the Party's destiny to that of the national economy. And no one really knew what would come of that union.

A few years after Mao's death, Deng put an end to the class struggle, epitomized by the Long March and the Communist Revolution, and established a new paradigm in which the legitimacy of the CCP depends on the population's well-being, just like in many democracies. This goal became the foundation of a new social pact between Party and citizens. It's a matter of radically reformulating two models, the Marxist and the capitalist, and yet in the West we didn't notice a thing. Why?

Because the world we live in remains steeped in the rhetoric of the Cold War, and Marxism remains ideologically linked to its Soviet incarnations: first Leninism and then Stalinism.

READING MARX IN BEIJING

In the mid 1980s it was impossible to find a local beer in Beijing, even though there was a giant brewery in the city. In bars and restaurants one could only find bottles from the most disparate regions of the country: Mongolia, Guangdong, even distant Guangxi. The only thing missing was beer from Tibet. And since these were imported products, the cost was higher than that of local beer. In this first phase of the opening up of Chinese markets, the system of prices imposed a ceiling on local products while leaving unregulated the prices of products imported from other provinces. The scarcity of local beer lasted only a season, but that was long enough to enrich the person responsible for it.

A group of Chinese entrepreneurs took advantage of local protectionism, an intermediate stage on the way toward the complete liberalization of prices, to make money. This group bought all the beer produced in Beijing and exported it to other regions. Meanwhile, they imported beer from these regions and sold it in the capital at a higher price. This little trick was repeated all over the country. The same trucks that left the brewery in Shenzhen for Beijing returned with bottles from the capital, creating an incessant traffic that for a season slaked the thirst of a nation.[26]

And the return? ¥300,000 (approximately €30,000) in just under six months, a small fortune in the China of those years, when people earned a fraction of that amount of money in a year of hard work.

Even if it had all the characteristics of the free market, that is, a group of entrepreneurs exploiting an opportunity, this beer speculation took place in a communist country, with an economy that was still predominantly Marxist—including state-owned breweries. And this was still the time of the Soviet Union and the Iron Curtain. But it's worthwhile to remember that even if we have difficulty distinguishing between Marxism and Bolshevism, the differences between the two are profound.

Indeed, after the Bolshevik Revolution, all the communist movements and parties absorbed the Leninist doctrine and its application by Stalin. Soon the experience of the USSR became the official interpretation and the empirical test of Marxism. This false identity was consolidated during the long years of the Cold War, when the Soviet fiasco dragged through the mud all the writings of Marx it never fully understood.

Unlike the Soviet Union, the modernization of China closely followed the economic prophecies of Marx. It is in the Chinese experience that we truly discover the originality and flexibility of his thought. Marx devoted almost his entire authorial production to an analysis of the faults of the capitalist system and only a very small part to a description of the communist society of the future. The two fundamental passages of the "future Marxist" theory concern the dictatorship of the proletariat and the classless society, the functioning of which the author could only imagine in the broadest terms. Marx was first and foremost a sociologist and an economist, and after spending his whole life in observation of the radical economic changes redesigning the world in which he lived, only timidly did he venture, almost as a common sensical conclusion to his economic analysis, into the field of political philosophy. He possessed neither the instruments nor the inclination to compete with Plato; his future vision of the world is thus in some ways merely an outline, not the detailed one you might expect had he been a political philosopher by training.

Lenin and Stalin, on the other hand, were politicians. They observed the reality surrounding them in order to shape it according to a very precise scheme they themselves developed: communism in a single country, Russia. Thus, they painted according to Marx's sketch the picture of Bolshevik Marxism. Lenin was no philosopher, and everyone knows who Stalin was—it's not surprising that it was difficult for them to conceive of the world beyond their borders, or that their vision lacked universality.

Mao didn't know what to make of this model. Even though China was like Russia, fundamentally an agricultural nation, the two peoples were radically different. Thus, the Chinese leader took what he needed from Marxist theory, the revolutionary element—the dictatorship of the proletariat that later became a permanent reality. And rereading Marx in Beijing, one is forcefully reminded of how the author had predicted that this form of government could also be oppressive, just like the bourgeois form was. In this instance, it would be the masses rather than the elite exercising tyrannical power. While a step forward with respect to the capitalist state, the dictatorship of the elite is, of course, not the final goal.

Let's pause for a moment on this word "dictatorship," chosen by Marx to describe this phase in the evolution of capitalism, and that presupposes the existence of a structure of exploitation. At this point, the means of production are in the hands of the people; thus, productive activity belongs to the entire population. And yet the state must remain an integral part of the process. Why? Because exploitation continues.

Removing profit from the hands of the capitalists doesn't mean destroying all the discrimination of the capitalist economy. It's true that, as the working class takes possession of the entire cake, rather than just receiving crumbs from the boss, wages become more equal. However, what's missing in this phase is a system of equal opportunity, the freedom of choice that in the neoliberal system is the soul of private initiative.

Deng's interpretation of Marx took the concept of equal opportunity into account. Marx never talked about abolishing profit; however, he did air the possibility that the state would disappear with the destruction of the economic inequalities that maintained it. A utopia? It certainly became an unattainable utopia to the Soviets. The Party became the domain of the new elite, those born of the Revolution, a permanent institution becoming ever more authoritarian, an oligarchy analogous to a new aristocracy and certainly not the vehicle for a transition from the dictatorship of the proletariat to a communist society. What arose in the USSR was not Marxism but a totalitarian regime created by Bolshevism.

The utopian classless society has no need of a party to

guide it; everything and everyone is in harmony. This was an image that corresponded incredibly well, as we will see, with the vision of Confucius and that of the emperor Zhu Di. An unattainable prospect, of course, and yet it was this utopia that motivated Deng.

The new leader decided that the evolution toward the classless society would have to pass through private initiative, a choice that reintroduced economic inequalities into China. At first glance, the road taken seemed to go against the principles of Marxism, and opposition within the Party was fierce. But the new leader reversed the equation: inequality is born from the lack of opportunity. If everyone takes off from the same starting blocks, someone will arrive first and someone last, according to their abilities, but this is not inequality—it's equal opportunity.

"I exploited the local protectionism to my advantage. But everyone had equal opportunities to do so, right?" recounts one of the beer speculators.[7] Up to this point, it would appear that we are heading for a scenario very similar to that of the West, whose fundamental points of reference are the market and competition. But what's different is the conception of the role of politics when the ideal horizon being aimed at is the disappearance of the state itself.

Once equal opportunities are guaranteed, the role of the state (that is, the Party) as guarantor of the interests of all against every abuse can, as a matter of fact, gradually diminish and, who knows, maybe even disappear. Power can be decentralized to the regions, to the provinces, to the small towns. Here's a specific design we can work with. And indeed, following the revolutionary phase of the dictatorship of the proletariat, the decentralization of power takes off.

Deng restructured China like a multinational corporation: "The central government is the board of directors and local governments are the managers that make it work,"[8] explains Liu Kaiming. Managing directors control the economy of their own region and pass on a percentage to the board of directors.

This program involved the progressive abolition of all inefficient state-owned companies and the introduction of private initiative. In 1998 in China, there were 64,737 state-owned companies, employing a total of 110 million workers. At the end of 2005, the state possessed only 27,477 companies and the number of workers had gone down by 40 percent, to 64 million. In the same period, the number of private businesses rose from 10,667 to 123,820; the number of workers employed in the private sector from 9.7 to 34.5 million.[9] In the short term, it must be said, the state industry restructuring process had a disastrous effect on employment and the workers were forced to reorganize themselves as best they could.

At the same time, the power of local authorities grew. Today, 7 percent of the central government's income comes from Shenzhen and 12 percent from Guangdong. These numbers alone explain why the SEZ local authorities are permitted nearly unlimited freedom, to the point that many of them are transformed into private businesses. Like the Blue Village.

Not far from Shenzhen, this town was born in the aftermath of the Maoist Revolution as a "rural brigade," as the first Chinese collective farms were known. In 1984 the local government established a manufacturing concern and in 1992 the village was transformed into a collective enterprise, a hybrid uniting the principles of socialist collectivism with those of the market economy. The village population became the owners, and thus was born the municipality of the Blue Village. Given that it was at this point a business, it asked for and obtained permission to become independent from the central government with regard to the management of foreign capital and trade—and this explains the incentive for the change.

It's easy to understand the frequency, during the 1980s and '90s, of such metamorphoses in the Special Economic Zones.[10]

And the local authorities were on hand to direct them. The transformation of rural villages into industrial enterprises was part of the country's modernization, which some have termed "local state corporatism."[11]

TIME IS MONEY

According to a modern Chinese saying, if you've never worked in Beijing, you'll never know how insignificant your job is; if you've never gone shopping in Shanghai, you'll never know how poor you are; and if you've never been with the girls of Shenzhen, you'll never know how little stamina you have. This last-named city is, for better or worse, the model on which contemporary China's evolution is based.

In the 1980s it was growing virtually before one's very eyes, thanks to foreign investments and migration. In 1995 it already had 3.45 million inhabitants, growing to 4.3 million by 2000. In 2007 it was estimated that more than 17 million people lived in the Special Economic Zone, approximately 70 percent of them migrant workers. In the 1990s its economy was growing at a rate of 28 percent annually, a real record even according to the standards of Southeast Asia. Soon skyscrapers, highways, restaurants, and fashionable stores transformed the abandoned villages of pearl divers and rice fields into a city that never sleeps.

All the Special Economic Zones became the engines of the Chinese economy, which thanks to them grew at a rate right out of the Industrial Revolution: from 1978 to 2007, Chinese GDP quadrupled. As more Zones opened, they followed Shenzhen's example, reproducing its structure down to the smallest detail.

On the other side of the world, in Eastern Europe and in the former Soviet Republics of Central Asia, where since the fall of the Berlin Wall the communist countries have begun their capitalist adventure, the scene is rather different. Post-communist modernism is called neoliberalism and democracy. It doesn't bring the quality of life everyone dreamed of; on the contrary, it relegated these countries to a secondary position with respect to Western economies. For example, in 2009 the Baltic Republics risked bankruptcy on account of the credit crisis; Hungary saw the growth of "democratic" dissidents lamenting the loss of communism; and from Western Europe rose up an antagonistic and racist wind against the immigrants from the East.

For the countries of the former Soviet bloc, being thrown into the "Super Democracy" reality show didn't mean improvements in the standard of living, which is what they expected in the euphoria of 1989. Instead, the Russian mafia took this opportunity to plunder both Soviet women and those unfortunate residents of Eastern Europe who found themselves unemployed after the economic collapse following the end of communism. Sold as commodities, they ended up on the sidewalks and in the brothels of the global village.[12]

Paradoxically, Chinese communism proved better able to navigate in the tumultuous waters of globalization. Recently red Europe might have imagined itself newly free, but meanwhile Asia had become rich. And for the first time this advantage weighed heavily because supremacy in the post–Cold War world was based not on military but economic power. Now, sustained growth is not a new phenomenon; we've already seen it during the Industrial Revolution and in the postwar period. However, it is only with the collapse of the Soviet system that it becomes capable of redrawing the equations of power and international political stability in favor of the Asian nations—the rich ones, of course.[13]

A similar experiment in Western Europe would be unthinkable; the neoliberal model that spread through democratic countries at the end of the 1980s is too rigid to allow this type of experiment. But the Chinese communist system is rigid as well and, paradoxically, it's the events of Tiananmen and three years of struggle inside the Party that renders it flexible enough to launch itself into the new capitalist adventure. To tell us this story we move to an unexpected parallel—between wretched Iceland and rich China.

CHAPTER 5

THE NEOLIBERAL DREAM OF MODERNIZATION

Among the most astonishing victims of the credit crisis is Iceland, a country bordering the Arctic Circle that has a population of just 320,000, the same number to be found in a neighborhood of Rome or Milan.

Is it possible that the origins of this tiny nation's bankruptcy can help us understand the choices made in distant 1989 by the leadership of the most populous country on earth, China? Could the Icelandic parable provide an interpretive lens through which to view the negative consequences of the collapse of the Berlin Wall on the part of the world that embraced the neoliberal credo?

Between these two exceptional events, in appearance so historically as well as geographically distant from each other, there is actually a subtle connection that we could in this case call the neoliberal dream of modernization.

At first glance, China and Iceland have absolutely nothing in common, but the resemblances are in fact numerous. In the second half of the last century, both nations burned with the desire for renewal; traumatized by colonization, they have sought to redeem themselves from this humiliation by means of their own recipe for modernity. They are also populations endowed with very strong national identities, characterized by the isolation that for centuries guaranteed them an internal equilibrium of which they have always been proud, destroyed by the arrival of the colonizers. And this national— we could almost say primitive—pride permeates above all the citizen's personal sphere, which revolves around the extended family and the community to which he or she belongs. The individual exists first and foremost as a function of the social realities in which he or she is inserted, and is lost without them. It is therefore easy to understand why, at a certain point in their history, these populations embraced the communitarian principles of socialism, which must have appeared to them as the natural evolution of the social dimension.

There are points of contact between the two nations on the economic level as well. World War II marked the end of colonization for both, but although free, China and Iceland remained poor countries with outdated agrarian economies, lacking any industry in step with the times. They are fully aware of this "historical lag," which they in part attribute to colonization. During the years of the Cold War they sought to overcome colonization in a misguided attempt to develop heavy industry. How can we not recall Mao's "Great Leap Forward," a plan for development that was to lead China to produce massive quantities of steel? It would have been better to rename the disastrous project the "Great Fiasco Ahead."

A final, crucial parallelism: in the 1980s, these two nations found themselves in a stage of profound transition, obliged to reconsider their industrial policies and their role in a globalizing world. It was a delicate process, influenced by the great upheavals taking place all over the world, which neither could control or change and which would bring Iceland and China to make diametrically opposed choices.

DESTINIES NO LONGER CROSSED

In response to the political storm of 1989, Iceland decided to enthusiastically embrace the neoliberal credo and transform the entire nation into a giant hedge fund. China, on the other hand, remained communist and distanced itself from the West. In the economic woods, the paths of the two countries diverged.

In the aftermath of 1989, Iceland became a neoliberal laboratory. In the next twenty years, daily papers and glossy magazines would describe it as the economic miracle of the century. They praised the local banks that competed with the giants of Wall Streets and exulted in 2005 when, three years before the bankruptcy, the United Nations declared it the country with the second highest per capita income in the world. Behold, spake the vox populi, the glaring proof that neoliberalism functioned as a model of economic development and modernization. Up until the explosion of the credit crisis, this is, in fact, what all the politicians said and what we read in the newspapers.

Let's leap ahead to Iceland's capital Reykjavik today. At this point, everything is for sale and only a few lucky ones have a job. The Icelanders' per capita debt has so many zeroes that no one any longer bothers to assess it. The country has gone bankrupt, entering the hit parade of the world's poorest. The fashionable boutiques are empty, so too are the bars where in the roaring years of neoliberalism the young lions of high finance guzzled till dawn. Today the compassion of the media and of governments is reserved for the Icelanders who beg money from the IMF for fishing boat fuel or containers in which to store the milk they have returned to using to produce that rich and flavorful butter the Scandinavians like so much. The island's economy once again depends on agriculture and on fish, precisely those productive assets that the neoliberal dream of modernization suggested they should abandon.

Let's jump back in time. A few months before the collapse of the Berlin Wall, Beijing filled the pages of newspapers around the world with its bloody repression of the demonstrations that had for weeks animated Tiananmen Square. In public opinion the world over, it was a gesture that confirmed the profoundly repressive nature of Chinese communism. As previously noted, from that moment on China assumed for the West a double face: a danger for humanity and a nation oppressed by communism. Thus began an ideological earthquake that would spare no one.

The Western Left, already weakened by the falling apart of the Soviet system, takes the blow very badly. Indeed, it has little idea how to respond to the accusations raining down from all sides against the Chinese regime, and so it cuts its ties with the communist dream and does everything possible to build a new identity around the word "democracy." The process that would strip the Marxist credo from Western communist and socialist parties thus began in the spring of 1989 with the events of Tiananmen and not with the collapse of the Berlin Wall. It was the end of an age, and the beginning of a new one in which the Chinese colossus would end up replacing the Soviets as the "Great Enemy."

On the flip side there was the Chinese population as object of the world's pity. Behold the latest innocent victims of communist totalitarianism, one read, not even particularly between the lines, in reports on the Tiananmen Square protests. The "compassion" we felt in the West for our eternally inscrutable Asian brothers, together with the anger we harbored against the single Party that oppressed them, fed a literature and a journalism of manners that, just like during the Cold War, was based essentially on ideology and on very few facts. And yet this vision became the founding stereotype of the relationship that we have maintained for the past twenty years with the inhabitants of this nation and with the Chinese communist regime—or, at least, of the relationship that our media and political class would have us maintain.

And yet today in Beijing, in Shanghai, and also in China's interior, where the new cities are shooting up like mushrooms, there's something entirely different in the air. The recession lasted hardly a trimester, the last of 2008, before the growth immediately resumed.

"China experienced merely a reflected crisis, because it wasn't a matter of an internal financial crisis. And then the plan to stimulate the economy was very effective, it maintained domestic demand," explains Mao Yushi, president of Unirule, an economic research institute in Beijing.[1]

In China, quality of life is tangible and the people know it. The automobile industry can't produce cars fast enough and future drivers must put themselves on waiting lists. Consensus, too, is tangible. During the sixtieth anniversary celebrations for the People's Republic of China in October 2009, the world watched in astonishment at the latest proof of the Chinese people's solidarity and national pride. Behind the parades and the parties wasn't the CCP alone but the entire nation.

As we have seen, it was the end of the Cold War and the advent of deregulation, which Iceland embraced and which China still today distrusts, that separated the crossed destinies of these two nations. And the results make it clear that the wariness with which China regards our model is today more than ever justified. A single example: in April 2009, the Chinese Institute of Accountancy and Certification blocked a Chinese consortium's proposed acquisition of Saab, owned by General Motors, because it found the company's balance sheets insufficiently transparent. They were afraid, in short, that behind those numbers there were losses, debts, and production inefficiencies that could damage the buyer.

Iceland, on the other hand, without noticing it, fell victim to the greed of high finance, foreign and local, and ended up sharing its fate. Meanwhile China began to ride the globalization tiger in earnest, which to this day has yet to unsaddle the country. The goal of the two nations is the same—to modernize. But while Iceland steers its own economy according to the financial logic of the Chicago Boys, the same that led Argentina into bankruptcy at the beginning of the century, China does the exact opposite, choosing a model—endogenous industrialization—regarded as obsolete in the West. And it does so without Wall Street's money and while still communist.

To understand the profound differences, ideological as well as cultural, concerning the roles and responsibilities that the Chinese and Icelandic states have with respect to their own citizens in the race toward modernization, we must take a step back, as well as a leap to another part of the globe, and revisit the horrors of the Pinochet dictatorship.

THE CHICAGO BOYS

In 1956 the Pontifical Catholic University of Chile signed a collaboration agreement with the Department of Economics at the University of Chicago. Thus began an exchange between Chilean students and US professors that would continue for two decades. At the end of the 1950s, roughly twenty students arrived in Chicago and enrolled in courses, at the time considered revolutionary, taught by Milton Friedman.

"What characterized the Chicago school was a strong belief in minimal government and an emphasis on free markets as a way to control the economy"—so Milton Friedman summarized his theory during an interview on PBS.[2]

Back in Chile, the students demonstrated their enthusiasm for the principles they had absorbed and began to meet together every Tuesday to discuss their plans. The goal was to reform the Chilean economy. Soon they would be christened the "Chicago Boys."

The ideas they promoted were in marked opposition to the policies of the socialist president Allende. The young economists mistrusted state interventions and state planning. They were against price controls, which they considered obsolete, even if according to the government this prevented the most disadvantaged among the population from falling below the poverty line. A fierce dialogue between government representatives and the Chicago Boys was born and continued up until the coup d'état of September 11, 1973.

It was a group of businessmen connected to Pinochet that unexpectedly ushered these young economists on to the political stage. At first the military was reluctant. "The generals preferred a controlled economy; that is, an economy that would obey orders," admitted Sergio De Castro, Chilean Finance Minister from 1974 to 1982.[3] Following extensive negotiation and with the help of the Chicago Boys, Javier Vial, head of the bank association, invited Milton Friedman to Chile to give a series of lectures on the Chilean economy. The first took place at the Catholic University in Santiago.

Friedman focused on the problems of inflation, which after the oil crisis of 1973–1974 were turning up everywhere, and sketched out a series of proposals for turning Chile into the first neoliberal nation. Pinochet received him privately and the American economist took the opportunity to explain to him his philosophy. If you cut the tail off a dog slowly, piece after piece, it will bleed to death, but if you remove the whole thing it will survive. Inflation is like the dog's tail, it should be lopped clean off with a single blow, Friedman explained to the dictator, who came away favorably impressed by his theory.

Months later the Chicago Boys were called upon to rescue the country's economy, and they applied Friedman's words to the letter: 500 state-owned businesses were privatized, import tariffs were abolished, government budgets were cut to the bone, and the markets were given free rein. Chile under Pinochet became, as Milton Friedman had hoped, the first nation guided by his neoliberal economic theory.

While the military swept away any opposition, the economy took off and Chile became the fastest-growing nation in all of Latin America. Paying the price was the Chilean population. The cost of living quadrupled, unemployment rose above 30 percent, and an unbridgeable gap opened up between rich and poor—a gap that remains extremely wide to this day. Few people realized that the success of the Chicago Boys' experiment was due to their anticipation by a few years of a trend that would soon revolutionize international markets. As we will see in part three of this book, in the 1980s Ronald Reagan and Margaret Thatcher introduced the same reforms that Pinochet experimented with in Chile.

The euphoria surrounding an economic model thought to have resolved the problems of galloping inflation in the 1970s and '80s got its start in Santiago and spread across the globe like a virus, reaching its apex with the fall of the Berlin Wall and deregulation. But the consequences of the triumph of Friedman's model were destined to reveal themselves in all their devastating force only years later.

The Chilean success established a perverse connection between free markets and political freedom, a connection that had never previously existed—and did not in fact exist in this case. In Chile, 2,400 people died or disappeared at the hands of the dictatorship during the coup; while the Chicago Boys were at work promoting free markets, Pinochet was effectively doing away with the last traces of political freedom. The country became an economic laboratory surrounded by an ocean of blood. In defense of his cooperation with one of the modern era's worst dictators, Milton Friedman declared: "Here was the first case in which you had a movement toward communism which was replaced by a movement toward free markets."[4]

The Chilean experiment allowed Friedman and his followers to contribute to the creation of a political mythology around supply-side economics. This became the bulwark of the free West against Soviet communism. But the economist didn't stop there, adding: "In the end, the Chilean military junta was replaced by a democratic society. Free markets did work their way in bringing about a free society."[5]

The Chilean experiment's influence changed the world. The

cultural movement the Chicago Boys were part of opened the way for financial leverage, the use of derivatives, and unfettered deregulation. It allowed the market heretofore unknown freedom of thought and action, freedom that the market was incapable of managing. It's startling to see how the culture of privatization and of tearing down statist systems, which today many people consider a dogma, was inaugurated without any common sense or regulations by a group of students passionate about supply-side economics and by a sanguinary South American dictator.

All this took place in an atmosphere of euphoria pervaded with the rhetoric of the prosperity of the postwar era, receiving plaudits and positive comments from illustrious economists and critics from all over the world.

The story of the Chicago Boys and of the cooperative relationship between the Chilean dictator and Friedman, whom the Swedish Academy's Economics Prize Committee praised for his courage and clear vision, marked the beginning of the decline of the Western nation-state. It represents only one of many striking examples of the climate characterizing recent decades, of how economic euphoria easily leads to the destruction of long-standing pillars on which stood entire systems of government, economic structures, and social equilibria—the socioeconomic supports that, even when indeed inefficient and outdated, were removed without analyzing possible outcomes first, while a careful evaluation would have allowed one to foresee and avoid the disasters connected with these collapses.

One imagined it was possible to wipe the slate clean and redesign the world. Instead, the hunt for fast and easy wealth via financial instruments has become so hysterical that we've stopped noticing the latest disasters these so-called free systems have been amply demonstrated to cause. The example of Iceland is only among the most recent examples.

COUNTRY FOR SALE

Iceland is a country in which legend and reality are separated by a particularly thin line. The nation's history is founded on sagas, ethnic fables that celebrate the greatness of a people on the edges of the earth, iced over for the majority of the year; a nation that has been obliged to develop its own strategies to survive in an often hostile environment.

In an article published in *Vanity Fair*, Michael Lewis tells how in 2004 Alcoa, the largest aluminum producer working in the country, when trying to obtain construction permits for a new facility, had to certify that the zone was not inhabited by elves, the "hidden people" of Iceland.[6] It's a claim many people smile at, but in a place where nature is dominant and views resembling inhospitable lunar landscapes abound, beliefs of this sort offer inhabitants a kind of psychological armor. More than ingenuousness, the existence of the elf population represents a proven strategy, however folkloristic, for overcoming the sense of profound isolation connected to the fact that Iceland finds itself near the top of the world, spends most of the winter months in the dark, and has so few inhabitants.

To understand how a nation that believes in elves plunged headfirst into a tank of Wall Street sharks, it is necessary to take a step back and look up one of the greatest of Icelandic poets, Einar Benediktsson. His dream became that of the entire nation: "To transform Iceland into a modern country with cities, factories, railroad lines, streets, ports, and mechanized farms."[7]

The modernity Benediktsson dreamed about was the same modernity pursued by their Nordic colonizers, Norway and Denmark, and by the greatest power in the world, the United States. At the end of the twentieth century it was a dream shared by all nations on both sides of the Atlantic, the dream of neoliberal modernization, which Europe and America succeeded in realizing but which at the end of the 1980s Iceland continued to pursue. In the meantime, on the other side of the world, China too was chasing the dream of modernity.

In the 1990s and 2000s, the Icelanders did not see their country's wealth in the surrounding sea, full of fish, or in the grasslands at the edges of the world, where cows grazed, but in hydroelectric energy, water power. The spectacular waterfalls and the large lava wells would transform Iceland into a great forge. This was and is the dream of the island's residents. But there are some logistical obstacles. Although the country has clean energy, so fashionable these days, hydroelectric energy cannot be exported. Whoever wants to use it has to do so on the island. And yet, in order to produce it, it is first necessary to find the money to transform lava and water into energy, and the finances have to come from outside, because this is a poor nation.

Like China, therefore, starting in the late 1970s and early '80s, Iceland tried to attract foreign capital in order to modernize. It did so by offering foreign entrepreneurs cheap energy, with particular attention to the industry that consumes the most, aluminum production. Up until the '90s international banks were very cautious and Iceland struggled to find sufficient credit, but everything changed with deregulation, and at this point a river of money began to flow toward Reykjavik.

However, heavy industry did not bring the hoped-for improvements in well-being. Profits were meager with respect to fixed investment costs and the immense consumption of energy. The capital returns were very low; that of Landsvirkjun, the national electric industry, was hardly 0.9 percent.

Aluminum production is such a capital- and energy-intensive industry that it did not even create many jobs. For example, the aluminum smelter built by Alcoa in Reyðarfjörður, on the island's east coast, consumes six times the energy of all the residential buildings in Iceland, but created only five hundred new jobs.[8]

Thus the industrial adventure turned out to be a fiasco. And yet the island's per capita income increased until it became the second highest in Europe. Why? Thanks to the financial bubble that, as we will see, transformed the country's astronomical debt into the illusion of wealth. Without realizing it, people were spending what they didn't have, and in the population's collective imagination the power plants, the factories, and the smoke from the furnaces were the economic shortcut to modernization.

The architect of this grotesque joke was international high finance. After the fall of the Berlin Wall, it became progressively easier to find bankers who were happy to finance extremely ambitious projects like Iceland's hydroelectric plants, and who would then convince themselves they had come up with an ideal modernization plan. It certainly isn't high finance that would propose the recycling of aluminum as a "clean" alternative to aluminum production, which is among other things one of the most polluting of industrial activities. It is widely acknowledged how much more economical, as well as more ecological, it is to recycle the millions of aluminum cans consumed every day: in the United States alone approximately seventeen million tons have been buried since 1972, equivalent to the entire amount of production at Iceland's Straumsvík plant for the next hundred years.

This is what the Icelandic writer, environment activist, and filmmaker Andri Snaer Magnason had to say on the subject:

It would suffice to incentivize recycling to reduce global production and pollute less. In 2004 the US threw away 800,000 tons of cans more than it recycled. If you add to this the aluminum containers and aluminum foil we use in the kitchen, you come up with 1,200,000 tons of aluminum a year, equal to four times the annual production of Alcoa's new plant in Reyðarfjörður.[9]

It's simple to recycle aluminum, because the metal doesn't easily corrode, but it costs so little as to be to considered a disposable product. Accordingly, the American food industry refuses to impose an added cost on those who don't recycle the cans, as occurs in some other countries, including Iceland. It goes without saying that the lobbies behind this metal are extremely powerful—Paul O'Neill, former president of Alcoa, was George W. Bush's first Secretary of the Treasury—and thus influence government decisions.

As previously suggested, the big bankers of the 1990s failed to consider the option of recycling primarily for reasons of personal gain. The profits generated by the financing of heavy industry in Iceland were far greater than those produced by the construction of recycling plants, obviously, given that the profit is directly proportional to the dimensions of the investment and the banks earn a percentage of this. If we then add fees for technical consultations, organizational costs, marketing costs, and all of the costs connected to the birth of new heavy industry, managed by the banks, we realize why international capital supported the unrealizable and absurd dream of Icelandic modernization.

Here is the great limit of a market where finance counts more than politics: the social—and also often the economic—aspect of the modernization process disappears to make room for the dividends of shareholders. But whereas it is normal for banks to pursue profit for their investors, governments ought to take responsibility for the well-being of the population. With deregulation, states become aiders and abettors of every whim of the banks, just like in Iceland.

Thus in 1995 these banks supported and encouraged the international marketing campaign launched by the Icelandic government, according to which all the country's present and future hydroelectric resources are put on sale. Iceland offered the lowest energy costs in Europe, an unbeatable invitation to all the giants of aluminum including the much talked-about Rio Tinto and the Russian businesses that had fallen into the hands of the oligarchs and mafiosi. The idea was to transform the island into a conglomerate of hydroelectric plants and aluminum smelters, erecting gigantic steel chimneystacks and glowing furnaces against the background of the polar nights. The environmentalists were horrified but nonetheless silenced by politicians who had learned the bankers' lingo and promised riches to a population confused and disoriented by the continually arriving strangers with blue double-breasted jackets and briefcases full of papers.

MILTON FRIEDMAN ON ICE

The former prime minister, Davíð Oddsson, is the Icelandic equivalent of Deng Xiaoping. He first came to power in 1991 and remained there until 2004, the key years of industrialization in which the speculative bubble would form. He was the one who redesigned the country's economic and financial structure according to the teachings of Milton Friedman; and also the one who used the sale of cheap energy to attract the world's heavy industry and incite the Chicago Boys to transform Iceland into a laboratory where credit leverage produced the money to finance an absurd dream of modernization.

In London, Tokyo, and New York they looked on in amusement at the heedlessness with which Reykjavik swelled the financial bubble. Indeed, it is only after the collapse of 2008 that the IMF issued any alarming declarations. Paul Thomsen, head of the bailout delegation, admitted that the lack of regulation had led to the development of an excessively large banking system, in which public and private debt amounted to 1,400 percent of the country's GDP.

Not only did the government of this Arctic island take the

advice of the Chicago Boys at face value, it also encouraged the entire nation to play the stock market. The cheap and easy credit flowing to the island in the 1990s became the spring-board for mad speculation on the part of local banks, the government, and a large part of the population, all of it under the aegis of a Central Bank always ready to meet the liquidity needs of the new speculators.

Let us now analyze some of the dynamics at work here.

Access to increasingly low interest rates convinced Icelandic banks to go into debt on the international market in order to invest in the local market in the medium and long term. Short-term rates are generally lower than long-term ones, and so the investment in heavy industry ended up being financed on the world market with regularly renewed three-month loans. Those who took them out had their backs covered because in case of any difficulty they could count on the Central Bank as creditor of last resort. The mechanism became jammed up when, due to the credit crisis, the Icelandic banks could no longer find anyone willing to offer them short-term credit, and the Central Bank did not have enough money to cover a national debt equal to 850 times GDP.

Thus in the 2000s, in order to build the hydroelectric plants and guarantee the public artificially low interest rates in the real estate market, both the government and the banks made use of short-term debt. Private citizens ended up employing the same practice to buy stakes in foreign companies, sold to them by the large merchant banks. Cheap and easy credit ended up supporting investments as well as consumption. On paper the value of both real estate and shares in heavy indus-try grew. Those who held them went further into debt by mortgaging what they had in order to acquire more of the same.

Initially, the two driving sectors were real estate and heavy industry, but in a few years finance took over and became the primary source of earnings and liquidity, to the point of absorbing a large part of the work force. Fishermen converted themselves into traders or bankers and, in a country of 320,000 inhabitants, there opened up no fewer than three business schools where young men and women could learn the art of easy profit.

"Every Icelander knew the magic formula for derivatives, the Black-Scholes,[10] and the engineering and mathematics departments offered courses in financial engineering," recounts Ragnar Arnason, professor of fisheries economics at the University of Iceland.[11]

RETURN TO TIANANMEN

Why is it that Beijing has avoided the recession Iceland fell victim to? Not only because the Chinese financial system remains strictly closed, the national currency isn't convertible, and capital flows are controlled, but also, and above all, because during the boom years, instead of going into debt, the country saved. In Iceland as well, before the advent of deregulation, the population saved. But this discipline was abandoned to follow the new fashion for indebtedness.

Indeed, neoliberalism can in every way be compared to a fashion, which after the fall of the Berlin Wall gained a footing everywhere and convinced the world to conform to a unique economic model, one no longer anchored to savings and production but to credit and consumption.

China and some other countries, such as the poor ones in Africa, didn't go in for it; irremediably "out of fashion," they were wearing flats when everyone else had moved on to high heels. The unfashionable nations were either two poor or too unfree to be neoliberal—or that is what we Westerners were told. Of course we felt sorry for them. Twenty years after the fall of the Berlin Wall, however, these "limitations" became the best defense against an economy destined to constantly oscillate between boom and recession, against debt defaults, as in the case of Iceland, and against the economic chaos of the countries of the former Soviet bloc. But let's return to our question: why did the crisis hardly touch China?

In 1989, Beijing, like Reykjavik, was at a crossroads. The entire political system of Soviet communism had been swept away, sparing nothing. And China too could have fallen for neoliberalism's indiscreet fascination. All the conditions for it to happen were there.

At the end of the 1980s, Deng Xiaoping's reforms were working, proof that a little bit of capitalism doesn't hurt. But the economy grew too quickly and the country felt the consequences. The modest liberalization of prices led to inflation and imbalances, such as that of the price of beer that made a few clever entrepreneurs rich at the expense of consumers, as we saw in the previous chapter. All developing countries have to confront such problems of growth sooner or later, but in the context of the collapse of Soviet communism these assumed new gravity. The danger is that the situation could slip out of the hands of those who were guiding the transition to an open economy, in this case the hands of the Party, and in China as in the Soviet Union the system could collapse in a flash. Let's try to imagine for a moment the consequences of this scenario.

To open up China in '89, as occurred in the USSR, would have brought hunger and chaos to the country. The first to collapse would have been agriculture, closely followed by industry, and from one day to the next 900 million people would have found themselves cut adrift. This is precisely what happened to Iceland at the end of 2008, after the bankruptcy, but fortunately this was "only" a matter of 320,000 people.

Can we imagine 900 million hungry refugees who want at all costs to reach the rich West? Just slightly under twice the sum of the American and European populations combined. This would have been the price of introducing democracy in the land that gave us silk, gunpowder, and spaghetti. After '89 the labor supply in the West, instead of doubling, would have quintupled, the cost of labor would have collapsed, and Western unions would not have been able to guarantee minimum wages to workers. And the disproportion between capital and labor would have been so great as to sweep away centuries of workers' struggles. Very likely, a democratic China in 1989, with the population free to move to the West, would have decimated our middle class.

Looking back on the decision to suppress the Tiananmen uprisings through this lens, it is only honest to make an extremely painful admission: maybe that sacrifice saved us all from catastrophe, and the one who made that terrible decision did so in the interest of the nation—of the China that would modernize following its own road and not that traced by the West, of the China that today prepares to step into the role of a superpower equal to the United States. It's not possible to wash away the blood of Tiananmen with the water of utility and the "common good," but it must be conceded that very likely this was one of those evils of history that avoided larger tragedies. With clear justification we condemned that decision; it is also thanks to it that we are still standing.

It is, however, important to be clear that both the repression of Tiananmen and the neoliberal shock therapy applied to the former Soviet bloc were the fruit of a wrong-headed approach to great historical changes. The blood of Tiananmen represented a serious blow to the opening process underway in the 1980s and put an end to important reforms, including those regarding unions. If the tumult of '89 had been confronted differently, it is very likely that today we would be facing a China both different and at the same time similar to the current one. Perhaps certain economic objectives would have been achieved sooner, perhaps the environmental and social price of the reforms would not have been so high, and perhaps we would find civil society and a press that is freer than it is today.

Fortunately, Tiananmen did not block the opening mechanism for good. The blood served to convince Deng Xiaoping that continuing along the path of economic reforms at a sustained pace was the only way to save the country from what befell the Soviets. And for nearly three years Deng struggled within the Party in defense of precisely what the young men and women in Tiananmen had been asking for, against the CCP's Maoist wing that pushed for a return to a planned economy. In the end, his resolution and a trip to the south of China, where he launched the "Enrich yourselves" motto, symbolized this victory—a triumph of modernization that might have seemed impossible in a civilization five thousand years old.

PART TWO

GLOBALIZATION AND CAPITALISM

CHAPTER 6

THE WORLD IS FLAT

Just over a year after the catastrophic credit crisis, J. P. Morgan and Goldman Sachs announced truly unbelievable profits. According to the headlines in the financial newspapers, we've gone back to 2007 levels, the golden year of globalized finance. And the entire planet wonders about the nature of this miracle as the world economy remains slow to recover.

And it is in Manhattan that we find an emblematic image of the incomprehensible gap that exists today between high finance and the rest of us. On January 14, 2011, photographers and reporters set up on Wall Street near the J. P. Morgan building. The board of directors had just announced 2011 fourth-quarter profits of $4.8 billion, up 47 percent from a year earlier.[1] Jamie Dimon, CEO, received $17 million in stock bonuses, a true record from every point of view.[2] The press lay in wait for the lucky mortals who worked here, wanting obviously to interrogate them about the multimillion-dollar bonuses they would receive at the end of the year. It was clear that no one would be responding to their questions.

A few subway stops north, a giant human snake wound its way around the corners of the municipal offices. The majority were in line to obtain the latest extension on their mortgage payments; in the last twelve months, nearly all had lost their jobs and ran the risk of ending up homeless. In fact, as bonuses were being paid in Wall Street, unemployment figures were published: 10.3 percent with four million people unemployed for over a year.[3] Unlike the investment bankers, these people all would have liked to speak with the press, to lay out the reasons for the collapse and to ask the state for help. No journalist, however, wanted to hear the same lamentably common story repeated again and again.

Here we observe the distance between finance and the real world. But there's another chasm that's opening, equally important, and it's between finance and the real *economy*. It is at this point impossible for any productive sector to compete with the financial sector in terms of profit. And this handicap is itself absurd in the light of all—truly all—economic theories of stability.

In the middle of 2011, it has become apparent that nothing has changed. The Federal Reserve is injecting huge amounts of money into the economy with quantitative easing, driving up inflation and commodities prices just for the sake of helping financial markets. They're the true beneficiaries of this policy; in fact until the Middle East revolutions broke out the stock market had been booming, while the economy had been suffering from higher costs due to inflation.[4]

What happened? It's simple: for years, in the West, finance has been contributing more and more to GDP. In the United Kingdom on the eve of the 2008 crisis, it amounted to as much as 14 percent of the nation's wealth. And we understand just how much the West has lost its way when we turn our gaze to the East; in China and in the Asian markets exactly the opposite is the case, and the engine of growth remains the real economy.

Even the Chinese bailout plan reflected this philosophy. Patrick Chovanec explains:

> In China, to combat the recession there were two economic stimulus plans introduced. In the first the government spent 4,000 million renminbi to strengthen infrastructure. With the second it injected 10,000 million renminbi into the commercial banks so that they would loan it to those in need; of this money,

2,000 million served to support the first stimulus. A part of the loans bestowed by the banks are so-called non-performing loans, investments that don't generate profit but develop the economy, as for example railroad construction. For the Chinese government, inciting the banks to behave in this way, that is to offer loans, is not a problem because it is rich and if necessary can easily recapitalize them.[5]

The same can't be said of our governments. The reason? The credit crisis that was unleashed by the fall of Lehman Brothers.

THE PURGES OF WALL STREET

Up until 5:00 PM on Friday, September 12, 2008, the activity in Lehman's trading rooms was frenetic. Aware that 2008 had been a lean year and bonuses would not be distributed, employees moved to acquire the bank's bonds on the open market, which at this point quoted them at heavily discounted prices, thinking to be able to later resell the bonds for twice or three times as much. And here would seem a good place for a brief technical explanation.

The markets quoted the Lehman bonds at a large discount and with a 40 percent probability that in the next five years they would not be honored. In short, they had sniffed out the fact that things were not going as they should. In the face of this scenario, it seems worrying that the attitude of the credit rating agencies was to ignore the obvious lack of confidence and maintain their A ratings that said the bank was rock solid. Indeed, the behavior of Standard & Poor's, Wall Street's most popular rating agency, is baffling—on September 9 it sounded an alarm concerning Lehman only to retract it precisely on that fateful Friday, September 12.

These technical premises explain why, scant hours before

the collapse, the Lehman employees were still convinced that their little speculations would compensate them for the loss of a bonus. No one interpreted the fall in the quotations as the warning sign that this was the last day of work at the bank, nor imagined that those purchase agreements would, the following Monday, be sucked into cyberspace by the Wall Street telecommunications system, reduced to blacked-out pages online. Institutions like Lehman, it was believed, don't fail.

Neither did the exalted efficiency and farsightedness of the markets foresee the worst; thus, less than seventy-two hours before the collapse, Lehman Brothers shares were trading in all markets with an A rating, and the bank's employees let themselves get carried away by financial bullishness, as one Italian trader recalls:

> Whoever went against the orders coming down from on high and pulled money out of Lehman, who sold the bank's shares, received phone calls from the bank's employees along the lines of "We know your bosses, these are things we don't forget and that sooner or later you'll have to answer for."[6]

Why, in this end-of-an-empire atmosphere, did the top management of the international banks call for the trading rooms to defend Lehman's shares at all costs? The Friday before the collapse, Credit Suisse sent an email to all its worried traders indicating that they should maintain the Lehman portions of their clients' portfolios, that is, not sell. The background of this order was revealed to us by the *Evening Standard* of August 22:

> In the US, the Federal Reserve phoned Credit Suisse to see if it had pulled a line of credit from Lehman Brothers. While the inquiry could be put down as a check

[-in] call in response to rumors that were swirling—and continue to swirl—around the embattled Lehman, that is not how it was interpreted on Wall Street. It was very much seen as the Fed leaning on Credit Suisse to hang in there, to stick with Lehman. Such calls have not been unknown in London either these past few months, as the authorities fought to save Northern Rock and subsequently Bradford & Bingley. What is never spelt out in these situations is what is the quid pro quo? What does Credit Suisse get for remaining loyal to Lehman? Isn't it also about time that the powers-that-be gave up their effort and let things be? Until one of the *big banks goes to the wall*, no banker will truly realize the mess they've got us into and recant their mistakes. (author's emphasis)[7]

It seems absurd, but that's exactly how it happened: the markets deliberately ignored the problems at Lehman because they were told to do so. This is why the passengers on finance's Titanic continued to dance in the bright ballrooms as the ship was going down. Nobody realized that it was time instead to leap for the lifeboats.

Just as incomprehensible is the speed with which the financial system recovered from this catastrophe, described by illustrious economists and politicians as the new '29. Not only did the banks swallow the blow, but some registered third-quarter profits greater than in the past. Unlike 2008, 2009, the year of the crisis, was by no means a lean year.

At this point it seems natural to ask if for Wall Street the crisis was simply an allegorical fresco, painted for the instruction of the masses standing beneath the windows of Bernard Madoff's office or in front of the former home of Lehman Brothers, or something more misleading. More than a year later, it increasingly seems less like the financial crash of the century and more like a Stalinist purge, and indeed the only effect was to get a few banks out of the way and to increase the power of the surviving ones. And, oddly enough, the victims belonged to that segment of the financial elite considered by those who run Wall Street to be "too independent."

This was the case of Bear Stearns, which J. P. Morgan used Troubled Asset Relief Program (TARP) funds to acquire in the spring of 2008, after it had been abandoned to its fate by its sister companies following the collapse of Carlyle Capital. In 1998, Bear Stearns declined to participate in the bailout of Long-Term Capital Management, the first hedge fund to go into crisis. And many think that the treatment it received ten years later was linked precisely to this incident.[8] Furthermore, the most illustrious victim of the credit crisis, Lehman Brothers, which was once the fourth-largest bank in the world, was run by Dick Fuld, who never hid his feelings of superiority over his Wall Street colleagues.

In a television documentary transmitted in England[9] on the first anniversary of the crash that retraced the last hours of the failed attempt to bail out Lehman, Henry "Hank" Paulson, former director of Goldman Sachs and Secretary of the Treasury at the time, complains about the stubbornness of Fuld. He recalls how during the summer he repeatedly invited him to find a buyer for the bank. But the other man didn't want to hear it, also refusing a few weeks before the collapse the offer of the Korean Development Bank as too low.

In the documentary, one picks up on a latent antipathy between Paulson and Fuld, who is completely excluded from the epic meeting—lasting an entire weekend—organized by the Treasury Secretary in the offices of the Federal Reserve of New York, in which all the big names of Wall Street take part. This summit, organized with the goal of saving Lehman, ends up facilitating the acquisitions of other banks, as in the case of Bank of America buying Merrill Lynch.

Many in the world of finance are convinced that Lehman Brothers paid a high price for its bad relations with Goldman

Sachs, and that Paulson's objective was precisely to push Fuld to sell off the bank in order to remove someone who had from the beginning contended with "his" men for the Olympus of global finance. It is a plausible interpretation, given that human nature plays an important role in every activity, finance included. It's also probable that Fuld's stubbornness was connected to precise calculations and that he didn't want to "sell off" the bank because he had predicted that the recovery—financial if not economic—would be swift. If that were the case, today no one could deny that he was right; twelve months after the storm, the shares of Goldman and of all the surviving banks are close to the heights of 2007, and many think Lehman's would be as well, if the bank had been saved.

In the British documentary, one gets the idea that Fuld didn't expect to be abandoned by the US Treasury, nor that the day after it would run to help his competitors, who were in just as critical conditions. If it is true that Lehman had exposed itself excessively, it is nevertheless true that none of its fellow companies were in any better shape. AIG, the world's largest insurance company, was practically insolvent, with $67 billion in debt. If it had failed, Goldman Sachs would have been $32 billion in the hole, enough to follow the unhappy fate of Lehman. But it was not to be.

The same day that Lehman Brothers closed their doors, the US Treasury injected tens of billions of dollars into AIG, becoming the majority stakeholder, and immediately afterward encouraged and financed the acquisition of small banks by the big ones. Also placed into conservatorship in the days to follow were Fannie Mae and Freddie Mac, the two largest American mortgage agencies, burdened with $1.5 trillion in toxic assets linked to American mortgages. And all this happened not only thanks to $700 billion from TARP, but also to quantitative easing, by which the government allowed the Federal Reserve to print money to bestow on the banks as it saw fit.

Not even the Lehman employees, who on that Friday in September were buying the bank's bonds at knockdown prices, could have imagined this scenario. They knew they were in crisis, but were sure that the Treasury and the Federal Reserve would come to their aid, given that these two institutions had been taking care of such troubles in the financial sector for the previous twenty years. Like in a John Ford Western, "our" men always turned up to clear out the Indians. This interventionism was part of globalization's standard procedure. Or at least it had been.

It's evident that there is another truth behind the "crisis." The summit that was supposed to save Lehman, in fact, met to redesign the financial order of the West, and those present were not the world powers but the cutting edge of globalized finance—the big American banks. The G8 and the G20 are only shiny decoys, positioned to dazzle us and make us believe that it's our politicians who pull the strings of the world. But the real power lies elsewhere.

The purges of finance's Olympus, therefore, restructure the financial markets and they do so thanks to the extraordinary powers that Congress and the White House grant to the Treasury and the Federal Reserve. Exercising them is a select group of people with fabulous offices on Wall Street, people who know how to whisper the right words in the president's ear. In just a few months, this elite transformed Western high finance into a small and extremely powerful oligarchy, which operates today on increasingly less competitive stock exchanges. And dictating the new rules of the game are no longer government institutions but a handful of banks, for whom access to credit at privileged rates (that is, very close to zero) becomes an added source of earnings rather than an incentive for extending credit to a population suffering from the recession, as the state would instead prefer.

To allow us to understand the enormity of this apparently technical detail, a pair of numbers will suffice. From September 2008 to August 2009 there was an increase in the bank spread (the difference between the interbank rate, the cost of supplying the banks, and the interest rate that the banks impose on clients). Thus for businesses, it is more expensive to access credit at a time when they have particular need of liquidity—precisely what the governments have tried desperately to avoid. Prior to the collapse of Lehman the spread was around 0.8 percent; a year later it oscillated between 2.8 percent and 3.5 percent, according to the activity to finance and the customer.

The spread is at the heart of the credit multiplier, the mechanism whereby banks, by gathering up savings and redistributing them, create money and therefore profits. These gains go into recapitalizing the banks and swelling speculation in the stock market. Thus in this crisis we the taxpayers have not only saved the banks and found ourselves poorer, but these same banks are enriching themselves at our expense.

In an article appearing in *Rolling Stone* in June 2009, Matt Taibbi describes Goldman Sachs as "a great vampire squid wrapped around the face of humanity, relentlessly jamming its blood funnel into anything that smells like money."[10] And some indicators tell us that this image is very close to reality. From the end of 2006 to October 2009, the bank's book value (assets less liabilities) doubled, while that of the entire US economy remained unchanged. Still in October 2009, Goldman's market value (equal to its quotations on the stock exchange) rose 140 percent with respect to November 2008, when it touched its lowest point, while that of the US market, that is the indices Dow Jones and NASDAQ, rose only 40 percent. The exceptional performance of Goldman compared with that of the American economy occurs precisely at the latter's expense. In fact, in 2009, the *Financial Times* writes: "The period of sharp outperformance has coincided with the departure from the market, or the hobbling, of almost all Goldman's strongest competitors. Companies make more money if they have fewer competitors."[11]

Thus financial profiteering was behind the fabulous bonuses of 2009. The new financial oligarchy profited from the management of the bailout policies, in other words benefiting from the very credit crisis that it had created. The big banks were charged with administering the government loans, TARP included. It's paradoxical, but Goldman Sachs is selling US Treasury Bonds in order to recover the $10 billion needed to keep it from failing, and on every transaction it pockets a handsome commission. Thus, in the first nine months of 2009, 78 percent of the bank's income was produced by its fixed income and currency divisions.[12]

At the same time, the bankers at J. P. Morgan, Goldman Sachs, and Bank of America are using government money to restructure troubled industries like General Motors (GM), in crisis precisely because of their misdeeds. These are the same firms that in the 1990s encouraged the American car industry to continue producing high-power vehicles like SUVs, who sold this sector's bonds and shares, and who offered positive forecasts concerning future industry trends. And giants like GM fell into the trap and unleashed their lobbyists to ensure that Congress was in agreement with this strategy. Meanwhile, Japanese companies like Toyota began to produce hybrid cars, boasting high energy savings, in the United States.

The same banks are advising governments on how to reorganize the financial sector, and all the proposals discussed in 2009 bear the signature of the financial oligarchy's legal experts. There is no productive activity in the world that does not fall within their province and there is no consulting company with professionals more in demand. Finance has us in its grip, today more than ever—there's less and less competition and the planet gets flatter and flatter.

LONG LIVE THE WEST!

In 2005 the well-known *New York Times* editorialist Thomas Friedman published *The World Is Flat*. The book, a magisterial summary of the Western vision of globalization, was an immediate best seller. Through this prism, the flattening of the earth appears as a positive phenomenon, and globalization becomes synonymous with Westernization, a process that should lead all countries to enjoy the political, economic, and financial appurtenances that up until the fall of the Berlin Wall were the monopoly of the rich countries. Every barrier between civilizations is pulverized—by the revolutions in telecommunications, in transportation, and naturally in finance, by fast food and by Google—and the inhabitants of the global village conform to a single model, the winner of the Cold War, inspired by the principles of neoliberalism and Western-style democracy. It goes without saying that capitalism wallows happily in this pond.

Now, a flat planet has always been Wall Street's dream. Thanks to the delocalization of the 1990s, American businesses relocated their factories in Asia, where labor costs were a fraction of the costs at home. At the same time interest rates, the cost of money, also fell. These two phenomena in turn produced a contraction in production costs; suddenly we could manufacture goods cheaper and cheaper.

Lower costs allowed businesses to sell products at more competitive prices, a phenomenon that together with cheap credit encouraged domestic consumption. The more we consumed the more the GDP and the stock market rose, pushing Wall Street indices to levels never reached before. From the beginning of the 1990s to the crash of September 2008, the Dow Jones climbed to increasingly higher peaks. Delocalization became the economy's Holy Grail because it broke down the natural limits of capitalism, which a mature economy such as ours had encountered. A shame that it was only an ephemeral dream!

In *Das Capital*, Marx writes that the capitalist's profits derive from human labor, which he defines as "living." This generates surplus value, which, not being paid to the worker, becomes profit. Machines that replace human capital do not produce the same surplus value. According to this logic, the rate of profit, or the percentage of return that one derives from investing capital, is higher when one employs more human labor and fewer machines. It follows that at the time of the Industrial Revolution this value was infinitely greater compared to the last century.

Technological progress and mechanization reduce the surplus value and therefore also the profit—this is in brief the thesis of the "tendential fall in the profit rate" enunciated by Marx.[13] The natural limit of capitalism is indeed progress that allows machines to replace human hands.

In the postwar period, Marx's predictions started to become apparent when the rate of growth of GDP per capita began to fall worldwide. Between 1973 and 2003 this indicator was half what it had been between 1950 and 1973, and if we exclude China, the gap between past and present increases further. Neither the fall of the Berlin Wall nor delocalization have altered this trend. Between 1960 and 1970 the rate of worldwide GDP growth never sunk below 4 percent, while in the 1990s it has permanently remained below this value. Delocalization provided only the illusion of new wealth; what boosted profits was cheap credit.

The GDP drop was felt particularly hard in Europe. In the wake of reconstruction, in the 1950s, the rate of profit only knew one direction, down, such that between the beginning of the 1960s and 2000 it was halved in Germany, France, and Italy. And confirmation of Italy's anemic growth came right from the mouth of Mario Draghi, governor of the Bank of Italy, who in his year-end report for 2009, declared that in the previous twenty years the history of Italy had been a story of stagnant productivity, with low investment, wages, and consumption, and high taxes.

Not even the United States, engine of the global village, was immune to Marx's predictions. Since 1940, average business profits, inclusive of taxes, have constantly decreased. On what basis, then, did the Wall Street indices increase? Thanks to financial bubbles: shares and bonds grow because they are constantly exchanged in the games of the great monopolies of globalized finance.

THE NEW WIZARDS

Thomas Friedman wrote that the relationship of interdependence established between Western entrepreneurs and Asian labor would standardize the economies of the two regions, causing them to align along an imaginary straight line whose extremes were the factors of production, capital, and labor. In fact, comparing those of the United States and China we realize that in the last twenty years the gap has been notably reduced; the Chinese economy has overcome a large part of its initial disadvantage.

In the collective imagination of the new wizards of the economy (experts, journalists, and political celebrities who reduce this social science to a handful of financial indices), these advantages represent giant steps in the direction of worldwide economic stability. But is it really so? Does shattering diversity help developing countries to grow, and not create imbalances in our own countries?

The "exportation of democracy" in Iraq and Afghanistan has been a fiasco that risks destabilizing the entire region; delocalizing production in Asia gave birth to the designer knockoff industry. And what if the attempt to flatten the world has instead set into motion an infernal mechanism, one that threatens the economic supremacy of us Westerners? If that were the case then there could exist another truth that describes a multipolar future, one in which the world is not at all flat, but is instead similar to a galaxy, where around some old and new superpowers move minor states absorbed into their orbit. It's what we will seek to discover in chapters 18 and 19, studying the presence of China in Africa.

For now, let's concentrate on the consequences of delocalization at home. *The World Is Flat* sums up the vision of the planet in 2005, three years before the outbreak of the credit crisis. And yet, rereading certain pages one has the impression that they refer to another era, to a remote past characterized by the naiveté and heedlessness of us citizens of democracy. Did we really believe that it would suffice to knock down some walls, entrust our savings to high finance, and flatten the earth under the banner of the Stars and Stripes in order to create a more just society? The Cold War ended twenty years ago and none of the much-exalted economic interdependencies became manifest. Nor have we witnessed the alignment of the factors of production—in the West wages have fallen precipitously and unemployment has shot up.

According to labor economist and Harvard professor Richard Freeman, delocalization following the fall of the Berlin Wall doubled the global labor pool.[14] Thanks to the Internet, a radiologist in Nigeria can analyze the X-ray of a patient in Boston and send him the diagnosis, all for a fraction of the cost that his Massachusetts colleague would ask. To stand up to the competition coming from Eastern Europe, or from Asia and the rest of the world, American and European labor finds itself forced to accept lower wages. If the planet continues to flatten, the wealth of families in the West is bound to diminish; according to US statistics, in America in the last ten years, family wealth has decreased by 15 percent.[15]

And if delocalization brings down costs everywhere, it does not necessarily lower the quality of products and services. An American hedge fund in need of someone to study trends in US society can hire an analyst from the Philippines rather than one from the United States, paying him much less for the same skills. We are also thus losing ground here in terms of competitiveness, as we witness a split in the Western production system, whereby according to the particular job delocalization is a source of wealth or poverty, as in the cases, respectively, of the Boston clinic or the American hedge fund, of the Nigerian radiologist or the Philippine analyst. And these examples suffice to make us understand why delocalization is one of the engines of both the Chinese miracle and the European tragedy.

Freeman argues that it will take another thirty years to align the lower and higher wages, that is, before the fees of the Nigerian and American radiologists become equal.[16] In the meantime, Asian and worldwide competition will become increasingly overwhelming and Western workers increasingly poor. Even demography is working against us. "Only" 10 percent of the Indian and Chinese populations is qualified to compete with Western labor, but this percentage represents two hundred million people, more than the entire US workforce, that are being added to the global labor pool. In other words, the numbers count, as the Chinese are perfectly aware. Western politicians, on the other hand, appear to have no idea what to do with them.

CHAPTER 7

FINANCIAL NEOLIBERALISM AS PREDATOR

At the end of October 2009, John Meriwether, founder of the first American hedge fund, Long-Term Capital Management (LTCM), which failed in 1998 due to excessive leverage, announced the opening of a third fund. The second, JWM Partners, had also closed following bankruptcy, leaving its clients with losses equal to 44 percent of the original investment.

Meriwether's new financial toy was, surprisingly enough, another hedge fund engaging in relative-value arbitrage, or quantitative analysis, an economic model based on historical data anticipating market fluctuations. Previously a mainstay of both LTCM and JWM Partners, the forecasts rest on the principle that historical series of prices follow a cycle that repeats over time. And the careers of people like Meriwether seem to follow the same course, to the point that we have to concede, notwithstanding the crises and the polemics concerning investment banker behavior, that old weeds never die—they just go to seed.

Myron Scholes, winner of the Nobel Prize in Economics for the option-pricing formula, the mother of all derivatives, described relative-value arbitrage as akin to a vacuum cleaner "sucking up nickels from all over the world."[1] This apparently works particularly well when the markets are confused, or "dislocated," as they say in financial circles. And in late 2009 they were, thanks to the constant showers of liquidity coming down from government bailout plans of banks and hedge funds. As we've seen, this money does not come in the form of loans to people, but is delivered directly to the banks that use it to play the market. Thus we are witnessing the formation of a new financial bubble.

Meriwether uses his econometric model to identify atypical price relations between one action and another. If those of either Volkswagen or BMW and those of Porsche move in diametrically opposite directions, while historically the contrary is true, then one presumes that sooner or later they will return to following the historical trend. By means of these complex mathematical formulas, technical analysis should be able to identify the precise moment in which that will happen. At this point making money is simple. It's enough to speculate using this information.

Relative-value arbitrage always generates ample profits in dislocated markets because the price fluctuations are often attributable to emotional factors; sooner or later the fundamental factors, that is the real data, gain the upper hand. Prior to the 2008 crisis, this strategy was used by all the banks, but no longer: many of the employees who knew how to use it have been fired, and in moments of profound crisis relative-value arbitrage doesn't work anyway. Thus we find ourselves in a situation where there is less competition in the market than in the past and the possibilities for making money are well above average. In the absence of any real competition, Meriwether's vacuum will suck up a large part of the speculative liquidity on the market.

The dark side of relative-value arbitrage is the ease with which profits turn into losses. This occurs every time the markets collapse, when panic spreads to all the stock exchanges and the historical relations between one action and another vanish, swallowed up by the emotional behavior of the market operators. Meriwether knows this well, having had it confirmed twice before. But given the facility with which someone who has failed not once but twice can return to speculating, this tiny detail does not seem to represent a significant obstacle. Why? Thanks to the absence of proper financial regulation.

FINANCE IS FLAT

The part of the world that has truly been flattened, and at light speed, is the financial sector. It may take thirty years for the costs of global production to converge and put a stop to Western wages' race to the bottom, but it only took two for financial costs to align the world over. This is one of the magical aspects of deregulation.

The ruble crisis, like that of the Asian markets we will look at in the next chapter, was a dress rehearsal for the credit crisis. Many believe that the former was a consequence of the latter, but what plunged the Russian economy into total chaos was the fall in commodity prices coupled with wild speculation on the ruble, which the government kept at artificially high levels to avoid social unrest.

All three crises were born from identical speculative bubbles, swelled by the same banks that today constitute the new financial oligarchy. This elite moved indiscriminately to New York, Moscow, and Kuala Lumpur, and given that profit is linked to risk, the so-called emerging markets of Moscow and Kuala Lumpur, as the most risky, became the most tempting.

Since the fall of the Berlin Wall, the frequency of crises has been connected to the imbalances of delocalization.[2] The increase in wealth produced in the emerging economies increases savings, which, however, do not find in their own countries a financial system sufficiently sophisticated to absorb them, and so they flow to the West. Indians, Chinese, Indonesians, and so on purchase shares and bonds from Western companies like IBM, Google, and Intel instead of investing in national enterprises. And these constant purchase requests cause quotations to rise. This is why the Wall Street indices rise while the industrial profit rate goes down.

Managing the anomalous wave of liquidity is Western finance, which does so without any control on the part of the state, pursuing its own profit and often running excessive risks. And the anomaly is by no means over. Once again the indices are pushing the economic indicators upward, telling us that the recession is finished, while the continuously decreasing profit rate argues for the exact opposite. The instability will continue until the system finds another equilibrium state—when the rich countries increase their savings and emergent countries offer their citizens investment opportunities similar to those in the West. Only then will people like Meriwether no longer be able to speculate with this mass of liquidity following the counsel of an econometric model run by a machine.

The one to pay the consequences of all these crises is always the taxpayer, even if procedures differ. The ruble crisis in the early 1990s pushed the Russian economy into depression, with disastrous effects for employment and the subsistence of large swaths of the population. The crisis in the Asian markets brought the economic growth of an entire continent to such an abrupt stop that some degree of social tension was produced just about everywhere: from Indonesia to Thailand to China. On a daily basis, we are all living the effects of the current recession: government debt, unemployment, decreased consumption, economic stagnation, increase in fiscal pressure. However, none of the recession's architects, that is, none of the big international banks, have paid a price as high as what we pay as individual citizens. Let's ask ourselves why. At least some indication may be found in the complex relationship that in the last twenty years Western democracies have developed with high finance, a relationship at time symbiotic, at others incestuous, a relationship that has conditioned the application of the neoliberal model, altering it profoundly.

Those in charge of government financial and economic

institutions, like the US Treasury, are increasingly often former Wall Street bankers, individuals like Hank Paulson, who comes from Goldman Sachs. This also holds true in Europe where, for example, Mario Draghi, prior to his nomination as Governor of the Bank of Italy, also worked for Goldman Sachs. These are thus people who earned handsome fortunes working for, with, and as part of precisely the same elite they are now expected to control.

Western public administration professionals all have behind them a brilliant career in the private sector. And this would not be a mistake if the only criterion were to guarantee client-citizens the best talents. But this is not the case. As we will see in chapter 13, since the times of Ronald Reagan, the dimensions of the Western state have been so reduced as to be insufficient for its running without continual recourse to the private sector, making necessary the revolving door employed by these professionals of the public and private sector.

The most serious consequence of the incestuous relationship that exists between finance and politics can be found in the connection between profit and financial risk, in which the latter no longer reflects the laws of the market, but rather the personal relationships between individuals belonging to the elite. In the spring of 2008, before the bailout of Fannie Mae and Freddie Mac, the legislative committees tasked with analyzing their management praised the soundness of the two government-sponsored mortgage giants. Representative Maxine Waters affirmed: "Through nearly a dozen hearings, we were frankly trying to fix something that wasn't broke. Mr. Chairman, we do not have a crisis at Freddie Mac, and particularly at Fannie Mae, under the outstanding leadership of Franklin Raines."[3]

Thus it is through the lens of oligarchy, rather than that of representational democracy, that we need to reconsider these events. Between 2003 and 2008, Goldman Sachs advised AIG's London office to issue credit default swaps, insurance policies against the risk of banks defaulting, for values many times its own capital, figures that brought the proportion between debit and credit on its books beyond acceptable limits, and yet the British Treasury didn't bat an eye. Between 2001 and 2007, Fannie Mae and Freddie Mac granted mortgages valued at thirty times more than its own capital, placing the country's economy at risk, and nobody in the White House or the Capitol paid any attention.

Not even the most illustrious American economists perceived the systemic risk of indebtedness of such biblical dimensions. In 2002 the Nobel Prize winner in Economics, Joseph E. Stiglitz, together with Johnathan Orszag and Peter Orszag, published a study, "Implications of the New Fannie Mae and Freddie Mac Risk-based Capital Standard," in which they declared that the risk of insolvency for the US government was effectively zero.[4]

The kernel of the problem is the transformation of risk into a commodity to be sold, according to Paolo Tosi, Institutional Clients Relationship Manager with Kairos Partners SGR, an Italian investment company, who explains:

> It was 1999 more or less, and in Italy I was already in the news as someone who was revolutionizing a national insurance body's investment decision-making process and so everyone wanted to speak with me. One of the many hyenas dressed up like polite City bankers, one of those types that get themselves the Porsche and the house in South Kensington with a single year's bonus, came up to me. He said: "Paolo, you absolutely have to buy yourself some volatility." This really puzzled me and I gave the only possible response in that moment: "You mean they're selling volatility?" "Of course, sure, in fact right now they're giving it away at sale prices." But I needed a bit of time to understand that we weren't talking about tel-

evisions or sofas, but about immaterial stuff, the most ethereal and intangible stuff in the world. If he had asked to borrow money to buy a ghost I would have felt much more in the real economy. Today despite myself I buy and sell volatility without a second thought, but the uneasiness is obvious when I return home, and at night I dream about producing the bolts used in scaffolding joints.[5]

The sale of volatility and the behavior, apparently irrational, of those who make their living off it find justification in the role assumed by the state in the globalized economic model as facilitator of financial activity to the point of assuming, in extreme situations such as the credit crisis, all the risk. Thus in the autumn of 2008, neither AIG nor Fannie Mae nor Freddie Mac defaulted; rather, their toxic assets, their debt, went to swell the US federal deficit.

The logic of "too big to fail" means that these giants with feet of clay have to be propped up at all costs; otherwise, the impact of their collapse could put the entire system at risk. More than a year after the crisis, nothing has been done to bring these institutions within acceptable limits, commensurate with their responsibility, every effort having been sabotaged by that same elite that enters and leaves the public and private sectors as it pleases. The proposal aired by Gordon Brown in November 2009, during the meeting of G20 finance ministers, to tax the banks on dividends and limit bonuses, has yet to come to anything. What's more, the example of John Meriwether, on his third hedge fund, tells us that even when financial companies are allowed to fail, like the phoenix, they are reborn from their own ashes.

THE NO-LONGER-INVISIBLE HAND

In his masterpiece the *Wealth of Nations*, published in 1776,

Adam Smith argues that the market is regulated by an invisible hand guided by the individual's egoistic instinct to maximize his own profits with the minimum of risk. It is a rational behavior, he adds, perfectly in keeping with human nature.

Smith, like Marx and David Ricardo for that matter, starts with the presupposition that at the center of society is the individual, and not the family or the collective. It is a vision shaped by Western philosophy that sees in the state a protective shield against the state of nature described by the English philosopher Thomas Hobbes, a lawless jungle where the strong triumph over the weak.

For Western philosophers and economists, the human instinct is closer to that of predatory beasts than of insects, who on the contrary need the community to survive. Now, this apparently simplistic conception of human interaction is in fact a pivot around which turn the profound cultural differences that divide us from, and at times oppose us to, other peoples, like the Chinese. It is also, as we will see in the next chapter, one of the greatest distinctions separating us from the Islamic world.

Thus, according to Smith, the sum of the egoistic behaviors of each individual enriches the community—this is the much vaunted "magic of the market." Exclusively following one's own interest with the minimum risk ensures the most efficient distribution of resources to those investments providing the highest profits and the lowest risks. Financial deregulation rests precisely on these postulates and extends them to global finance: the state ought to allow the market, through competition, to find its own equilibrium.

Blind faith in the market is born of its presumed rationality. In 2005, the former head of the US Federal Reserve, Alan Greenspan, one of the major theorists of deregulation, affirmed in a commemorative speech in honor of Adam Smith that:

The vast majority of economic decisions today fit those earlier presumptions of individuals acting more or less in their rational self-interest. Were it otherwise, economic variables would fluctuate more than we observe in markets at most times. Indeed, without the presumption of rational self-interest, the supply and demand curves of classical economics might not inter-sect, eliminating the possibility of market-determined prices. For example, one could hardly imagine that today's awesome array of international transactions would produce the relative economic stability that we experience daily if they were not led by some interna-tional version of Smith's invisible hand.[6]

In reality, the economic stability referred to by Greenspan only applies to the giants of Western finance; the little fish are regularly swept away by financial crises, as banks in Asia, Argentina, and Iceland know only too well. The "magic of the market" has a great deal to do with the deflationist monetary policy pursued by the US Federal Reserve and little or nothing to do with the invisible hand of the market described by Adam Smith.

We've seen how crises are confronted: cutting rates so that the banks and financial companies who created the crises are not swept away. This is no passive state simply leaving the market be, but rather an active institution in the service of Western capital. The monetary policy pursued in the wake of the Berlin Wall's collapse is thus interventionist to the point of influencing the functioning of major market segments, those controlled by European and American high finance. It is an extremely dangerous recipe, applied to ensure the tri-umph at all costs of an approach irreparably contaminated by the neoliberal model. The rate cuts aid the banks even when they take on excessive risks or go against the logic of the mar-ket, and the countries in which high finance creates bubbles are the ones that pay the price: Russia, several Asian nations, Argentina (which went bankrupt in 2001), and Iceland, victim of the same fate in 2008.

We find ourselves in unknown territory for economic theory, since not only is this practice not foreseen in any economic doctrine, but it is also profoundly discriminatory. This is not the behavior described by the neoliberal model, which on the contrary severely punishes those who take on excessive risk. It is thus wrong to claim that in the last twenty years Western economies and those linked to them have followed the teachings of Smith; exactly the opposite is the case. Flattening the world, knocking down all the walls, has facilitated the exportation of a neoliberal economic model in name only; the model in question is in fact elitist and predatory.

The exchange between politics and finance thus facilitates the latter's tendency to structure itself as an oligarchy. Such a metamorphosis has only become possible due to the erosion of the powers of the state in the twenty-first century. In fact, the phenomenon has occurred before in the past, and led to the crisis of '29; the advent of globalization has simply brought it back.

THE FIRST RENEGOTIATION OF THE AMERICAN SOCIAL CONTRACT

The crisis of '29 exploded during a period of great economic instability, similar to the current one. The first faults in the liberalist system had begun to appear forty years earlier and, like today, the manipulation of Smith's model was what aggravated them.

Nineteenth-century economic liberalism celebrated the nonintervention of the state in the economy in the name of the superiority of the market, which was considered sufficient regulation. Smith in truth enunciated these principles in a particularly positive period for the English economy, in which the market had managed to self-regulate thanks to a series of contingent and exceptional conditions, such as the gold standard. Smith was well aware of this. And in the *Wealth of Nations* he warns against the abuses of the market by the invisible hand; it is rather in man's resourcefulness that he places his trust. Economic liberalism, on the other hand, constructed on the basis of Smith's theories the dogma of the market's infallibility, around which developed, at the end of the nineteenth century, the policy of laissez faire. Thus Smith's recommendations became right and proper, unbreakable economic laws, and liberalism was transformed into a messianic doctrine preaching "man's secular salvation through the self-regulated market."[7]

The first thirty years of the twentieth century were catastrophic because this economic model did not work. The indifference of the state facilitated the concentration of wealth into the hands of a small elite caste running the economy and the financial system in exclusive pursuit of their own advantage; exactly like today if we consider that 1 percent of the American population controls a quarter of the country's wealth. This led to increasingly violent financial crises, up until the collapse of the fixed exchange rate system on the eve of World War I. Like today, the economic system acted as a predator.

Contrary to Marx's prediction, in the 1930s what led to the loss of faith in economic liberalism was not the Western working class's rebellion against the capitalists exploiting the means of production to their exclusive advantage, but a powerful coalition composed of the middle class, industrialists, banks, and businessmen, all of whose interests were continually threatened by a highly unstable economy. This alliance began to assemble in the wake of World War I, amidst the failure of desperate attempts to return to the liberalist system. Little by little, as it became increasingly clear that the postulates underlying the old system, first among them the gold standard, were not to be recovered, the desire for change became acute. And every failed attempt eroded the financial system further, decreasing its competitiveness.[8]

Therefore, the crisis of '29 arose from the cracks emerging in the liberalist model during the preceding forty years. It's easy to understand why the rhetoric of the new president Franklin Delano Roosevelt was steeped in a new economic doctrine, one diametrically opposed to that of the past: the economic and political debate had had four decades to develop an alternative vision of the world, and men like John Maynard Keynes were formed in such an environment. Today as well a new model is emerging from the cracks in the neoliberal system and those formulating it are looking with growing interest at alternative systems, those that have resisted the flattening of the world: the Chinese model and the model of Islamic finance.

Roosevelt too was formed politically during the years of economic instability; when he came to power he was convinced that the catastrophe of the Great Depression was provoked by an excess of individualism. Thus he repositioned the rational and social behavior promoted by a benevolent government at the center of the economy, in place of the egoistic behavior of the individual and the corporation. The new president renegotiated the terms of the American social contract: the state would no longer guarantee only the protection of the natural and political rights of the individual, as stipulated by the Founding Fathers. In fact, the danger was no longer tyranny, it was the hidden, informal power of the "economic aristocracy."

Faced with this new internal enemy, the powers of the government had to change; they could not be limited, because the social problems to be resolved were unlimited. The lines of unemployed Americans in the 1930s, begging the government for a bowl of soup, come to mind, but so too do the images of suicides on Wall Street, bodies flying from the windows of the centers of American financial power. The government redefines the concept of liberty, connecting it to the protection of economic rights, making it synonymous with human needs.

"Necessitous men are not free men,"[9] said Roosevelt—a sentiment that could also sum up Deng Xiaoping's strategy in China.

Laissez faire and the welfare state of Roosevelt, in other words the liberalist and Keynesian models, are effectively the only two economic systems expressed and applied by the West. At bottom, even the Soviet system belongs to the latter category with the state replacing the economic system and expanding its welfare dimension to the point of managing the life of the individual in toto. Here as well we find the formation of privileged elites. Both models turn on the individual and the elite, people who know how to take full advantage of the system. And if liberalism and neoliberalism triumph in the expansion phases of the economy and guarantee maximum liberty to the individual, the Keynesian model returns to the stage whenever the economy runs up against a crisis, to protect the individual from the errors committed by the elite.

Tearing the rhetorical veil from the "free market" we have thus brought a paradox to light. The nineteenth century's ideological archenemies, Western capitalism and Soviet communism, conceal similar realities and economic structures—and the same errors. So where does one have to go to find truly alternative models? To the East, for an exploration of Islamic finance and Chinese Marxism.

CHAPTER 8

IN UNION THERE IS STRENGTH

In September 2009, the Italian talk show *Porta a Porta* dedicated an episode to the customs and traditions of the Muslims in Italy. During the program, the host, Bruno Vespa, interviewed an eighteen-year-old Muslim woman living in Milan. Several times he asked her why she didn't go out in the evenings to parties; she responded that it did not seem right to do so from 11 p.m. to 4 a.m., and agreed with her parents who prohibited this "Western" behavior. The journalist's attitude was that of a friend who wanted the young woman to give vent to her feelings, but the result was just the opposite: with conviction and intelligence, the woman defended a way of life that some of us consider obsolete, without, however, judging us negatively for this. One had the impression that the program's young guest was not all that interested in our opinion anyway.

In the multiethnic Europe born out of the fall of the Berlin Wall, the Muslims have erected behavioral walls against total Westernization, but we would like to pull these walls down because diversity makes us uneasy. Beyond the violent incidents filling the newspapers, the basic ideological problem is that, in a flat world, not only does it seem absurd to put up walls, but whoever wants to do so seems suspect.

Now, given that the economy functions as a mirror of society, a look at the globe reveals that the two areas in which the financial storm produced the least devastation are those still protected by "barriers" against the flattening of the world: the Chinese economy and Islamic finance. What's kept them up

in the past twenty years has been the culture, history, and religion of those who built them centuries ago. It's a question of
ancient values that are characteristic of these societies and that
distinguish them from others, of cultures for whom the planet
has remained round. It was capitalism that was obliged to
adapt itself to their demands, and not the other way around.

ALTERNATIVE GLOBALIZATION

Geert Hofstede's framework for assessing the influence of
national culture on organizational culture represents the bond
that exists among national cultural values, the globalized
economy, and the business world. The framework confirms
the diversity of peoples with respect to the Western model and
reaffirms that, in general, Muslims, while not fearing other
cultures, don't want to be assimilated into them. When their
presence in the West is guided by the desire to live peacefully
with others, the result is that mix of tolerance and indifference displayed by the eighteen-year-old Muslim during the
Porta a Porta episode when faced with typically "Western"
behaviors.

The Chinese, according to Hofstede's framework, though
less rigid and more disposed to change than Muslims, are a
people that tend to maintain their distance from strangers, the
"barbarians" identified by the emperor Zhu Di, and this is
also how the Chinese describe us today. Muslims and Chinese
possess a cultural reluctance to open themselves up to cultures
different from their own, and above all to globalized culture.[1]
We should add that it is possible that we in the West would
behave in the same way if globalization were not synonymous
with Westernization, but instead imposed different usages and
customs than we are used to. We too, like the Chinese and the
Muslims, would fortify the barriers that protect us from
assimilation.

It is not necessary, however, to believe that the desire to preserve one's own cultural identity from the great melting pot of globalization necessarily leads to open hostility, as Samuel Huntington theorized in coining the famous expression "clash of civilizations."[2] What's more, one finds very few Chinese and Muslims in the no-global movement, which fights the exportation of neoliberal capitalism to every corner of the earth. To the extent that Chinese and Muslims benefit from the flattening of the global economy, we could call them champions of a kind of "alternative globalization." As we will see, it is possible that in the long term—if, as many imagine, the new world proves to be multipolar—this will turn out to be the winning choice.

As we have seen, the long-term impact of globalization on China is positive; without the emergence of the market and the foreigner's exploitation of Chinese labor, there would not have been the great leap forward of the last years. Islamic finance also owes its success to globalization, and in particular to the wild speculation of the Western banks in Asia during the 1990s. Everyone knows how this story finished: with the great collapse of the Asian markets in 1997. But, paradoxically, in the long term this crisis was transformed into a unique opportunity for the Islamic financial system and those who applied it.

The force of the Chinese model is similar to that of Islamic finance and can be summarized with the motto: "In union there is strength."

THE ASIAN FINANCIAL CRISIS

In the mid-1990s, Western high finance discovered that there was money to be made in Asia. Thus began the race to open markets there, starting in Malaysia, Thailand, and Indonesia. A great deal of the liquidity to which Western financial institutions all over the planet aspired ended up in Asia. Growth in the demand for Asian financial products, from securities to shares, attracted increasing bids. A financial whirlwind was formed, dragging all prices higher, including those of real estate and the exchange rates of Asian currencies. At the center of this vortex was born the financial bubble, because this is exactly what it was. The economic growth of those Asian countries singled out by the Wall Street giants was indeed fruit of a collective race toward these markets, not anything born of the real economy—something everyone knew but did nothing about.

In 1997, inevitably, the bubble burst and panic spread to all markets, just as would happen following the default of Lehman Brothers. Traders hurried to sell off their own portfolios and to close positions in Asia. In a few days the flow of capital is reversed, from $100 billion in, equal at the time to a third of global flows, to $12 billion out. It was a general stampede, share prices collapsed along with those of real estate, currencies were devalued, and the GDP of many nations shrunk by 10 percent.[2]

Confronted with this cataclysm, Alan Greenspan, the great puppet master at the head of the Federal Reserve, moved the "invisible hand of the market," slashing American interest rates, which in turn guided the descent of rates worldwide. Thus all the international business banks covered their own losses by drawing on a credit market with extremely advantageous rates. Without this deflationist maneuver, the losses would have gobbled up all the profits, weakening the banks and perhaps leading some to close.

However, the rate cut did not help the Asian nations battered by the crisis, and in fact no one was disposed to offer them a line of credit. It was at this point that the International Monetary Fund came on the scene, offering a bailout plan with exceptionally severe terms, since, from its perspective, a large part of the responsibility for what happened belonged to the Asian governments, who had not proven able to manage globalized finance. Certainly, they were guilty of overconfidence and greed, but the Western bankers who had been so convincing, were they completely innocent? So it appeared, and the countries "to blame for the crisis" had little choice.

Among the Asian nations, Malaysia was the only one to refuse the IMF package and publicly accuse international high finance of having created the financial bubble.[3] The prime minister Mahathir bin Mohamad turned to his Muslim brothers in the Gulf, who immediately closed ranks around him. The Islamic Development Bank, together with rich Saudi investors, created an alternative to the IMF bailout package consisting of loans and investments. At the same time, Malaysia definitively turned its back on traditional finance and hastened to complete the process of Islamicizing its banking and financial system. Iran, following the 1979 Revolution, had Islamicized its financial system for political reasons; Malaysia was the first country to do so for economic reasons.

The Muslim bailout lifesaver worked. Not only did Malaysia emerge from the crisis before any of the other Asian countries, but, immediately afterwards, it initiated a period of sustained growth.

The Islamicization of finance in Malaysia and in the countries of the Persian Gulf laid the foundation for an alternative international finance system and prepared the ground for the great repatriation of Muslim capital, which occurred in the wake of 9/11. The attacks on the Twin Towers and Bush's response, the "war on terror," pushed a large portion of Muslim investors to liquidate their own portfolios in the West, fearing the strict capital controls introduced by the Patriot Act, the restrictions on visas for Muslims, and the possible freezing of accounts following new policies against the financing of terrorism. Thus began the hunt for alternative investments in the most sophisticated Islamic markets: in Malaysia and Dubai, but also in emerging markets like Saudi Arabia and in traditional ones like Iran.

THE MAGIC OF MICROCREDIT

In 2003 Asare-Boateng, a woman living in Jeikrodua, a city in central Ghana, with her husband and newborn daughter, borrowed fifty-five dollars from a microcredit agency and used the money to sell mineral water from a refrigerator in front of her house. In less than a year, and with the help of another sixteen microloans, the woman built a clean water supply that the inhabitants of the neighborhood drew on with their buckets. Asare also expanded, becoming the owner of a small emporium of products essential for her community: insecticides, antidehydration tablets, and condoms.[4]

Asare-Boateng is one of the hundreds of millions of beneficiaries of microcredit. Born in the 1960s in Bangladesh thanks to the work of Muhammad Yunus, the Nobel Peace Prize winner in 2006, this form of credit fights poverty with the weapon of small business. Many think that it sprung from the rib of Islamic finance; it's possible. The inspiration for microcredit was, in fact, the opposite of liberalist egoism, social conscience, and Islam has always placed an emphasis on community. For this reason, Islamic finance places no faith in the invisible hand of the market, nor in the laws pronounced by classical economists.

Let us take a step back and return to the genesis of this form of finance. The first Islamic banks were born of an extraordinary joint venture between rich Muslims and men of faith, between cash and Koran. This union goes back to the 1950s, when economists, bankers, intellectuals, and religious men began to concretely explore the possibility of creating a banking system without *riba* (interest), considered a form of usury. The original concept was that money cannot generate money, but ought to be a productive tool; it ought, in other words, to give life to real, tangible wealth.

Among the most popular products is *murabaha*, which is an ingenious way to avoid applying interest to bank loans.

Instead of lending money, the bank buys a product, for example some piece of machinery, that it then sells to the client on an installment plan at cost plus a profit established in advance together with the client.

Up until the mid-1960s, however, due to the chronic lack of capital in the Muslim world, Islamic finance remained in an embryonic state and was regarded by traditional finance with great skepticism. "To the people, the idea of an Islamic bank sounds as absurd as a Muslim whiskey," recalls the sheikh Hussein Hamid Hassa, a Sharia scholar. It is only during the second half of the 1960s, thanks to the immense influx of money produced by the two oil crises, that a group of aggressive bankers managed to dispose of the capital necessary to establish credit institutions based on these principles.

The task of laying out the corporate structure was entrusted to a group of religious authorities, experts in Sharia, who designed it according to Islamic principles. Today these experts are on the Sharia supervision board of these same banks, with the task of verifying the conformity to Islamic law of the financial instruments offered. They do by issuing fatwas, religious rulings, which become a sort of good housekeeping seal of approval.

This experimental fusion between financial techniques and religious principles was in turn based on the concept of *umma*, the community of believers. *Umma* is the body and at the same time the soul of Islam, a composite but unified entity that breathes, thinks, and prays in unison and where there is no place for the egoistical instincts of the individual. Individualism is an extraneous concept for the tribal culture in which Islam was born and rooted, characterized by traditional values such as a strong sense of group identity, the obligation to help friends in times of need, an acceptance of the authority of religious leaders, and submission to Koranic law.

It's good to remember that Islam developed in a region of the world every bit as inhospitable as Iceland, the Arabian

Desert. It took root among the Bedouins there, in an environment where it is not possible to survive without the support of the tribe, to which the individual is of necessity doubly bound. The ethical values and code of behavior of Sharia are an expression of the principles of societal life that, over the centuries, permitted the Bedouins to survive in the desert. These same precepts, from the prohibition on usury to that on investing in sectors, like the alcohol industry, that damage society, are formulated to protect the individual from an equally hostile environment—contemporary finance.

Those who created this financial system had a vision different from that of Adam Smith and the classical economists. Man chooses to live in society not to protect himself from the violence of his fellow men, but to survive in a hostile environment thanks to reciprocal aid. The state of nature is not a jungle populated by savage beasts, but a space open to the construction of beehives and anthills. Man bears more resemblance to the bees and the ants, insects who must be part of a tribe to survive, than to the great predators of the animal world.

The success of microcredit in the West, for example in California where it is increasingly widespread, seems to say there is a need for these values at home as well.

"This is something that people want: a sense of connection and a sense of community. Because it's decreasing in our daily lives," explained Bob Graham, founder of NamasteDirect, a microcredit organization in San Francisco.[5]

Microcredit is breaking into China as well. Mao Yushi, president of the Unirule Institute of Economics, had this to say about it in an interview:

> The government supports and finances it, even if the organizations involved in microcredit do not have a defined legal status in China. Microcredit can help the economy during financial crises, for example the

migrant workers who return home can use it to start small businesses. In China the potential is enormous because the financial system is not very developed. And these activities will continue to grow because the demand is strong, but above all because there is a critical mass of people well off enough to loan the money.[6]

Returning to Islamic finance, the absence of liberalist egoism transforms its philosophical significance, transcending wealth and profit. Thus those who are rich must not forget those who are poor, the same message contained in the *zaqat*, one of the five pillars of Islam, effectively a kind of religious tax self-imposed on annual earnings in order to help the less fortunate.

Among the stories from the life of the Prophet Muhammad, there is one that well represents the duty to spread the wealth that one in possession of it ought to assume.

> The Prophet once saw a wealthy Muslim gathering up his loose garments so that a certain distance would be kept between himself and a poor Muslim sitting close by. He remarked: "Do you fear that his poverty will cling to you?"[7]

According to this tradition, wealth belongs to all even if some have more than others; thus one ought to use it so that not a few but many benefit. In a certain sense, this anecdote recalls the previously cited aphorism from Deng Xiaoping: "Let's let some get rich before the others and then help them do the same."

If *umma* is the heart, cooperation is the heartbeat of the Islamic economy. At the base of this banking system we find the coparticipation in risk: the bank shares it with the client—always. The two are business partners. A client in difficulty becomes a partner in need of help.

"If someone cannot manage to pay the installments on any item that the bank has acquired in his name, due to contingencies such as a sudden illness or the loss of a job, the bank ought to be understanding and make dispensations," explains Edham Yaqoobi, member of the Sharia board of many banks as well as the Dow Jones Islamic Market Indexes.[8]

The lending institution thus comes to assume a social role, providing its community the liquidity it needs to grow, which is prioritized over its commercial role—drawing a profit from its intermediation. Here is a fundamental difference with Western finance, whose goal is instead to optimize profits while minimizing risk. Risk sharing is the ethical foundation capable of preventing Islamic finance from following traditional finance into misadventures in junk bonds, which on the contrary are based precisely on the decomposition and sale of risk.

Paradoxically, the presence of a Sharia supervision board gives Islamic finance a flexibility and creativity lacking in Western finance. In theory, any product can be designed according to the principles of Sharia, from microcredit to mortgages, from oil drilling to bridge construction; even sponsorship of sporting events can be part of the Islamic banking package, as long as the Sharia supervision board issues a favorable fatwa. Many argue that its success is bound up precisely with this characteristic, the ease with which Islamic banks create ad hoc tools to satisfy the specific needs of clients, whether it be the reduction of tax burdens in the country where they operate, or the raising of funds needed to self-finance.

In many aspects—social cohesion, a great degree of cultural homogeneity, and population size—the Islamic world resembles its Chinese counterpart.

"What can you do with a finger?" asks a Chinese man seated at the green tables of the Venice casino Ca' Noghera, speaking to the Italian journalists Riccardo Staglianò and Raffaele Oriani. "Look, I can't even pick up a chip. But if you've got a hand you can do what you want. If you don't have relatives you're nobody, if you're not part of a hand you're done for."[9]

CHAPTER 9

FROM MUHAMMAD TO CONFUCIUS

Islam acts as the cultural glue of the Arab and Muslim worlds for better and for worse. The suicide bombers who struck London on July 7, 2005, were motivated by the daily humiliation suffered by their Iraqi "brothers" at the hands of coalition forces—this was the gist of the message left by one of the perpetrators in his video testament. The word "brother" speaks effectively to the relationship that runs between European Muslims, Iraqis, Pakistanis, or Somalis; the force of the cultural and religious identity of *umma* is in fact analogous to blood ties.

This relationship is difficult to understand for us Westerners, who subordinate our political identity to the concept of "homeland," an entity in turn superimposed on the nation-state, achieved thanks to the blood spilled by our "brother" patriots. Thus the Americans have the myth of the Revolution against the British Empire; the Italians look to the Risorgimento as the force that opposed the Italian nation to their neighbor and colonizer Austria; the French look to the Revolution of 1789 as creator of the first state in modern history.

Muslims and Chinese do not recognize these criteria and instead go back to the "civilization-state": the caliphate for the former, and five thousand years of civilization for the latter. It is a way of conceiving the world that transcends space and time and thus also politics, a concept that in the case of Muslims rests on Muhammad, and in the case of the Chinese on Confucius.[1]

Little is known in the West about the thought of the latter, whom many mistake for a sort of prophet or guru. In reality Confucius was a philosopher and, as was the case in our culture with Socrates, Plato, and Aristotle, his thought laid the foundations of Chinese civilization and influenced its intellectual development for centuries. As in Muslim society, at the center of Chinese society we find the extended family to which the individual owes not only respect, but also his identity.

THE FAMILY, COCOON OF CHINESE CIVILIZATION

The family represents the nucleus of Confucian ethics. Confucius traces the architecture of society back to five relationships: ruler to subject, father to son, elder brother to younger brother, husband to wife, and friend to friend. Apart from the first and last, all can be traced back to blood ties. The relationships are never equal, not even that between friends, but are based on precise, well-codified social values and norms; and on the Confucian ideal of *ren*.

Ren is a concept bound to the way the Chinese conceive of the individual that can be very effectively explained by describing the corresponding Chinese ideogram. This is composed of two parts: a man standing and the number two, plurality. The meaning could be "the condition of one who is such only in relation to the other," or "man does not become human if not in his relationships with others."[2]

Thus, for the Chinese, the individual does not count in itself, but only in its relational quality. In this context ancestor veneration reveals the importance of family cohesion, in which there is no clear separation between life and death; it is rather a matter of a circular process. Here we do not find ourselves in a Hegelian dialectic of opposing forces, which clash and alternately exclude one another in search of a synthesis, but in a cycle similar to the alternation of day and night.[3]

Li Juan, a coordinator for Global Call to Action Against Poverty, a nongovernmental organization (NGO) fighting poverty in China, successfully conveys the importance of the social dimension to the Chinese: "More and more Chinese want to become volunteers. Especially after the Sichuan earthquake. The government is working on a proposal to regularize the position of volunteers, a law on voluntary service."[4] The government serves as a framework for man's passions, conceived as an administrative structure managing the community, maintaining its unity and stability.

The ideal ruler is "like the polestar, which by keeping its place makes all the other stars revolve round it." With this maxim Confucius intended to emphasize the importance of the example of rulers to their subjects, regardless of the rigidity of the laws. As if to say, if the sovereign is good and virtuous, so will his subjects be, and the society harmonious. This is the theoretical basis of the dichotomy between "government of man" (to which China tends) and "government of law" (prevalent in the West).

Thus unity and stability depend on hierarchy. Individual, family, and state follow an ethical code valid for all levels: in the family, where children respect their parents; in society, where the young honor the old; and in the state, where submission of administrator to ruler prevails. Confucius defined all these behaviors as *ren*, virtuous, the quality essential to the individual.

Unlike Hobbes, in this vision human nature remains essentially positive.[5] It is possible that with the right schooling and family guidance, the individual may assimilate a system of values and ethical behavior that permit him to interact properly in society. At the same time, anyone can rise to the top of the social scale on his own merits. In China, our notion of a divine right that sanctions the legitimacy of kings and emperors has never even existed. Anyone could become emperor and anyone could maintain this status if he did not abuse it.

The theory of the "Mandate of Heaven" invoked by Mencius, the most important follower of Confucius, affirms that emperors and dynasties do not receive the right to rule by virtue of birth; rather, they have to deserve it. If they are not successful, then Heaven will punish them, striking the country with natural disasters. And the people are authorized to rebel and replace the old dynasty with a new one, "under the eyes of Heaven, which legitimates this revolution."

Centuries before the birth of Jesus, then, the Chinese were more democratic than us Westerners.

The optimism of Confucius also issues from the absence of one of the cornerstones of Western thought: individual egoism. Outside the community, the individual has no reason to exist. Thus the Western philosophical imperative "know thyself" becomes "know humanity." The sense of social unity, as in the case of *umma*, is tremendously strong, and man has the duty to act to transform and improve the context in which he lives, with the help of his fellow men. Here there is no room for the pursuit of self-realization, not even in the service of eternal salvation—Confucian thought is neither metaphysical nor transcendental but pragmatic. "Paradise" is living together, something to build in this world, not in the other.

Many are unaware that Confucian thought also has a golden rule, that of "do not do unto others what you would not have them do unto you," a maxim closely recalling the teachings of Jesus. And this exhortation, which constitutes the nucleus of Confucianism's social philosophy, precedes the birth of Jesus by some five centuries.

FROM CONFUCIUS TO MACHIAVELLI

Confucius lived during a period of great political instability. To a people torn apart by fratricidal wars and weary of violence, his philosophy offered an ethical code going well beyond mere survival. The most famous work in which he expressed this thought is the *Analects*, written by his disciples, in which the wisdom of Confucius is placed at the service of the emperor. It is a political manual that became an irresistible alternative to the struggles that raged in the country and advanced the harmony of collective life. And since it turns on universal themes such as good government, it is still highly relevant 2,500 years later.

Niccolò Machiavelli lived in a similarly tumultuous period and his most famous work, *The Prince*, also still has much to say to us today. Machiavelli wrote it for Lorenzo de' Medici in the hopes of regaining the position of counselor that he had lost. Like the *Analects*, *The Prince* is a manual for he who holds the reins of power. But Lorenzo de' Medici did not appreciate the work and Machiavelli never returned to court. Nevertheless, generations of politicians would be fascinated by his theory.

Confucius and Machiavelli both lived under aristocratic regimes characterized by disorder, in which relationships were managed on the basis of personal convenience. And yet they arrived at diametrically opposed conclusions. The former deplored the political chaos and lack of morality in the running of the state; the latter encouraged the use of lying for political ends. Is it possible that this discrepancy, a cultural gap that still today separates West from East, is a matter of different conceptions of the world? The end justifies the means is the mantra of the latter, whereas the key work for the former is harmony. And these principles became the emblems of two schools of thought that continue on into our own times, Machiavelli in the West and Confucius in the East.

"Confucius said, 'Harmony is something to be cherished,'" affirmed Chinese President Hu Jintao in February 2005.[6] At the same time, the fabrication of evidence against Saddam Hussein in order to justify the preemptive strike in Iraq is of a piece with Machiavelli's maxim: "The end justifies the means."

However, it is a mistake to consider Machiavelli the theorist of corruption, or to see in *The Prince* the expression of a barbarian civilization in which force and cunning triumph over ethics as primary components of the state. It is at the same time inappropriate to consider Confucius the theorist of peace merely because he maintained that rulers ought to act as examples to the population and oppose the use of force to promote morality.

Both Machiavelli and Confucius took to heart the good of the community (the city-state of Florence and China, respectively), an end so important as to relegate to second-class status, in the eyes of Machiavelli, morality and ethical values, and to justify, for Confucius, even armed intervention. Their major differences are intrinsic to the societies themselves, about which the two intellectuals offered a comment: one lived in an egalitarian nation, and indeed celebrated meritocracy; the other operated within the oligarchic schemes of his time and thus encouraged "special" relationships.

Confucius can freely admit that when a sovereign becomes a tyrant he loses his sovereignty and returns to being a common man, and as such he can be executed. This is the basic outlook of the Chinese people. Machiavelli, prevented by divine right, cannot accept tyrannicide. In modern terms we could say the former is a comrade and the second is a subject.

This could offer a key to understanding the success that communism had in China and the idea that for the Chinese the Revolution was a democratic phenomenon, which removed a tyrannical government. And oddly enough the communist principles most easily assimilated by the Chinese were precisely those that Marxism shares with Confucianism: meritocracy, well-being of the population, and aversion toward the elite. Where Maoism failed was in the imposition of behaviors that went against this philosophy, like the Cultural Revolution. The attempt to substitute the values of the family with those of the Party were not successful, and in fact they created strong opposition. Filial piety, preached by Confucius, is still profoundly rooted in the Chinese family today.[7]

THE CHINESE CIVILIZATION-STATE

No one can deny that Confucianism has given to Chinese civilization the same theoretical continuity that Greek metaphysics gave to Western civilization. We are all children of our history. The Chinese, however, are more aware of this. Among the famous faces of the new China there is Yu Dan, author of a self-help book based on the teachings of Confucius that has sold more than a million copies. Yu has become a real star and often appears on television to popularize the benefits of Confucianism. It is difficult to imagine an analogous arrangement in the West, with a diva committed to the application of Aristotelian philosophy to everyday problems. More inconceivable still would be the idea of a television program in which we are taught to apply the principles of Machiavelli in our day-to-day life, and yet these are exactly what our politicians follow.

The Chinese are more in touch with their history because their political structure has remained substantially unchanged for five thousand years; Chinese civilization is not fragmented like the West's is, having survived within its original geographical borders. Inside one can find the roots of some fundamental differences with our culture, according to Arthur Kroeber, managing director of Dragonomics, whom we have already met:

> Much of what is happening today in China is built on an inheritance from the past. China developed the idea of a currency well before Europe. And the Chinese state played a much more important role in the creation of this currency with respect to the European

states. The concept of private cooperation, on the other hand, goes back to Roman times. In China it was really only talked about in the 1990s, even if there had been some attempts in the '20s. The power of state participation in China is thus stronger than in Europe, whereas private participation is weak to the point that no institution for this type of activity exists.[8]

Unlike China, ancient Greece, the splendor of the Roman Empire, and all the age-old manifestations of Western civilization, including the Florence of the Medicis, have been destroyed. What remains and unites us, beyond the ruins of past splendor, is the political culture from which we come. But this is recent history, traceable back to the birth of the nation-state, which is only this civilization's most recent manifestation.

And here we are spontaneously led to ask if the extraordinary longevity of the Chinese state is not tightly bound up with the Chinese and Confucian vision of the world. Confucian thought conceives the state as the symbol and guardian of Chinese civilization, whose unity it is committed to maintain; this means that, unlike the nation-state, its range of intervention is infinite, going well beyond national security and respect for the law. The most appropriate, and widespread, comparison is with the father, whose authority is limitless. Thus the state is like a father: it protects and at the same time demands respect from its children/subjects.

While in the West the Roman Empire crumbled—thanks to the guidance of a decadent elite who had taken on excessive military and political risks—the Chinese were safe behind their Great Wall. Within this closed space occurred many great upheavals similar to our own, including the Chinese Middle Ages (206–581), which strongly resembled their European counterparts. Like the latter, it was a period in which religious currents and regional fragmentation exercised a growing influence, and yet it did not conclude with the emergence of different nation-states, but rather with the reunification of the empire under the Sui and Tang dynasties. Even the revolutions in China ended up redrawing modern versions of the same nation, since none of the metamorphoses undermined the popularity of the Confucian message.

Even the Maoist Revolution was born under the sign of a strong continuity with the Confucian concept of the state. Thus the inevitable political elites, though distant from the people, are responsible in this regard. The role of the Chinese Communist Party as supreme arbiter is nothing other than the latest incarnation of the same values, the father-state. If we want to understand China we must account for its people's fidelity and pride in the state—their model, not ours.

"During Maoism, Chinese society was permeated by Confucian philosophy just as much as today," confirmed Wang Dong, a professor at the Center for Strategic and International Studies at the University of Beijing, in an interview.[9]

And once again the writings of Confucius throw light on the scarce inclination that the Chinese have for *our* democracy. Jiang Qing, a contemporary Confucian intellectual, argues that the Confucian concept of politics, as compared to the model of Western democracy, is more appropriate to China. It is based on harmony, very different from the conformity at the core of democracy.[10]

This is not to say that China doesn't believe in the rule of law; as we saw in the preceding chapters, Deng proposed the creation of a state where there is respect for the law. What Confucius wanted to say was quite different: the law does not suffice to guarantee good government; what is also needed is the commitment of the rulers, the virtue *ren*. Without it, the state degenerates into the personal realm of whoever is at its head. Prophetic words that seem extremely appropriate in our present.

The Confucian concept of the state, naturally, is strictly

hierarchical, and the government responds only to itself; however, it is also committed to a form of self-criticism in which members are viewed as model workers obliged to serve as examples. It is, moreover, in their interest to do so since the people have the power to overturn them, and the Chinese, have a number of times, done exactly that in the last five thousand years. Thus Mao launched the Cultural Revolution in order to cleanse the Party of the Western influences that were poisoning it, and this, to his eyes, was an act of self-criticism.[11]

The failure of political activity is in fact a source of great shame that often leads to public humiliation. The authorities involved in the reconstruction fiasco following the Sichuan earthquake, and in the milk scandal, asked the population for forgiveness before resigning publicly. In the West this type of behavior would be inconceivable; the humiliation of politicians is a rare sight, especially if they are members of the current government. Did someone in Tony Blair's government ever ask forgiveness for having willfully altered the parliamentary report on Iraq? No, on the contrary: in January 2010, in front of the Chilcot Inquiry into the Iraq War, Alastair Campbell strenuously defended the lies contained in the famous report Blair sent to the Americans. Has Berlusconi ever made amends for his shameless use of public money and offices? In China he would have had to: the central values of a politician in a communist state are the trust and security that he guarantees to the people.[12] The corresponding Western values are instead responsibility, representation, and participation—the people themselves are the ultimate arbiters.

THE TRADITIONAL ECONOMY IN A MODERN KEY

The cultural gulf between the China of Confucius and Europe in the fifth century BCE, even if it has in the course of millennia been reduced somewhat, remains the greatest obstacle to understanding the Chinese people's way of thinking.

It is a mistake to believe that the economy is not influenced by cultural values and that any model could be exported from one part of the world to another. The great walls exist also and above all in the minds of those who build and use them.

Perhaps some peoples, like the Chinese and the Arabs, have resisted amalgamation precisely because of the role that culture and religion occupy in their economy. And this had led them to modernize the traditional economy rather than embrace that of the market.

In China, fifty years of communism and nearly three thousand years of Confucianism have also laid the foundation for their business culture. Analogous, in the Arab and Muslim world, was the profound influence of Islam in the daily life of *umma*.

The business world in China has always turned on the family-like networks constituting *guanxi* (a system of relationships or web of interpersonal connections) and rests on solid Confucian ethical principles. The concept of *guanxi* also plays an important role for Chinese immigrants in the West. The community offers its members the support necessary to prosper, above all in terms of economic assistance. Inside the *guanxi* the individual finds, but at more advantageous terms, the same range of services, including banking services, offered by the Western state.

In his book written with Raffaele Oriani, *I cinesi non muoiono mai* (The Chinese Never Die), Riccardo Stagliano, a journalist with the Italian magazine *Venerdì*, a weekly supplement to the newspaper *La Repubblica*, gathered this testimony concerning *guanxi*:

> It's much better than a bank, because it depends on the human factor. Around the time of SARS [severe acute respiratory syndrome], many restaurants had huge liquidity problems: full of debts, with empty

tables. If they had been exposed with the banks they would have lost the restaurants, instead among ourselves in these cases we give each other a hand: the important thing is that your creditors see you're giving it all you've got.[13]

Then, further on, Stagliano describes the clandestine banking network of *guanxi* in these terms:

The relationships that unite every single Chinese to a web of family members, partners, colleagues, and friends are failure-proof because they are based on loans granted by acquaintances to acquaintances, who would never think about not paying them back. The penalty is perpetual ostracism from every economic activity, civil death, which means becoming a *heiren*, a "black person," one who has lost the respect of his own people. As a qualification it is incommensurable, as far as dishonor goes, with the bank's term "insolvent." For a Chinese it is shame that cannot easily be washed away.[14]

In Western culture there has developed a concept of guilt that we find again in Christianity, in which alongside the possibility of erring, repenting, and starting over, there is an original sin, a sort of "fall." In China, the equivalent of guilt is the shame derived from social censure, automatic exclusion from the group to which one belongs. And this attitude is comprehensible to the extent that without the social dimension, *ren* cannot exist. What's more, confession does not exist in Chinese culture; shame is a one-way street. In Chinese the concept of "honor" is made up of two characters, *mianzi* and *lianzi*. Whereas *mianzi* refers to social prestige, the status of the individual, *lianzi* signifies personal moral integrity, on which the group places its trust, and if one loses it there is no way to recover it; one is no longer able to perform one's role in society.

Given that everyone revolves around the group, it should come as no surprise that weddings are an assured source of financing, a kind of teller window in the *guanxi* banking system. At a friend's wedding, a young Chinese man told Staglianò, €46,000 was collected from 106 guests. The procedure is always the same: you arrive for the banquet and there's someone who takes your coat, someone who tells you where to sit, and someone who collects the red bags full of money. The bookkeeper opens them and diligently takes down the amount and name of the donor.

Guanxi functions like a social bank, where instead of interest there's trust, *xinyang*, the other face of *guanxi*, along with shame. A young entrepreneur in Prato told Staglianò:

> My uncle just opened a restaurant in Verbania. He invested 200,000 euro, I gave him 16,000 of it. Without interest, without a due date, without anything. The next time it will be someone else helping me, even though I'd prefer it to be my parents making the phone calls, because, well . . . I'm still too young to be asking for money.[15]

Facilitating the transition of the Chinese model from a communist economy to a new entrepreneurial economy was precisely *guanxi*, a concept that is perfectly integrable into the communist system, in which, in fact, it survived without creating shocks. But in the long term this web of personal connections could impede the development of a more sophisticated capitalist economy, if one ends up preferring *guanxi* to financial institutions.

CHAPTER 10

THE GREAT WALL OF RENEWABLE ENERGY

From Beijing, a comfortable half-hour ride aboard an ultra-high-speed "bullet" train takes one to Tianjin, "the city of wind," among the most important centers of wind energy in China. Suspended centimeters above the ground, one truly seems to be traveling into the future, arriving at a space station out of *Star Wars*, in a forest of gigantic windmills. Only the sea, an immense reservoir of clean energy, reminds us that we're on planet Earth.

China abounds with such landscapes, many belonging to the desert zones of central Asia, where the structures producing green energy are visually monitored by the Chinese army. In the province of Gansu, flat and arid like southern Iraq, rises a Parthenon of photovoltaic panels: column after column, the reflective panes run along a perimeter the size of three football fields. In every direction white sand dunes conspire to give the area a lunar aspect. This image is only reinforced by satellite views of the Xinjiang and Inner Mongolian deserts, which show us how Beijing is turning over to clean energy immense expanses of inhospitable and completely uninhabited land.

As Professor Can Li, head of the National Laboratory for Clean Energy, explains:

> Solar is most important for the future of China . . . We have a lot of land that is not suitable for farming. Gansu and Xinjiang are all desert. We estimate that if

we covered a third-to-half of the area in solar cells and caught only a tenth of the energy, then we would be able to meet the current energy requirements of the whole country.[1]

The solar energy industry has grown steadily at rates of 20 to 30 percent a year, in tandem with wind energy. By the end of 2011, the capacity of solar installations is projected to increase fifteenfold from 2009 to reach 2 gigawatts.[2] The country's first "sun city" is in Dezhou, south of Beijing in Shandong; in September 2010, it hosted the international conference "Solar City," dedicated exclusively to this type of energy. In this prototype of the city of the future, developed over more than 330 hectares and sustained by photovoltaic panels, every structure, even water heaters and air conditioners, runs on solar energy. The city was built by Himin, a Chinese company at the forefront of photovoltaic production that sells two million square meters of solar water heaters a year, a real record. Before the end of 2010, it is estimated that this type of heating will save Beijing 22.5 million tons of carbon a year.[3]

But it is the arid and lonely heart of central Asia that is witnessing the swift construction of a new Great Wall: an energy belt composed of wind turbines, photovoltaic panels, biomass reservoirs, and hydroelectric and nuclear power plants, a monumental edifice as spectacular to our eyes as was the original to the Arab merchants who ten centuries ago traveled the Silk Road. The goal of the new Wall is not to keep out the Mongol hordes, but rather to guarantee the country a constant flow of energy, the vital nourishment necessary in order to complete the ambitious process of Chinese modernization. Without this barrier, the dream of Deng Xiaoping will not be achieved and the very foundations of the Chinese Communist Party's political credibility could crumble.

The Great Wall of renewable energy thus protects China

from one of the modern era's principal threats: the struggle to secure increasingly scarce resources. As in the past, the peril comes from the West.

ALL TOGETHER NOW UNDER THE GREEN BANNER

Army surveillance notwithstanding, it is possible to approach the new Great Wall to form an idea of its dimensions and capacity. Even more than America, for so long the country of "go large," modern China thinks, develops, and produces on a giant scale.

On the outskirts of Wuwei, a city in Gansu, one can look through the cages of zoo animals on their way to extinction and catch a glimpse of a photovoltaic plant. Behind a family of pandas, it is possible to make out the panels of a cathedral of reflective surfaces surrounded by a garden of large-blade turbines, three times more efficient than ordinary turbines. The Wuwei plant generates 500 kilowatts; it is not the country's largest, but it is the first of such dimensions to be tested in the desert and also the first to be connected to a transmission grid.

One of the fundamental problems with renewable energy is the impossibility of storing it and transporting it from one end of the earth to another. Oil, natural gas (in the form of liquid gas, LNG), and coal are easily loaded on boats; solar and wind power are not resources that can be transported or stored—they must be transformed into electrical energy on the spot.[4] This limits the range of action to a few thousand kilometers. The same restrictions apply to nuclear power. No existing technology is capable of catapulting this type of energy from one continent to another, as is possible with hydrocarbon. We have already seen the negative consequences of this limitation in Iceland, where the need to use the island's energy locally led the government to make some execrable choices.

In China, there are yet other technical and political problems. Not all the wind and solar power production is accessible from the grid, a good 30 percent remaining outside. And if it's not possible to connect it to a transmission system, no one can buy the energy produced. The Chinese companies that control access to the national grid, a web that Beijing is still weaving, are very powerful and often maintain a "special" relationship with the coal plants, which have fed the grid for years. More than 70 percent of the electricity consumed in China comes from coal, far and away the most polluting source of energy, which certainly explains the country's environmental degradation. It goes without saying that whoever produces coal does not look kindly on clean energy.[5] But the government is resolved to reduce the consumption of hydrocarbons.

What's more, it is precisely in China's phantasmagorical metropolises that the problem of energy becomes most pressing. Apart from the pollution, the cost of hydrocarbons represents in the long run a serious obstacle to economic growth. In megalopolises of tens of millions of inhabitants, energy consumption can reach dangerously high levels and even approach the supply capacity of existing systems. Recurrent blackouts would constitute not just an inconvenience for citizens but a humiliation for the central government and a dangerous spur to dissent. Energy conversion is therefore an urgent political question and will necessarily be characterized by internal power struggles, whose arbiter will not be the CCP alone, but also, and above all, local authorities.

Behind the construction of a national transmission grid it is possible to glimpse Beijing's intention to create a new model. The idea comes from economists such as Jeremy Rifkin, who speak of a worldwide grid, a web of intelligent mutual exchange capable of distributing and exchanging energy at the same time. "In the cities of the future every building will be part of it, will at the same time be a producer and transmitter of energy," Rifkin explains.[6] We can imagine skyscrapers as enormous rechargeable batteries; when one is depleted another next door allows it to recharge and vice versa. In such a scenario, green energy could easily travel from one building to another, from one village to another, from one city to another. A science fiction fantasy that modern technology has yet to find a way to realize, perhaps, but one at which the Chinese are already hard at work. It is easy to imagine the spectacular skyscrapers of Shanghai as enormous deposits of solar energy, or of the wind energy produced by turbines strewn along the coast, and at the same time conceive of them as switchboards for the grid.

For now, however, both the Chinese and Westerners have to be content with a short-range renewable-energy transmission system, meaning that the race for a green planet is, above all, taking place at home, not globally. And Beijing is well aware of this—all investment in new sources of energy is managed internally by Chinese banks.

As Claudio Vescovo, analyst with an international business bank in London, explains: "Anyone wishing to participate in the energy conversion that the CCP is orchestrating, has to do so through local bank intermediaries, and indeed the large international investment banks do not have easy access to this sector."[7] China has at its disposal the money to undertake a very ambitious green conversion but fears a Western presence in such a strategic sector. This doesn't stop the foreign giants of clean energy, which are on the contrary present en masse in the country. In Inner Mongolia, First Solar from Tempe, Arizona, the largest US producer of solar modules, is building a power plant combining wind, solar, and biomass energy, boasting a productive capacity of twelve gigawatts, approximately ten times greater than that of a natural gas or coal plant. General Electric, together with the Elion Chemical Industry of Ordos, the business capital of Inner Mongolia, has completed a project to cut traditional industry's wastewater discharge into the Yellow River.

The restoration of the environment goes hand in hand with the expansion of clean energy, but more than an achievable objective, it represents a very powerful tool of propaganda to give weight and force to the green conversion. Everyone is familiar with the environmental degradation and destruction that industrialization has wreaked on China. The images of devastation in black and white—not because they are taken with black and white film but because pollution has wiped out all color—have gone around the world; now they are a weapon in the campaign for the transition to renewable energy sources.

The current vice minister of Environmental Protection, Pan Yue, has led a green movement since 2003; recently it obtained the full support of the Chinese Communist Party. In 2008 he launched an initiative to awaken public opinion to environmental problems and make the people's voice heard all the way to Beijing.

"By increasing the transparency of environmental information, the force of public opinion can put pressure on those who destroy the environment," explained Pan Yue to the *New York Times*.[8] Public opinion is essential: in 2006 alone there were sixty thousand protests related to the environment. And the new green campaigns coming out of Beijing are a confirmation of the CCP's ability to reinvent itself. The same body that in the first half of 2000, in Dongzhou, a small fishing village near Hong Kong, violently repressed demonstrations against the construction of the umpteenth coal plant is today the champion of clean energy.[9]

After having ignored the problems of pollution associated with industrialization for thirty years, today China marches united under the green flag. Again Pan Yue:

There has been a flaw in our thinking: the belief that the economy decides everything. If the economy is booming, we thought, political stability will follow; if the economy is booming, we hoped, people will have enough to eat and live contented lives; if the economy is booming, we believed, there will be money everywhere and materialism will be enough to stave off the looming crises posed by our population, resources, environment, society, economy, and culture. But now it seems this will not be enough.[10]

Green fever has spread west from Beijing to take over the entire country. Inner Mongolia is only one of the many regions and provinces that now compete to finance clean energy sources, among them Gansu and Qinghai. All three regions have declared their hopes to build solar power plants of more than twenty megawatts each. Of course, these good intentions are still in need of approval and financing from Beijing, as the investments are considerable: the wind plant under construction in Gansu, which will be the world's largest with a capacity of twenty gigawatts, is set to cost $17.6 billion. In the summer of 2009, the central government set aside $218 billion for green projects, 34 percent of the national antirecessionary stimulus package. The corresponding figure in the US is barely 12 percent.[11] China, in other words, has responded to the greatest global economic crisis of the postwar period by investing more in projects of environmental sustainability than any other country in the world.

For the period 2011–2015, China plans to have hydropower energy reach 324 gigawatts, solar energy 2 gigawatts, and wind energy 200 gigawatts. Presently hydropower fuels 6 percent of China's energy requirement, versus 3 percent in the US and 1 percent in Germany. But the most important data is the amount of money it intends to spend on energy efficient projects: Y5 trillion, or $600 billion, an investment which will create fifteen million jobs in the next ten years.[12]

Naturally, the central government expects individual

regions to contribute financially. Ordos, the city responsible for a large portion of the Inner Mongolian economy, is among the richest areas in the country, home to a sixth of China's coal reserves and a third of its natural gas. With a population of barely 1.6 million inhabitants, it has a per capita income of ¥100,000, the third highest in the country. Ordos, like hundreds of other municipalities, considers environmental projects such as the expansion of clean energy a means of growing the local economy and reaching the affluence and level of development of Shanghai, Beijing, and Shenzhen.

THE SECOND PHASE OF THE CHINESE INDUSTRIAL REVOLUTION

The involvement of local authorities in the green crusade is part of the second phase of the Chinese industrial revolution, meant to modernize the most remote parts of the country. In the first phase, Deng Xiaoping looked beyond the Great Wall and did so from Hong Kong, a window on the West ably exploited by China to open itself to the world. The leading edge of his plan was the Special Economic Zones scattered along the southern coast; the growth engine was the cheap labor exploited by foreign capital. As we've seen, in this phase China becomes the workshop of the world, producing low-cost products for the global village's consumption. With the experiment comes tremendous wealth: between 1978 and 1994, Chinese per capita income triples, GDP quadruples, and exports increase tenfold.

At the time of Deng's death in 1997, the still-developing Chinese economy is among the most powerful in the world. But, as we have seen, the price of this economic miracle is very high, paid in workers' lives and environmental devastation. In attempts to drive down manufacturing costs further and further, Beijing ignores the potential ecological damage of forced industrialization, and the first areas to suffer the consequences are the Special Economic Zones. It's here that the pollution reaches critical levels, here that the first concentration of popular protests against the environmental degradation appears. Geographically, this industrial season, which has lasted more than two decades, brings more wealth to the coastal zones than to the interior of the country. And it's easy to understand why: the economy's great leap forward rests on exports, and the ships full of low-cost "Made in China" products set sail from coastal ports.

The second phase, on the contrary, looks not west from the Great Wall but east, to the country's interior. Energy and internal consumption are the new key words for Beijing these days. The international business situation, in forcing the West to plead mea culpa with regard to a lifestyle that it could not and certainly can no longer afford, has unexpectedly favored the process of Chinese modernization by prompting Beijing to take notice of the imbalance between savings and consumption. If we spend what we don't have, the Chinese save even when they should spend. In particular, the timing of the crisis, and of the recession it produced, has pushed the CCP to make drastic economic decisions that it would perhaps have had difficulty making in other, more favorable circumstances. The fact remains that the sector into which they have chosen to channel surplus capital is alternative energy, and the area where they have decided to concentrate that capital is Central Asia—precisely where, to date, there has been the least development.

We have here a situation in many ways diametrically opposed to that characterizing the immediate post-Mao period: where once a lack of capital was the problem, now there is an excess of liquidity, connected to the high savings rates of families and businesses, to the extent that the government blocks participation by foreign banks in energy projects. The country no longer needs to accumulate but to spend, and internal spending is still too low for a nation with such a large trade surplus.

Once again Claudio Vescovo explains:

> By 2020 the Chinese government intends to build
> seven wind-power mega-plants of at least ten
> gigawatts each. Just to give some context, the largest
> such facility currently in operation, near Roscoe,
> Texas, has a capacity of less than a gigawatt. The
> plants, to be located in the provinces of Gansu, Hebei,
> Jilin, Jiangsu, Xinjiang, and in Inner Mongolia, will
> together have a total capacity of 120 gigawatts, mean-
> ing that in the government's plans, wind energy will
> contribute more to the country's needs than nuclear
> energy, whose capacity by 2020 will be 60–70
> gigawatts.[13]

Given the difficulty of exporting renewable energy, investing in the most remote regions means bringing industry and
infrastructure to these areas. And that is what is happening.
Central Asia's Chinese territories are being modernized, a phenomenon that should stimulate energy consumption. As if
peeling an onion, Deng Xiaoping's policies have developed the
external layers, the southern coast and the peripheral zones,
while the second phase starts from the heart of the onion,
Central Asia, and works toward the outside. The green energy
generated in the deserts will serve to modernize the surrounding regions and then will be transported via the grid to the
coastal cities.

The Great Wall of renewable energy sources, therefore,
marks the borders of the new China and traces the geography
of its modernity; there's no going beyond it, nor any desire to
do so.

THE CHINESE PARADOX

The transition between the first and second phases of Chinese industrialization means that, for the time being, the world's greenest country is also its blackest. This is the Chinese paradox. China is the greatest producer of renewable energy in the world, with roughly seventy-six gigawatts of capacity, nearly twice that of the United States (with forty). It is also first in producing energy from small-scale hydroelectric plants, fourth in wind energy, and the nation in which energy consumption per unit of GDP has decreased the most: 10 percent between 2006 and 2008. Its ecological objectives are among the world's most ambitious, such as the aforementioned goal of obtaining 15 percent of the nation's energy from renewable sources by 2020. Going further, in November 2009 an ad hoc government task force presented a plan by which 50 percent of energy consumption in 2030 will have to come from clean (renewable and nuclear) sources.

In 2008, meanwhile, China became the world's greatest polluter in absolute terms, and the environmental degradation is visible nearly everywhere. This dubious distinction had since 1880, the time of the Second Industrial Revolution, belonged to the Americans, who nevertheless, due to their lifestyle, remain the greatest per capita polluters. In China it is industry that pollutes, because it contributes 48 percent of GDP (the government promises to reduce this figure to 41 percent by 2030), a much higher level than in contemporary Western service-based economies. What's more, Chinese industry is in large part heavy industry (chemical, metallurgical), thus requiring high levels of energy consumption, and 70 percent of the electricity produced comes from coal.

In America and throughout the West, the pollution is linked to a lifestyle that, in the face of global warming, appears shocking and bizarre. In the Arizona desert there are entire small towns inhabited for just a few months in the fall by the new American superrich. In many cases these are gated communities, monitored by security forces, complete with golf courses, pools, and fitness centers. In summer, when temperatures rise above 110° Fahrenheit, the towns empty out and the golf courses return to their original sand-dune state; but every fall, when the residents return, the grass must be regrown. The water required to do so in the desert is extremely precious and the energy cost of supplying it is nearly prohibitive. Such is one example of how we Westerners waste energy.

In China, where no such luxuries exist, energy consumption is still linked to the modernization process. This is why the air quality in the coastal cities, where most of the factories built during the first phase are located, is often hazardous. To guarantee a blue sky during the 2008 Olympic Games, the government had to shut down the factories of Beijing and the neighboring areas for three months. To date, the American ambassador maintains a Twitter feed reporting on the air quality in Beijing, in which the word "hazardous" often appears.

The environmental crusade wants to change this scenario and make China the first clean-energy nation. But let's not fool ourselves; Beijing is hardly motivated by intentions any nobler than those of Washington, DC, which for 120 years thought only of growth, ignoring the environmental problems linked to increasing its GDP. The same lack of responsibility for its role as a superpower, the same egoism that characterized American administrations in the last century, is found in the Chinese government. The CCP thinks only of China and its own survival, and the development of clean energy is linked to economic calculations. But is there really nothing new under the sun? Something has changed: if all great empires have always been exclusively concentrated on themselves, it's also true that the processes they set in motion alter ways of living beyond their own borders and control. And the energy revolution, the technological ventures Beijing has embarked upon, could also revolutionize our world in a positive way.

A STEP BACK

After the Industrial Revolution, the heavy use of hydrocarbons redesigned the planet from every point of view, including those of population growth and environmental conditions. Industrialization put an end to Malthusian cycles, rural inhabitants stopped dying of hunger, medicine made great strides, the quality of life of huge numbers of people improved, and population growth took off dramatically. In the year 1000, the world population amounted to 300 million, slightly less than the American population today. In the next 750 years, up to the eve of the Industrial Revolution, we arrived at 700 million, growing at 57 percent. It was a billion in 1800. In the next 100 years population growth nearly doubled. In 1900, there were 1.6 billion of us; in 1927, 2 billion; and so on.

Progress leads us to multiply. Since 1950 we are increasing by a billion every ten years, meaning that every thirteen years, a population equal to that of China today is added to the world population. Population growth poses as great a danger as global warming, and the Chinese know this better than anyone, since for decades their leaders have sought to limit births with the one child policy. Nonetheless, their country's population continues to place an awful pressure on the environment.

The technological triumphs that have made the West so powerful have proven both a blessing and a curse. In the contradictions of the Industrial Revolution we can rediscover some aspects of the Chinese paradox. In the 1950s and '60s, cities like London, whose homes were heated by coal, were constantly covered by a canopy of smog, as seen in the appalling images of a famous 1966 film starring Alberto Sordi, *Smoke Over London.* Our indifference to the environment was linked as well to the conviction that the resources of hydrocarbon were infinite. It is only in the fall of 1973, when the Arab members of OPEC impose the oil embargo, and oil becomes an economic weapon capable of dragging rich countries into crisis, that serious discussion of alternative and renewable energy sources begins. And yet ever since the end of World War II, estimates concerning hydrocarbons have hardly been encouraging.

In 1949, M. King Hubbert, an American geoscientist, warns of the end. He calculates that US oil production will reach its peak in 1970 and from there begin to decline, while the demand for energy will rise. The prediction provokes little fuss until 1971, the year in which production from American oilfields begins to decrease. To date, the so-called Hubbert peak theory has proven accurate and by now everyone agrees it has revealed the greatest obstacle to future development of the planet.

The race for clean energy is a question of life and death—that's why everyone is getting involved. As we have seen in the preceding paragraphs, by 2010 China became the world's largest consumer of energy;[14] given its status as a developing country with a population of 1.3 billion, the energy problems of the future are particularly pressing for Beijing. Just a few figures suffice to describe why. If China and India were to increase per capita oil consumption to the level of South Korea, they alone would require 119 million barrels of oil a day, roughly twice the entire current global demand, according to Rifkin's estimates. And if China were to consume the same quantity of oil per capita as the United States, it would require 81 million barrels a day. Clearly, if China wants to reach a level of wealth comparable to that of the West, it must find energy sources other than oil.

The resources, therefore, are insufficient, and China is not the only country to invest in clean energy. The United States, Germany, and Spain are at the forefront in this sector.[15] In 2008, with respect to the previous year, the productive capacity of the world's solar power plants tripled, and that deriving from wind power rose nearly 30 percent, while the annual production of ethanol fuel increased 34 percent. And a historic milestone has been reached, as once again Claudio Vescovo explains:

> For the first time in modern history, in Europe and in the U.S. there has been established a productive capacity of electrical energy coming from renewable sources (sun, wind, biomass) greater than that coming from conventional sources (natural gas, oil, coal).[16]

Also responsible for this growth is the enthusiastic support of international finance, whose investment in green productive capacity between 2004 and 2008 climbed from $20 billion to $120 billion. According to *New Energy Finance*, the magazine of the Italian Association of Capital Market Brokers (Associazione italiana operatori mercati dei capitali, or ASSOIM), $97 billion comes directly from financial markets.[17]

THE LAW OF THE BIG NUMBERS

For some years, China has been the largest producer of rare metals; in 2009, 95 percent of worldwide consumption came from its mines. The most important among them are in Baotou, in Inner Mongolia, a town recalling those of the American Gold Rush; only here do the mines belong to the state. It's a business that generates hardly a billion dollars a year, from 95,000 tons (for the sake of comparison, the area's iron mines alone annually produce a billion tons).

The rare metals, however, play a strategic role. The green energy industry uses them in solar panels, in wind turbines, in the catalytic mufflers and batteries of hybrid cars (every Toyota Prius has twelve kilograms of neodymium in its rechargeable battery). Rare metals are also essential for electronics: every cell phone, computer, and plasma television has a handful of them inside, to say nothing of precision-guided, "smart" weapons. Already in the 1990s, Deng Xiaoping recognized the importance of these metals: "The Middle East has oil, China has rare metals."

In 1994, China controlled 46 percent of worldwide production, but in the last fifteen years Beijing has acquired a large share of foreign mines, as well as associated strategic industries. In 1995, two Chinese companies, San Huan New Materials and China Nonferrous Metals, together with two American partners, bought Magnequench in Indiana, which manufactures 85 percent of the rare metal components used by the arms industry in smart weapons. Since then, the manufacturing has moved piece by piece to China, and at the moment there is no production of this kind in the United States.[18]

Thus the Western world today is terrorized by the possibility of drastic reductions in rare metal exports. Beijing has yet to declare itself, but it seems clear that the goal is to relocate to China a large part of the industries that make use of them, including those producing smart weapons. Toyota, which has an arrangement with China for neodymium, has already agreed to relocate some assembly lines near the mines. Rare metals will prove useful in the accomplishment of China's extremely ambitious plan for energy conversion. Green energy could thus be the key to the Chinese industrial revolution, and in this way sanction the nation's supremacy, a susceptibility for historic milestones based on the concept of "multitude."

What transformed the eighteenth century's innovations in technology and energy into the Industrial Revolution was the magnitude of the changes. For the first time, we began to produce and to think on a large scale. This is why "industrial" and "multitude" are two faces of the same concept. The writings of not only Marx, but also of Smith and of Ricardo, tell us so. The very birth of economics as a social science coincides with industrialization, because it was at this point that economic and industrial choices began to condition the life of the masses. The motor that drives this relation is profit, for the first time within reach of a new class of individuals that is larger and more easily joined compared to preceding oligarchies, a group that can and wants to arrogate some of this profit to themselves.

Similarly, in the second phase of the Chinese industrial revolution, the multitude has a central role to play. China is the most populous, and one of the vastest, countries on earth, characteristics that have already given it a great advantage in the process of globalization. Now, in order to avoid ecological catastrophe, it is necessary to think precisely in planetary terms, to put the multitude, in other words, before the privileged few who live in the rich countries. To overturn the political paradigm is not simple, as we are realizing precisely during this recession. But in ecological terms, the limits of a planet dominated by an elite become very clear.

Will communist China save us from an environmental holocaust? This is the question many are asking themselves at this point. Certainly, no nation today is in a position to think and to act on a greater scale. If this country were to become the new green energy model and succeed in creating an intelligent and efficient grid, then everyone else would have to adapt, just as it happened in the Industrial Revolution. And this would mark the end of Western supremacy and the start of a new era, with the world's center of gravity shifting from Washington, DC, to Beijing.

PART THREE

GLOBALIZATION AND DEMOCRACY: A SHOTGUN WEDDING

CHAPTER 11

LOOKING AT WASHINGTON AND BEIJING THROUGH CHINESE EYES

At the end of 2009, Barack Obama made a visit to China.[1] This was hardly a step with the historical proportions of the meeting between Nixon and Mao in 1972, nor a media event like Bill Clinton's visit, televised around the world, nor was it like the presence of Bush among the VIP spectators at the Beijing Olympics. The current president's trip was full of ambiguity, a key term in any description of the relations that have prevailed for some time between Washington, DC, and Beijing.[2]

One had the impression during the brief visit that Obama was treading on eggshells. He measured his words and, even if armed with his usual joviality, maintained a certain distance from his interlocutor, Hu Jintao. A chill emanated from the Chinese side as well, becoming particularly evident when talk turned to human rights, the old stalking horse of every American president visiting the country. Indeed, it is tradition that on the occasion of a visit from a US head of state, the Party frees a dissident or two, imprisoned for having displayed "excessive" enthusiasm with regard to Western democracy; Obama's visit, however, became an exception to the rule.

On the economic and political fronts, as well, results were hardly brilliant. America's request for support for economic sanctions against Iran fell on deaf ears. Hu Jintao offered an identical response when, during a press conference, Obama criticized China for again pegging the national currency to the dollar, an unpopular maneuver in Washington because it keeps Chinese products in America and throughout the world artificially competitive. To the dismay of his constituents, the US president returned home virtually empty-handed.

Also palpable was the disappointment of the Chinese. According to a Beijing journalist who preferred to remain anonymous, and who we will call Li Chan:

> The Chinese adored Clinton because they were unaware of the social problems in the United States at the time. Today the students have access to more information about this country. And even though everyone knows that our system has problems, they also know that the others aren't in any better shape. President Obama's visit seems more like an exercise in diplomatic relations between the two countries than an opening to the Chinese people. And even though the scandals of Abu Ghraib and torture were widely reported in the media, Bush had a better relationship with China.[3]

The international press also noted the difference and could not fail to compare Obama's brief visit with the longer and more fruitful trips of his predecessors, and the picture that emerged was humiliating for the United States. Some attributed the coldness of the Chinese to the role the country has assumed vis-à-vis America, that of the banker who has issued too many lines of credit and now fears he'll never see his money again. China has drastically reduced its purchases of American Treasury bills: in 2006 it financed 47 percent of the US debt; in 2008 this percentage had gone down to 20.2; and in 2009 it amounted to a modest 5 percent.[4]

There were also those who saw in the CCP's lack of deference a confirmation of the weakness of the American president as an institution compared to the Chinese Communist Party. The most popular American blogs talked about it, but so too did the traditional press like the *New York Times* and the *Wall Street Journal*. What's more, everyone knows that the first citizen of the United States is in office for a limited period of time, during which he remains hostage to Congress, constantly forced to make compromises with various political and economic forces, as in the battle to reform health care. The Chinese Communist Party, on the contrary, considers itself the unanimous, indisputable, and solid expression of the People's Republic of China.

The weight of consensus, in short, is not to be underestimated. Chinese economic growth in the face of worldwide recession has increased the popularity of Hu Jintao and the government he represents. This new reality became apparent when the Chinese leader visited Washington, DC in 2010. The narrative appeared totally different from what many had expected. Illuminating is a picture which portrays the Obama couple welcoming Hu Jintao at the gala dinner at the White House. While the president and his wife wear glittering black tie, projecting the image of wealth and prosperity, and have surrounded themselves with Hollywood stars and Wall Street's moguls, many of Chinese descent, the Chinese leader wears a dark suit and arrives alone. Two worlds, one still in the past and the other projected into a future we do not understand, are portrayed side by side.[5]

The economic crisis, two wars, and the many difficulties involved in fulfilling campaign promises such as the closing of Guantánamo have eroded the faith that the American people had placed in one of the most popular presidents since the times of John F. Kennedy. In other words, the red star of the CCP is ascending, while Obama's stars and stripes appear to be in decline.

CHINA AND AMERICA AS SEEN FROM THE EAST

The meeting between Obama and Jintao was thus emblematic because it summed up the shift in the power relationship, in less than two years, between China and the United States of America. Contributing to this shift has doubtless been the increasing freedom of the press and of information in China. As Li Chan explains:

> News from abroad comes more frequently. Before it was fifteen times a day, now it's fifty or more. And since there's no censorship, they're much more informative. The credit crisis was widely followed in China, in part because we were afraid it would pull us into the recession too. The Chinese press did a good job; you can't say the same of the Western press. In discussions about it with foreign colleagues, you have the impression that the Western media "sells" the news while the Chinese media provides information and is interested in the country's development. And maybe the basic reason for this is that in the West they want to criticize the government, while here we want to educate the reader.[6]

At the origin of the chill between China and America we thus find the diametrically opposed effects of the credit crisis and the recession in the two countries. It is useful to analyze this diplomatic drift from the unaccustomed—for us—point of view of the Chinese.

In comparison with the China that Barack Obama would visit at the end of 2009, the nation that hosted George Bush in August 2008 was very similar to the one that ten years earlier had welcomed Bill Clinton. And America was not the same either. Clinton was in office during the "roaring '90s," when the euphoria of the victory over communism blinded everyone and the world was shaken by deregulation; Bush rode the tiger of the "war on terror," as neoconservatives instilled a sense of patriotism in the people summed up well by the mantra "with us or with the terrorists." Obama came to power in the middle of a full-on economic crisis, and became the leader of a country beset with the specter of recession and a military stalemate in both the extremely unpopular wars it was fighting.

But it would be a mistake to consider these three presidents as three separate realities. The crisis in the economy and the crisis in values, including perhaps that of identity, inherited by Obama, had already begun to take shape the day after the fall of the Berlin Wall, and all the residents of the White House made their contribution. Early in the new millennium, it was already clear that Washington was struggling to maintain the hegemony it had enjoyed since the end of World War II. Globalization, promoted by Clinton, confused the issue, and the power that according to Reagan brought down the Berlin Wall slipped from his grasp. In addition, deregulation offered other countries, like China, unimaginable opportunities. But no one noticed what was happening until 2007, when the recession began.

No one, in the upper reaches of power in particular, intuited that in order to maintain superpower status in the global village it was first of all necessary to reinvent the very concept of power. The future universal problems of modern society go by the names environment and health, not military supremacy or, for that matter, democracy. Thus, to recreate in the new international context the hegemonic equilibriums of the Cold War is a dream—not only unrealizable but anachronistic and even dangerous. And yet this was precisely the objective that the Bush administration resolved to pursue. Paradoxically, after 9/11 it also became a goal shared by other Western countries. It wasn't a question of nostalgia but of arrogance and inertia; in the end no one had the desire to reinvent themselves.

In the eyes of the Chinese and of the majority of Asians, the American president, once upon a time considered the most powerful man in the world, is also the symbol of a country that has lived, and continues to do so, beyond its means. In the eyes of those who in 1997, at the outbreak of the Asian financial crisis, watched the exodus of the big American banks and suffered humiliation at the hands of the IMF, today the US is paying for past errors—as well as for those of the present. How can anyone ignore the continued growth in unemployment, the persistence of a brutal financial system that has brought the world to the brink of a new Great Depression? And the president lacks the strength to alter the situation, despite his promises during the epic electoral campaign to reform high finance. The Volcker Plan, designed to regulate what the banks can do with our savings, is certainly not looked upon kindly in a Washington where the fight between the financial lobby and the White House continues to rage. But even if it were to come to fruition, it would be useless, because it is too vague and incomplete to avoid future abuses.

Barack Obama is also a president at war in two countries, Iraq and Afghanistan, wars financed with Chinese savings. And it matters little if he inherited them from his predecessor; now they belong to him. For more than a year, the Chinese press has been hammering readers with articles describing these absurd situations and cataloguing American defeats. China, on the other hand, is infinitely stronger thanks to globalization, something about which the average American has no idea. The average Chinese, however, guesses it, and finds it difficult to look at America and see the superpower that was in the twentieth century; it's easier to classify it as a nation held hostage to Wall Street and to the neoconservative ghosts of the past.

The destinies of these two nations appear to be intimately

connected, like two sides of the same coin, such that at times China's rising economic, diplomatic, and social fortunes seem to inversely mirror America's decline.

THE CHINESE NEW DEAL

Beijing has used the immense monetary reserves accumulated in the last twenty years to launch an economic bailout plan along the lines of the old American New Deal: roads, schools, hospitals, a "futuristic" railway network (like the train connecting Wuhan and Guangzhou at the speed of 350 kilometers per hour), and an extensive highway system. All these innovations have gone hand in hand with generous investments in the renewable energy sector. It is, in short, a "revised and updated" version of the policy Keynes produced for Roosevelt—but in a communist country. How is this possible? Patrick Chovanec explains:

> The government did a good job doling out resources. First it gave support to the companies about to go bankrupt, a matter of short-term loans that also shored up employment. Then it turned to the long term and here mortgages and business loans entered the picture.[7]

Just like the "original" New Deal, the economic bailout strategy enjoyed great success, stimulating domestic demand that, contrary to Western expectations, compensated for the fall in foreign demand to the extent that economic growth, though slowed, did not stop. From the *Financial Times* to the *Economist*, from analysts at the big Western banks to those working for hedge funds, extremely few economists had predicted this miracle. On the financial front, the Chinese bailout plan certainly enjoyed more success than its US counterpart. Rather than boosting bank reserves, as was the case in the

West, the monetary stimulus injected into the banks ended up in the hands of the Chinese, thanks to the control the government exercised over the financial and banking systems.

The Chinese state is always watching over the economy. Thus, when in early 2010 and later on in 2011 the specter of inflation appeared on the horizon, the CCP raised interest rates and imposed restrictions on credit. According to the previously cited Arthur Kroeber, managing director of Dragonomics:

> The stimulus package, as in the West, was monetary rather than fiscal. The government brought liquidity to the banks. And it's likely that in the future there'll be bank loans that won't be repaid; it's inevitable, and the government will have to intervene. But the way the Chinese managed this was smarter than what the West did. When they buy toxic loans from the banks, they don't pay full price, and the more a bank finds itself in the situation of having to ask for help, the worse the credit terms they'll receive.[8]

China is still far, far away from Western deregulation. And this has been a good thing, even if in order to grow, the country will still have to reduce controls on capital flows. Kroeber continues:

> There's a need for a market where capital can be accumulated more efficiently. In the United Sates the regulatory system has failed. And this failure lead to inacceptable banking practices that caused the market crash. The Chinese system today won't crumble, but that doesn't mean it's not inefficient. China needs a bond market; the instruments are already there and used by the local authorities. The crisis has certainly accelerated the Treasury's decision-making process

toward a financial reform in this direction.[9]

What leaps out is the alacrity with which the Chinese government is battling the economic crisis. Less freedom? It's an open question, given the degree to which our political forces are hostages to the lobbies. In Britain, the governor of the Bank of England clashes openly with the government on monetary policy: the former would like to increase interest rates in order to prevent inflation; the latter is opposed to this, in the name of the wishes of the market and of its sponsors.

If we look at Washington and Beijing through Chinese eyes, we see how to be engaged on the world scene also means to observe the balance of power leaning inexorably to the East. Let's return for a moment to the days immediately following the American president's visit. Back in Washington, DC, Obama imposed further protectionist measures against China, his "banker-state." In November 2009, he approved new import tariffs on Chinese tires, both to give a boost to the domestic economy and to placate the opposition, who had been unhappy with the treatment the US received in the East. The reaction from Beijing? None. American protectionism is incapable of troubling an ever more stable Chinese economy: America becomes increasingly less important to China as the latter's dependency on an export economy diminishes. It is now the domestic market that supports a large part of the national economy.

Washington, on the other hand, needs Beijing more than ever. Not only is Barack Obama president of a nation that has since 9/11 financed costly military follies with the savings of Chinese workers, but he also relies on Asia to support, in addition to its military efforts, the economic recovery. Past, present, and future debts are inseparable, all going back to the deregulation and political hegemony of Bush; the Obama administration, however, seems incapable of changing course. The legacy that George W. Bush has left his successor appears unmanageable. Thus, to understand the current weakness of Washington, it is necessary to revisit the "war on terror," the mother of all recent American political follies.

THE WAR AGAINST TERRORISM

After September 11, 2001, the Bush administration launched the war against terrorism, assigning Osama bin Laden and his followers the status of irregular combatants, an unprecedented gesture on the part of a state, with important institutional consequences. Terrorists, prior to the fall of the Twin Towers, were the responsibility of the judiciary: police tracked them down and courts judged them, a treatment just like that received by common criminals. Its criminal nature, in fact, has always been central to the universally accepted interpretation of the concept of terrorism. This doesn't mean it constitutes a unified and well-defined threat for the modern state. On the contrary, its "political" aim, directed in general against the entire system, presents the state with a difficult problem: how to respond to the attack? Is it a threat to national security, as Bush considered it? Or is it a crime, even if sui generis, as European states have considered it throughout the second half of the twentieth century?

The problem's solution was provided to us by a British professor of political philosophy, Paul Gilbert: terrorism is a crime with war aims.[10] It is a simple but useful definition that can be applied to all forms of political violence, including the transnational terrorism of al-Qaeda; and in fact, it is the one all countries used prior to the tragedy of 9/11. Including the United States: Ramzi Yousef, one of the perpetrators of the first attack on the World Trade Center in 1993, is serving a life sentence in a US maximum-security prison.[11] For Beijing, criminals with war aims also describes the groups of Uyghurs, Chinese Muslim populations, behind the series of deadly riots in 2009.

Let's return to the immediate post-9/11 period. Bush launched the war against terrorism and, from one day to the next, Osama bin Laden became America's public enemy number one, an adversary so powerful as to require two conflicts, one in Iraq and one in Afghanistan, to wipe him out. Today we know that al-Qaeda lacked the strength to represent a threat to American national security; we also know that behind the decision to go to war was the will of the Bush administration to reintroduce the US as the hegemonic power in strategic areas of the planet, among them Iraq. In the minds of neoconservatives, this would have resolved Washington's difficulties in managing a world no longer divided into the "comfortable" spheres of influence of the Cold War.

9/11 thus became the casus belli for the recreation of a world order that belongs to the past, an unrealizable goal. The neoconservatives' propaganda machine was so well oiled, however, that everyone, truly everyone, fell into their trap. Even Muslims, who like huge numbers of other inhabitants of the planet had never heard of Osama bin Laden, were convinced that he possessed the strength to threaten the most powerful country on earth.

The consequences of this propaganda were dramatic on every front, from economics to politics. To make it easier to sell US Treasury bonds on the international market, Bush knocked down interest rates, which decreased from 6 percent on the eve of 9/11 to 1.2 percent at the beginning of summer 2003, when Washington, DC, still echoed with the famous "mission accomplished" phrase. The federal deficit, swelling like a balloon, was financing two wars, and declining tax revenues in turn created the ideal conditions for the junk bond bubble to expand to giant proportions and speculation fever to become a pandemic—all this thanks to the savings of the Chinese, with which the national banks underwrote the US federal deficit. And if indebtedness eroded the US world-leadership role, the status conferred on the threat of al-Qaeda, as the world's greatest military power's public enemy number one, gave new impetus to Islamic terrorism, while the war in Iraq proved to be an extremely powerful factor in recruiting young Muslim martyrs.

Since 9/11, Islamic fundamentalist terrorism, instead of disappearing, has spread across the world like wildfire. But the hardest blow inflicted on America by the "war on terror" is the impossibility of bringing home the troops and closing this sad chapter. It is difficult to plausibly declare victory over an enemy that doesn't exist, one created by the propaganda machine of the neoconservatives. Would there be any point in leaving Afghanistan without capturing bin Laden? Or abandoning Iraq with bombs still raining down on neighborhood markets?

A war against what is not a regular army, nor an enemy state, but rather an intangible adversary with ever-shifting features, is a potentially endless conflict. And "to bring democracy to Iraq and Afghanistan" is too vague an objective to be achievable—what does it mean? Universal suffrage, direct participation of the population in the republic, removal of the dictator Saddam Hussein? Retaking Kabul? We soon became aware of these incongruities and so too did Washington, but no one knows how to resolve them.

The few objectives that have been achieved, driving out the Taliban (on paper) and executing Saddam Hussein, have complicated the overall picture rather than improving the situation. A Pandora's box has been opened, and so today the war rages on at both fronts. The error was committed at the source, as was demonstrated for us by the Pentagon experts and Blackwater mercenaries who reminded us that the "war on terror" belongs to what the *Marine Corps Gazette* defined as the last generation of wars, those that the modern state cannot win on the battlefield, conflicts that should be avoided or at least approached in a different way.

In broad terms, fourth generation warfare seems likely to be widely dispersed and largely undefined; the distinction between war and peace will be blurred to the vanishing point. It will be nonlinear, possibly to the point of having no definable battlefields or fronts. The distinction between "civilian" and "military" may disappear. Actions will occur concurrently throughout all participants' depth, including their society as a cultural, not just a physical, entity.[12]

China's ascent of the Olympus of superpowers has much to do with the strategic errors of recent US presidents. And if we want to understand the connection between these two factors we should start by asking ourselves some questions. Why does the heart of the empire stubbornly persist in trying to recreate a world that no longer exists, setting the propaganda machine in motion to transform 9/11 into something it's not? To attribute these errors simply to neoconservative folly is not a good answer. Societies implode and disintegrate because those in charge of running them don't know how to keep up with the times, not because a group of fanatics succeeds in seizing power for a few years. Thus the Soviet bloc collapsed because the politburo and the *nomenklatura* failed to understand that a system that functioned during the first decades of the USSR's existence had become obsolete and needed to change. The KGB was aware of the fact and prepared itself for the new order. Thus today the man in charge of the new Russia is Putin, former chief of the Soviet secret services. Deng Xiaoping possessed rare foresight that he used to trace a new course for China while communism crumbled all over the world.

Washington at the beginning of the new millennium, like Moscow in the 1970s, lacked the foresight that characterized Beijing. And this was true for both the neoconservatives and their adversaries, the Democratic Party. The political machine that revolves around the administration is a rusty and out-of-date institution which doesn't understand or know how to adapt itself to international changes. The neoconservatives were convinced that military intervention was the winning strategy for opposing the international forces contending with Washington for supremacy. And they didn't even take the trouble to figure out how much all this would cost the country and who would pick up the tab. They only knew they needed a conflagration similar to the one in the past, a clash between good and evil:

> Americans expect their wars to be grand heroic crusades on a worldwide scale, a struggle between light and darkness with the fate of the world hanging on the outcome.[13]

Are we unknowingly witnessing the dying flames of the American empire? Will it collapse like the Roman Empire under the eyes of the court, which hardly seems to notice as Rome is burning. Only the future will be able to answer this question, and only the past can help us understand the significance of the parallel. So let us review and revisit.

CHAPTER 12

LATE IMPERIAL SPIN

OSAMA BIN LADEN AS THE MODERN ATTILA

We know almost nothing about the origins of the Huns. The most common interpretation is that they were descendants of the Xiongnu, Central Asian nomadic warrior tribes that threatened the Chinese empire for nearly a thousand years, up until the fourth century CE. It is said that the first Chinese emperor, Shi Huangdi, began the construction of the Great Wall in the second century BCE precisely to keep this warrior horde far away from Beijing.

The Xiongnu did not create a civilization, much less an empire, like the Chinese, and they certainly did not have a well-organized army; they were tribal populations devoted to hunting and war. And yet they conquered parts of present-day Mongolia, Manchuria, and Chinese Siberia. However, unlike their descendants, the Huns that would lay siege to Rome, the Xiongnu never reached Beijing. What stopped them was precisely the Great Wall.

Suddenly, at the beginning of the fifth century CE, these nomadic populations disappeared from the books of ancient Chinese history; at the same time, the Huns made their appearance in the annals of the Roman Empire. They show up as pillagers in southeastern Europe, and it is precisely their methods, so similar to that of the Xiongnu, that led many anthropologists to propose a blood tie between the two peoples. Before long the military tactics of the Huns defeated the Visigoths and the Ostrogoths, whose realms served as buffers for the Roman Empire from West to East. Soon after, the new barbarians, as they called them in Rome, marched toward Constantinople.

The Eastern Emperor Theodosius, fearing the Huns, made an agreement to save his empire, offering them an annual tribute. This pact obliged them to stop for a few years in the vast fields of present-day Hungary. It is here that in 432, King Rugila united all the Hunnic tribes and created a new kingdom. At his death two years later, power passed to his nephews Bleda and Attila, who took up again the advance toward the heart of the Roman Empire.

At the gates of Rome, Pope Leo I stopped the man the inhabitants of the Empire already called the "Scourge of God." Attila agreed not to sack the city and retired. Not long after, in 453, he died of natural causes, and without his leadership the kingdom of the Huns dissolved.

The court in Ravenna thought the Roman Empire was safe, but it was only an illusion. The fact that the Huns had put to flight the Roman troops and struck at the heart of the Empire destroyed the idea that Roman power was invincible in the eyes of those living in the East, and also of the conquered and subject populations. In the collective imagination, Rome had lost the status of superpower it had held for centuries.

WASHINGTON, THE MODERN RAVENNA

A quick glance at Washington, DC, suffices to draw the parallel—is the American capital the modern Ravenna? The bureaucratic machine has swallowed even the promises of the candidate Obama, and of that mantra that resounded everywhere to the rhythm of the word "change" there is no longer the least echo. The current president has not managed to refuse Bush's legacy of war aims, nor does he know how to shatter the neoconservatives' unrealizable dream of hegemony. The needs and hopes of those who elected him remain outside the door of the White House.

The parallels are multiple. Robert Straus-Hupé describes the similarity between the concentration of power in the hands of the modern US oligarchy and what prevailed at the twilight of the Roman Empire at the Ravenna court. While aware that we cannot return to the democracy of independent yeoman farmers conceived by Thomas Jefferson, it's not clear if we have understood better than the Romans the problems inherent in the concentration of immense power in the hands of the executive.[1] During the victories of the Huns, a profound resentment welled up among the population of the Empire, fed by the inequalities created by a system of taxation that took from the poor and the weak to lighten the tax burden of the rich.[2] Fiscal policy discriminated in favor of the rich during the eight years of the Bush administration as well. At the beginning of the new millennium, the United States is the industrialized country with the highest rate of social inequality (1 percent of the population collects more than 60 percent of GDP),[3] a situation that worsened during the Bush presidency to the point of threatening the very survival of the middle class. And even Obama's eagerly awaited fiscal reform did not erase these injustices. The architect of Bush's policies, Karl Rove, nicknamed "Bush's brain," went so far as to celebrate these inequalities when he promoted the concept of the "undeserving poor," society's trash. The "social rejects" of 1960s urban ghettoes, they are associated with liberal welfare policies and the "victim culture" promoted by the Democrats.[4] People with no desire to work, who live off the charity of the state. Of course, neoconservatives don't mind using these same people as soldiers in the wars they launch to recreate the Great America of the Cold War. The statistics are clear: the new recruits come from the lowest socioeconomic strata of the population.

OSAMA BIN LADEN AS THE NEW ATTILA

Attila was not the first barbarian to arrive at the gates of Rome; in 410, Alaric had gone even further and sacked the city, prompting the court's move to the more easily defensible Ravenna. Attila and his warriors were, however, the first to militarily triumph over the Roman army of both the Eastern and Western Empires. The greatness of the Roman Empire was in decline and, paradoxically, heroism on the battlefield belonged to the followers of Attila and their captains.

> The Huns learn from the cradle to the grave to endure hunger and thirst. . . . The key to understanding the success of these successful nomadic warrior societies rests in the effectiveness of their leadership: only great leaders were able to overcome internecine conflicts. These leaders were highly respected by those they led: not necessarily the case with more conventional bureaucratic militaries.[5]

This is what historians of the period tell us. The emperor, on the other hand, maintained power through an army of mercenary soldiers for whom the *solidus* (pay) had replaced Roman patriotism. The use of barbarian mercenaries can be traced back to the time of Constantine (305–337). Thus, the loyalty of the most powerful army in the world depended not on birth or on citizenship but on riches.

The Imperial army had far greater means at their disposal than did the Huns, and yet they failed to defeat them. Why? The victories of the nomad warriors demonstrate that military supremacy does not necessarily belong to the richest and best-equipped nations, but to those who force their adversary to fight on a ground or with procedures that are foreign to them. Frequently, it is a question of asymmetrical conflict.

Returning to our parallel, Bush was convinced that the

invasion of Iraq would be brief and lead to certain victory because the United States is the greatest military power in the world. And little more than a month after the start of the war in Iraq he officially declared "mission accomplished." But he was wrong. The war has been transformed into an infinite conflict swallowing up immense human and financial resources, and the Iraqi insurrection, unlike the US Army, knows how to fight it. The B-52s and Pentagon technology are not enough to win it; the insurgents have to be confronted on the battlefield, door to door, and the American soldiers are not trained for this. And this is not to speak of the cost in terms of human lives, which is unacceptable for highly civilized Western society. In fact, Bush behaved like the Emperor Valentinian and his court who, faced with the threat of the Huns, overestimated their own strength and responded to the emergency as if nothing had changed since the Empire's golden age, thus sending a colossal military machine to its destruction.[6]

But the place where the destinies of Washington and Ravenna truly cross is Afghanistan. In addition to overestimating the pacifying and stabilizing role of the "democratic" forces it promoted in the region, Washington gravely underestimated the tactical abilities of the Taliban and of the followers of al-Qaeda, abilities that undeniably recall those of the Huns, whose superior mobility allowed them to outmaneuver the Roman troops.[7]

Similar complaints can be read in the politburo's reports on the advance of the mujahideen, documents produced by Soviet generals deployed in the 1980s during the occupation of Afghanistan, and in those sent to Washington, DC, by American generals fighting the Taliban in the same regions today. When coalition forces conquer a village the enemies disappear into the mountains, where it is impossible to follow them, only to return as soon as the troops leave. Like the Soviet Army before them, the coalition forces never manage to declare victory, an ephemeral and unreachable goal.

Thus in Afghanistan for the past ten years, a ragged band of fighters has held the world's most powerful troops and richest nations in check. The United States alone spends $12 billion a month in Iraq and Afghanistan, money that it doesn't have and must borrow. The situation is as absurd and incomprehensible as the Hun's victory over the Romans nearly sixteen centuries ago. And in the eyes of his followers, the Saudi Osama bin Laden, like Attila the Hun, is a legendary character, an icon capable of guaranteeing victory.

KNOW YOUR ENEMY

Nine years after their retreat from Kandahar, the Taliban remain a cunning and invincible enemy, in a war that is economically ruining America. How is this possible? "Know your enemy," said von Clausewitz, but in the Pentagon today no one is paying any attention to this maxim. How is it that this irregular army has managed to finance a decade-long war? The answer is heroin.

The Taliban are by now an integral part of the narcotics industry; the potential export value of their opium cultivation and processing activities averaging roughly $3 billion a year since 2006, according to the United Nations. Following the fall of Mullah Omar's regime in 2001, their "sales" increased exponentially.[8] In "democratic" Afghanistan, drug trafficking has provided the Taliban with previously unheard of economic power. Prior to 2001, Pakistan's Inter-Services Intelligence agency (ISI) paid the stipends of the Kandahar public administration so that the government would not allow extensive drug trafficking. Taliban Afghanistan's balance sheet was less complex than the average household budget: apart from modest opium production, which the rulers tolerated and taxed, its income sources consisted of rent from al-Qaeda training camps and taxes on the transit of contraband. At that point, yes, they could have been called a ragged band; today, however, the situation is quite different.

A secret Pentagon report from June 2006, cited by the *Washington Post*, claims that the Taliban earn a percentage at every stage of the drug's production, from planting to the export of the finished product.[9] They impose taxes even on the importation of the chemical agents used in local laboratories to transform the opium into heroin. They do so because, in reality, they are the ones who created the conditions allowing this industry to develop in Afghanistan. And the growers, the drug lords, the traffickers, and the entire criminal world that thrives on this business in Central Asia are perfectly aware of and grateful for it. No one would dream of not paying. It was, therefore, the territorial advance of the Taliban army that removed all the obstacles to drug trafficking. The 2009 United Nations Afghanistan Opium Survey refers to a correlation between lack of security and opium cultivation.[10]

Since 2006 the Taliban have led the transformation of the country from opium producer to heroin exporter. According to the same United Nations report, they have become business partners with segments of local organized crime precisely for this reason. This joint venture has financed the spread of heroin-production laboratories into the territories under their control. Thus approximately two-thirds of the opium produced annually today, as opposed to one-half just a few years ago, becomes white powder *before* being smuggled abroad. Soon Afghanistan will export more heroin than opium. This is doubtless the goal of the Taliban, given that they earn more if they tax the finished product, heroin, with a value six or seven times that of opium. Turnover in 2007 came to nearly $3 billion; in the coming years it could easily double.

In ten years, under fire by the coalition forces and under the noses of the Americans, the Taliban have learned to take advantage of the wealth of their country—the poppy plantations—to win back the territories lost at the end of 2001. For the West, the balance sheet is decidedly negative.

While the Taliban get rich, the West is floundering in the most serious economic crisis since the Great Depression. Let's recall that the coup de grâce Attila inflicted on Ravenna was more financial than military. To maintain an army of four hundred thousand men, mercenaries for the most part, is expensive, and already in the times of Septimus Severus, at the turn of the third century CE, the taxes imposed on the population had become extremely heavy precisely for this reason. The cost of empire security was too high, and the countryside—saddled with 90 percent of the tax burden—struggled to pay it. With the spread of corruption among the tax collectors, it soon became clear that even the entire system could not support the expense of war.[11] And the population legitimately wondered if dying, maybe, from a barbarian invasion at some unspecified future date, wasn't better than dying, immediately, from hunger.

In order to confront barbarian attacks and to pay for the loyalty of the German tribes who acted as buffers on the Western border, the Roman court eventually used up its gold reserves. In 476, Ravenna no longer had the financial muscle to repel the umpteenth barbarian invasion and the Empire fell. The work begun thirty years earlier by Attila was completed.

It's not possible to equate the fall of the Roman Empire with the end of US supremacy, which is in fact still in existence to some degree, in part because it would be necessary to consider the recourse to credit, nonexistent at the time of the Empire. But an account of the errors committed by our ancestors can help us understand why those living in the East perceive in the West a weakness that escapes us. In the East they see an army that fights, but doesn't want to leave too many bodies on the battlefield; a bankrupt financial system, which pays for the war by getting into debt with China and other Asian nations; an imbalance between rich and poor that impoverishes the nations; an oligarchic democracy run by a privileged elite that thinks only of its own interests; and a propaganda machine that alters the perception of reality.

How can it be that the wonderful dream of our progress, celebrated as the Berlin Wall crumbled, has turned into the nightmare of our decadence? But that is exactly what is happening. And at the beginning of it all, as in Genesis, we find the story of two progenitors, those of the neoliberal revolution: Ronald Reagan and Margaret Thatcher, saboteurs of the nation-state.

CHAPTER 13

SABOTEURS OF THE NATION-STATE

Deng Xiaoping, a victim of the Cultural Revolution, ended up under house arrest, and from this sui generis observatory witnessed the evolution of the first oil crisis of 1973–1974. It was precisely the shrewdness of the capitalist system's initial response to the oil embargo that convinced him that Chinese communism had to renew itself by adapting to a rapidly changing world. Thus began the long march of reforms that, as we saw in the first chapters, was at one point suspended on account of the events of Tiananmen Square, but then took off again with new impetus in the early 1990s.

Meanwhile, in the "free" world, the political reasoning of Margaret Thatcher and Ronald Reagan was strikingly similar: if Western democracy wants to survive it must renew itself. The fierce, crusadelike, anticommunist campaign waged by both heads of state was only one aspect of the new path to triumphing in a globalized and postideological world. The second energy earthquake, produced by the Iranian Revolution, offered them the launch pad for overturning the way politics was done in the West. And it was an out-and-out revolution: it would in fact be reductive to speak of reforms made by Reagan in America and the Iron Lady in the United Kingdom, because the policies pursued by each redesigned the role of the Western state.

Instead of the nation-state, which protected the citizen from the anarchic jungle, they substituted the market-state, which creates for the citizen the best conditions to enrich themselves and nothing else. Too bad that, for the globalized world, there's no question of an improvement with respect to post-war democracy. Let's have a look at why.

THE THREE SABOTEURS

In the East as in the West, the energy crisis became the catalyst for shedding obsolete political paradigms stuck in the past. The sudden rise in the price of oil modified, for good, economic equilibriums going back to the Industrial Revolution. The nation-state and Western democracy, expressions of these equilibriums, began to misfire. It is emblematic that what convinced a group of farsighted politicians of the need for change was precisely the transformation of oil—the energy that made the Industrial Revolution possible—into a weapon in the hands of the countries producing it, nations that until then had lived in the shadow of either the Western or the communist system. Their entry onto the world stage first changed the number of players and then, with the collapse of the Berlin Wall, also the rules of the political game.

Thus at the end of the 1970s, Thatcher and Reagan were preparing to turn the page on the historical calendar and destroy the two-hundred-year-old nation-state in the West, as Deng Xiaoping was with Maoism in the East. The work of the three great saboteurs began with the slogan of Deng Xiaoping: "Mao was right 70 percent of the time and wrong 30 percent"; and that of Reagan and Thatcher in their election campaigns: "Government is not a solution to our problem, government is the problem."

In the West, therefore, government became the enemy of the people; not since the French Revolution had there been such a political cataclysm. Instilled in the citizen was a gnawing distrust of the political machine, such that they came to look to the market as the representative of their own interests. In the East, the people are encouraged to get rich, opening the first glimpse of freedom through the thick communist curtain. In both cases it is the economy that comes out on top: on one side under the newly victorious neoliberal banner, and on the other in the form of a channel in which the individual can freely express the best (and also the worst) of himself, far from the watchful eye of the big brother state.

The intuition of the three saboteurs was ahead of their time: at the end of the 1970s there was truly a need to prepare the ground for the new modernity that would allow globalization to take off. The classic filters in the relationship between citizen and state, like political parties, were slowly losing relevance in favor of the various manifestations of an increasingly dense and far-reaching social net, a direct expression of civil society, unimaginable only thirty years earlier. Indeed, Beijing reminds us of the power of global citizenship whenever it imposes censorship on the Internet.

From London to Tokyo, from New York to Buenos Aires, the issues that are the most important to us are the same: the environment, health, terrorism, problems that—like, for that matter, the economy—no longer belong to one nation or another, but to the entire planet. As we will see below, parties cannot express these problems nor respond to them. This is in part because they have been transformed into instruments in the hands of the executive and in part, simply, because they have been emptied of their content and their power. This void has been filled by transnational organizations such as the antiglobalization movement and the World Social Forum or Greenpeace, but also NGOs. Direct expressions of civil society, they are more suitable to the needs of the globalized world and represent a channel for the expression of the real voice of modern politics. It's too bad that the contemporary Western ruling class cannot or will not hear them.

What is happening in the East? In China the Communist Party seems less deaf to the voice of civil society even if, in many respects, it is less "politically" developed than our own.

In the last ten years, the first NGOs have appeared in China. According to Yu Fangqiang, chief coordinator for Yirenping, a Beijing-based nongovernmental group that fights to eradicate hepatitis B:

> There are two types of NGO in China, ones financed by the government and independent ones, but all of them are registered as private businesses. It is more expensive to run them because they have to pay taxes like any other company, 8 percent in the first three years and then 25 percent of revenue. Naturally, being registered as a business is risky, the government can close you down whenever it wants to. But it's a question of differences in form that don't affect the substance of the operation. Between 1999 and 2008, the number of both types of NGO went up. For example, we receive subsidies from abroad, from international organizations that are fighting hepatitis B. The majority are American, but recently we've also started to receive assistance from European businesses and universities.[1]

Official data counts ninety-three million people in China affected by hepatitis B, but, according to Yirenping's information, the number is closer to one hundred million, more than 7 percent of the population. The highest concentration live in the south of the country, in Guangdong, Hainan, and Jiangsu. The problem is very serious.

Yu Fangqiang insists that the government listens to advice and suggestions from the NGOs, and that even if dialogue does not exist, channels of communication are open. Yirenping regularly sends the government its studies and uses a series of alternative channels to influence national health policy including the press, people close to the government, university professors, lawyers, and anyone occupied with health-related matters. His NGO also works with the University of Beijing and organizes seminars and lectures.

The growth of NGOs in the health field has become a source of support for the government, which often uses these organizations' work to formulate the right policy.[2] And here it seems appropriate to make a brief aside and speak about poverty. What is the Chinese government doing for the poor? According to Li Juan, whom we have already met:

> In China there are three categories, requiring different kinds of help: people without the resources to improve their own condition, for example the sick and disabled, who need health care; poor people who work in the countryside have some resources but have to be helped in order to take advantage of those resources, for example instructing them in what kind of crop to produce and then sell; then there are the indigent in urban areas, those who've been unemployed for a while, homeless who need financial assistance, a house, and health care.
>
> In the last ten years, the government has done a lot for all three of these categories, and at the moment is working on a law for the eradication of poverty. Many foreigners don't know these things and think that China is a totalitarian country, but that's not the case. The central government works. For now, the single-party system is better suited to the country than a multiparty one.[3]

Thus, while the intuition of Margaret and Ronald failed to produce the desired results, as confirmed by the malaise spreading through the West thirty years later, in China the engine of growth continues to move in the direction glimpsed by Deng, to the point that NGOs have a voice and the war against poverty makes progress.

Why has our democracy failed? Why does it seem so deaf to the needs of the general public? Owing to a misunderstanding: the voice of civil society has come to be confused with, or in the worst of cases reduced to, the mere voice of the market. And this confusion persists, even if the credit crisis and the recession have made us understand that completely abandoning the economy to market forces, thinking that these forces were one of the principal channels through which civil society was manifested, was pure folly.

This strategy has left the citizenry exposed to the abuses of power. It's enough to glance at the federal deficits of the Western countries, swollen enormously to save the big business banks, or to examine the boxes on our paychecks, from which social security benefits have virtually disappeared, or exchange a few words on the subject with our children, condemned to a lifetime of precarious work. These signs surely indicate that it is the elites, and certainly not civil society, who control the market, the same elites who run the political parties and the unions. Such powerful groups have no interest in bringing about the renewal that the base of the political pyramid demands, and in fact they often work against it.

On the other side of the world, the economic success of China, a communist country, reminds us that the state exists first of all to promote the well-being of its citizens, not that of the elite, and that its presence is as necessary in the economy as in foreign policy. It is the duty of the state to safeguard economic as well as national security. Would you trust the defense of the country to the "invisible hand"? Would you trust mercenaries to defend the national borders? Then why have we put our well-being in their hands? The saboteur Deng has paved the way for a series of gradual reforms, under the alert and vigilant gaze of the government. And so far the experiment has worked. The Chinese are freer and better off than they were twenty years ago. And us?

Even if we do not agree with this type of government, even

if we condemn the social repression that has occurred in China in the name of progress, we cannot fail to notice that our own democracy is increasingly open to abuse by those wielding political and economic power. And we should hope that our state too looks after us rather than leaving us "freedom" that translates into slavery to the market. This is what China has to teach us. Somewhere, the right formula for a new modernity exists. Since Deng's time, the Chinese have kept themselves busy looking for it, trying out political alternatives; we don't even look anymore. The successors of Thatcher and Reagan have continued to sabotage the nation-state with the mad aim of replacing it with the market. The sad fate of Iceland reminds us of the dangers hidden in this model.

But in order to appreciate how the Chinese experience can help us to understand where we have done wrong and how to visualize what lays ahead for us if we persist down the slope of political negligence, we must venture on one last voyage back into contemporary history: the rise of Margaret Thatcher and Ronald Reagan. We do this, above all, in order to reflect on the urgent need for new strategies to take back what is ours: politics.

RONALD AND MARGARET, ADAM AND EVE OF THE MARKET-STATE

The Bible tells us that our world was born from original sin: Eve offered Adam the apple from the forbidden tree and from that moment on, everything changed. Without knowing it, Adam and Eve created the concept of modernity, or the desire to try new things and the need for change, the two faces of progress.

Like Adam and Eve, the alliance between Ronald and Margaret resembles a genuine idyll. It is said that their first meeting was for both of them a case of love at first sight. It was April 9, 1975, and Thatcher had recently been elected secretary of the British opposition party, the Tories; Reagan had just left the position of governor of California and was preparing for his presidential campaign, he too in the opposition. They were both conservative politicians in transition, looking for alliances. The meeting lasted twice as long as the planned forty-five minutes: to the bewilderment of their aides, both continued to ask for more time. This is how the future US head of state described the meeting with his political soul mate: "We found that we were really akin with regard to our views of government and economics and government's place in people's lives and all that sort of thing."[4]

Indeed, the Atlantic alliance with Thatcher turned out to be extremely powerful, even revolutionary for Reagan. In clear contrast with members of their own parties, which continued to profess the Keynesian creed, both were obsessed with the monetary theory of Milton Friedman, the same theory Pinochet experimented with in Chile. But there's nothing surprising in that; neither one, in fact, expressed the majority view of his or her own political group, both came from the periphery. Not by chance, among their primary objectives was the fight against communism, which neither Republicans nor Conservatives considered at all a priority.[5]

The electoral success of "outsider," nonaligned politicians at the end of the 1970s was no coincidence. For some years both the Tories and the Republicans had struggled to win majorities, a particularly worrying unpopularity in a historical moment in which those in office, Labour in the UK and the Democrats in the US, enjoyed very little support. Why be surprised? On both sides of the Atlantic in the 1970s, progressive ungovernability and economic decline reigned. The postwar formula—sustained growth, controlled inflation, and increased international competitiveness—was at that point an unrealizable dream. And those who suffered the most were in fact Great Britain and the United States, where between 1962 and 1972, annual US (3 percent) and UK growth (2.2 percent) were the lowest among the G6 countries. Between 1972 and 1979, the gap between the US and the UK and France, West Germany, Italy, and Japan increased.[6]

The slowdown in growth pushed the welfare state into crisis, and in order to take care of public spending the government went into debt. In 1975, the budget deficit represented 50 percent of British GDP, a level, according to then–Minister of the Interior Roy Jenkins, incompatible with a free society. In the United States the federal deficit passed from $63 million in the 1960s to $420 million ten years later.[7]

But inflation was this decade's obscure sickness. In Western countries it jumped from 2 percent in the 1960s to 6 percent in 1970. At the end of 1973, the time of the first energy crisis, it rose to above 10 percent in the United States, reaching 14 percent in the spring of 1980. In Great Britain the situation was even worse: in autumn 1973 inflation was already at 13 percent; eighteen months later it doubled and reached 27 percent. At this point, people not only began to worry about the advent of hyperinflation, but also to fear for the very stability of the worldwide economic system.[8]

Rising prices and decreasing GDP eroded wealth, and this created discontent among the population, especially with regards to the parties in power. Even more serious, between the middle of the 1960s and the advent of the Thatcher-Reagan revolution, as much in Great Britain as in the US, a crisis of faith in the Western political system continued to spread.

According to the American National Elections Studies Center, in the United States the percentage of so-called cynical voters went from 16.4 percent in 1964 to 50 percent in 1978. In the same period, the percentage of those who still had faith in the system fell from 57.1 percent to 15.1 percent.[9]

The relationship of the citizens to party politics deteriorated. Investigations conducted by CBS and by the *New York Times* revealed that in America between 1967 and 1980 the proportion of citizens who had trust in the functioning of the party system fell by a third among Democrats and by half among Republicans. The same thing happened in Great Britain where the number of those voting for one of the two major parties contracted from 96.8 percent in 1951 to 76.8 percent in 1974.

In the West, electoral participation fell everywhere, but it did so in a particularly worrying fashion in the US and the UK. In America, a country with traditionally low voter participation rates, 62.2 percent of the population voted in the presidential elections of 1960; sixteen years later only 54.4 percent exercised this right. In 1974, less than 72 percent of the English went to the polls, among the lowest levels in Europe. And the population displaced political participation outside traditional structures. The 1960s produced a boom in pressure groups, lobbies, and political action committees. Extraparliamentary parties were born, student movements, and the Greens. This was civil society's political debut, a new force born out of the profound uncertainty into which the energy crisis had thrown Western democracy.[10]

By now it is clear that, unlike Adam and Eve, Ronald and Margaret did not live in an earthly paradise, but rather in a swamp that often swallows up politicians. Jimmy Carter is one of these: elected triumphantly, after four years he was a very unpopular president. But Thatcher and Reagan were ready to risk everything to reclaim the swamp and put a new brand of cunning in the field. During the electoral campaign that would bring them to power, they didn't attack the adversary as someone incompetent to run the state machinery; they attacked the state itself. They attributed the crisis and the sense of insecurity that spread through the population to the political system. The welfare state was presented as an old motor, costly and obsolete, that prevented society from modernizing—the state and those administering it became the enemies of the citizens and reformist politicians. And this ideological revolution, fed by the fictitious sense of well-being during the 1990s, was destined to become the lens, or perhaps the cage, through which we still look at the world today. What bothers us most about China is not the single party (how many of us believe in the real differences between our political parties?), but the omnipresence of the state.

Completely overturning the nation-state equation, Margaret and Ronald insisted that the role of public administration had to be cut to the bone and the citizen left completely free to decide how to live. Health, education, pensions all migrated from the public to the private sphere and thus required individual decisions. And here the parents of the neoliberal revolution committed their first error, failing to understand that in the long term the historical changes that national policy would have to confront would be identical to the challenges of the globe, like the environment and health issues, that cannot be resolved by individuals, much less by the market. But in distant 1983, global warming and the spread of cancer appeared to be the problems of the extreme few, irrelevant phenomena.

Thus, state assets are put on the auction block through the process of privatization, becoming the "private property of the citizens." And the emerging business banks handled the sales, drawing mind-boggling commissions. Thus the Wall Street banks got fat making merry with the carcasses of state services.

The social contract, which for more than two hundred years had brought stability and prosperity to the West, was smashed because it was "no longer of use," and in its place was introduced, with fanfare, the market-state, an infinitely smaller and thus more agile and, above all, less expensive apparatus, whose ultimate aim is precisely to facilitate the functioning of the market. The citizens are invited to trust in the market, an institution as old as the world. The laws introduced after 1929 to limit the abuses of Wall Street, protect the savings of citizens, and ensure the soundness of the economy are abolished one by one. The first to disappear was the Glass-Steagall Act. Thus fell the prohibition on playing the financial market after hours and on participating in foreign stock exchanges. The market, now open twenty-four hours a day, became the motor of Western society.

Reducing the state to the bone allowed the launch of a campaign that remains invincible at the level of political propaganda: the tax cut. It's enough to make the promise of a tax cut to fool the voters into thinking that all the problems that assail them can be put down to the poor functioning of the machinery of the state, a predatory organism that squanders their earnings. Paradoxically, the government became the champion of the people against the state.

CHAPTER 14

SUPPLY-SIDE ECONOMICS

At the core of the crusade against the state, what essentially legitimates it, is monetarism, which both Reagan and Thatcher supported and which they summed up in the slogan that the progressive reduction of the role of government and the tax burden improves the functioning of business.

Supply-side economics, or monetarism, was born as an alternative economic theory to Keynesianism, which in the 1970s failed to curb inflation connected to the energy crisis and ensuing degeneration: stagflation. A mix of high inflation and absence of growth, the phenomenon eroded the wealth of Western nations and left them with no way out. Neither monetary maneuvering (the variation of interest rates), nor fiscal adjustments (changes in tax rates), seemed to work.

But if it is true that Keynesian theory was unable to stop the crisis, it is also true that monetarism did not work either. Not only is the latter a theory that studies a single aspect of the economic system (the supply and demand of money), but unlike Keynesian theory, applied after the Great Depression, it has never been put to the test.

Opposition to the welfare state was Thatcher and Reagan's game, however, and thus it was immediately adopted as a "doctrine of renewal" and adapted to the new political course by a group of individuals defined as supply-siders, whose principle characteristic, surprisingly, was their scant knowledge of economics and politics. This from a Nobel Prize winner in economics, Paul Krugman. In 1992, some journalists asked him to mention the names of some prominent academic exponents of supply-side economics. Krugman was silent. Not only does there not exist an American university where monetarism is studied, but there are no economists who could be defined supply-siders. So who were these people?[1]

The answer is to be found in the world of the media, on the periphery of the US Congress where the lobbyists graze, in the consultancy firms and research centers that, like mushrooms after a night of rain, appear among the political undergrowth. The leading edge of the monetarist movement is the group of "reformers" put together by Robert Bartley in 1972, when he was asked to become the editor of the *Wall Street Journal*'s editorial page. For the most part these were journalists and a handful of iconoclast economists, among them Jude Wanniski, who together transformed the financial daily into a monetarist manifesto.

In addition to the supply-siders there were a few conservative voices such as Arthur Laffer and Robert Mundell. Laffer, specifically, was the father of the theory that if taxes go down, the motivation of citizens to work more goes up, because they pocket a higher percentage of what they earn, a postulate never verified empirically.[2] No one, in fact, among the supply-siders was an empiricist; on the contrary, they all kept well away from any testing of their theses. These were thinkers who, in the intimacy of their offices, far from the real problems of a world changing to the disadvantage of the West, imagined theoretical solutions.

The monetarist position rests on a series of assumptions and logical arguments that confirm the postulates and make use of mathematics to back them up.[3] It is, therefore, profoundly self-referential. The motto seems to be that reality must adapt itself to the theory. This is the message that Friedman carried to Pinochet when he convinced him to transform Chile into the laboratory of the new economy, a transformation that succeeded at gunpoint.

We are thus far, far away from the philosophy of Deng Xiaoping and from the methodology applied in reforming the Chinese economy. If Deng placed one foot after another into the riverbed in order to cross it, Friedman and his followers ensured they'd be swept away by the current.

IT'S THE GOVERNMENT'S FAULT

Thus the key to the monetarist revolution's success is to be sought not in the theory's modernity but in the dissatisfaction of the 1970s. It was a difficult moment for the West. Everyone realized that the growth mechanism was jammed, but how to repair it? How to return to the splendors of the postwar period? Nobody knew, including the saboteurs, who nevertheless made sure to give the opposite impression.

In the same way, it hardly mattered if Milton Friedman lacked the winning formula to pull the West out of its economic mess; the supply-siders took care to invent the right slogans, enough to win over the majority of voters. Thus the actual existence of the mess was pushed into the background, or rather was hidden by the new winning political-economic "strategy." And this is why, with infinite dismay, we are only discovering this today, thirty years later.

As we will see below, part of this work of obscuring, of making things less and less visible, falls to spin, the art of manipulating information. The conservative press acted as an echo chamber for the new course, ensuring that the absurd ideas of the supply-siders would bounce from one coast of the Atlantic to the other. Cohorts of recent graduates, frustrated by the meager job prospects offered by an economy in crisis, would devour the editorials on the subject. And little by little the drab, cautious, and competent men who had until then run our state institutions, including the banks, began to be pushed out by the ambitious young go-getters who would in due course bring about all the economic megacrises of the global village.

Unlike Deng Xiaoping, who sabotaged Maoism with the aim of reforming the system and saving Chinese communism, once in power Reagan and Thatcher were limited in their destruction because they didn't have a plan. But the ferocity with which they swept down on the nation-state, aided above all by the jackhammer that was the *Wall Street Journal*, managed to fool many: such ardor had to be connected to a well-defined project, a new political system.

Thus, in the wake of the fall of the Berlin Wall, the supply-siders appeared more like knights of the neoliberal Round Table than of the political-economic apocalypse of the West. As far as the progressive press goes, the events of 1989 caused them to completely lose their ideological equilibrium, rendering them mute before the revolutionary advance of the conservatives, and no one had the strength to oppose the gushing euphoria of the victory over communism.

In *Peddling Prosperity*, Paul Krugman asks how it was possible that two politicians whose programs, even just on paper, privileged only the rich, were elected by the majority. Many find an answer in the simplicity of the neoliberal formula, which singles out the state as the enemy and the market as the solution to all problems. But neither the antistate propaganda, nor the helpless confusion in which progressive forces found themselves unable to mount a cogent response, can explain the persistent popularity of this ideology. What is then the real answer?

Today we realize that the other face of the fictitious well-being produced by the monetarist revolution is indebtedness, but at the end of the 1980s this aspect was overshadowed by what appeared to be the success of the new doctrine. The possibility of going into debt temporarily obscured the West's economic problems, and the sale of state assets and the events of Berlin revived the agonizing capitalist system. A perfect correlation was established between the federal deficit and

GDP: both only went up. On paper there was a recovery, but it turned out to be ephemeral. Above all it produced a generation of individuals motivated solely by money and uninterested in social problems, rending the socioeconomic fabric of the modern democracies.

LOADSAMONEY

In the 1980s the English comedian Harry Enfield created a number of different characters for the Channel 4 program *Saturday Live* that incarnated these changes. Among these was Stavros, a Greek restaurant owner, the young politician Tory Boy, and the yuppie who waves wads of cash around while shouting happily "loadsamoney," which became his nickname. Stavros is of Greek origin, but apart from the name is the stereotypical Englishman from a working class background, just like Loadsamoney. The latter, a great beer-drinker, speaks the incomprehensible dialect of Essex, the county northeast of Greater London from which the city's nonprofessional staff traditionally come. Like Stavros, he was born in one of the squalid working-class neighborhoods that flourished in the areas destroyed by Nazi bombing during World War II.

Thanks to Thatcher's reforms, Stavros becomes rich selling kebabs and Loadsamoney makes deals more or less everywhere. The former doesn't pay much in taxes, because he runs a private business; both are without family, and both have at their disposal a much higher income than they would have in the past. The young yuppies working in the city of London in the 1980s, coming from all over the West, belong to the generation of Stavros and Loadsamoney. They're noisy, arrogant, and vulgar, but they work hard and above all they are ruthless. For them the end always justifies the means and there is just one goal: to make loads of money. They are the heirs of Machiavelli and the financial industry, the sector that derived the most advantage from the neoliberal reforms, became their stomping ground.

The Iron Lady's gift of well-being allowed many to improve their social status: they bought fancy cars, went to live in neighborhoods previously reserved for the upper classes, and frequented expensive restaurants and bars. Money becomes the aphrodisiac of an entire generation; wealth is to be paraded; and saving is replaced by unfettered consumerism.

Stavros and Loadsamoney remind us that, thanks to Thatcher, social mobility became a reality in England for the first time, and the working class achieved success not through education but thanks to business. The daughter of a grocer, Maggie, openly promoted the class of merchants, business-men, and bankers. Unpopular with the nobility, openly opposed to the monarchy, the scourge of intellectuals, she encouraged the common people to raise their head and seek in money the social redemption denied them for centuries under the reign of His Majesty.

This social revolution, however, does not bring about lasting well-being nor modernize the country, as had been promised; only inequality continued to grow. Stavros and Loadsamoney belong to a minority, the fortunate ones who, following the Machiavellian motto, end up on the right side of the barricade. Those who don't manage to clear this hurdle sink into the mud.

Between 1979 and 1994–1995, the rate of income growth among the English poor is the lowest since the end of World War II; while that of the richest 10 percent is the highest. If we also take into consideration the cost of housing, which took off in this period, the gap becomes even greater. For the poorest 10 percent, per capita net income, in fact, contracts.

These inequalities were willfully ignored not only by the new generation of yuppies, but also by the opposition party, which, through the metamorphoses orchestrated by Tony Blair, became New Labour. In order to win elections the future prime minister didn't hesitate to propose to this newly well-to-do class better tax and economic incentives than those offered by the Tories. No one spoke about the socioeconomic problems faced by an increasingly large part of the population. On the contrary, first Thatcher's model and then Blair's more recent version end up being exported all over Europe. That is, naturally, up until the credit crisis and the recession.

Things went very differently in China. The magic formula resides not in the market but in the state. Let's listen once again to Maurice Ohana, head of Ohanasia:

> The German chancellor Gerhard Schröder attended the inauguration of the maglev train, which carries passengers at supersonic speeds from Shanghai to the Pudong Airport. The press asked him how that train, produced by the German company Siemens, came to be built in China rather than in Germany. "Because in Germany," he answered, "there would have been infinite disputes, first about prices, then with the environmentalists, and so on. In China the government does things. The train was necessary and so they did it. In China the government works for the people, in the interests of the population." In 1998 we didn't even have Coca-Cola here. Everyone got around on bikes. Today we're buying more cars than the Americans. In ten years we have built 30,000 kilometers of highways and all the big cities have an extensive and efficient subway system.
>
> The central government has guaranteed the country food, schools, and progress. Guess who the people would vote for if there were elections? You Westerners don't want to understand that the government guides development by means of enthusiasm, not a whip.[4]

It would be difficult today to find a Westerner prepared to

describe the neoliberal "miracle" in analogous terms. But China is no earthly paradise, it's a country like so many others, with big problems—but they are not the ones we imagine. The people aren't dreaming about our democracy but instead talk about economic inequality, equal opportunity, and the corruption of politicians, exactly like in the rest of the world. Let's hear again from Mao Yushi, president of Unirule:

> The rich evade taxes. The internal revenue office doesn't know who they are because a large part of their income comes from abroad, from profits generated by investments, not wages. This is why the government isn't informed. Thus only salaried employees pay taxes. When there was the planned economy, no one paid taxes. And so institutions don't have the proper tradition, and people aren't used to paying taxes. It's a bit like in Russia. In China the internal revenue derived from taxes is barely 1 or 2 percent of GDP and the objective is to bring it up to 20 percent.[5]

But trust in the government's development policy and in the state apparatus is still strong. And the results are undeniable, especially if compared with those of other Asian countries. As Patrick Chovanec reminds us:

> China has chosen the long road of development. Vietnam took the shortcut. The Vietnamese government tried to take all the money and bribes it could from investors in as little time as possible. Although this tendency is also present in China, it's not the line taken by the government, which instead pushes investors to stay and invest more. The effectiveness of the pursuit of this type of policy was proved by China's entry into the WTO, which has been immensely positive for the country. Up to now, the

Chinese government has moved in a sensible way: planning for the future and promoting solid policies to support the economy. Deng's promises have in large part come true.[6]

We cannot say the same of Margaret Thatcher. When she was removed from government everyone realized that her promises were worthless; even those relative to public spending didn't come to anything. In 1979 she had declared: "Public spending is at the root of the nation's economic difficulties,"[7] an assumed truth on which was founded the privatization of state assets. When more than ten years later she left the political arena, public spending considered as a percentage of GDP had gone down by an extremely modest 1 percent with respect to 1979. Where did the privatization money go?[8] To swell the balances of the business banks, which thanks to Thatcher transformed themselves into exceedingly powerful conglomerates, with earnings greater than the GDP of entire nations.

In the United States the well-being was also illusory. GDP growth in the 1980s was lower than that registered between 1974 and 1980, during the two oil crises. Despite government being slashed to the bone, between 1980 and 1992, during Reagan's two terms and George H. W. Bush's one, the federal deficit quadrupled to exceed $3 trillion. Benefiting from this was the military industry, made more powerful by two presidents for whom national security was among the few tasks still left to the state.

Thus, the destruction of the welfare system did not radically alter the size of public spending, just modified its priorities and prevented the redistribution of wealth.

While, in the East, Deng Xiaoping was opening the economy and encouraging farmers to become workers, and China was taking its first steps into the realm of private property, the West was getting poorer. And the classic mechanisms of democratic political participation suffered a heavy blow.

CHAPTER 15

THE FULL MONTY

The expression "the full monty" was coined during World War II to describe the immense appetite of General Montgomery, nicknamed Monty, who every morning would devour a full English breakfast without leaving behind so much as a crumb, in the midst of the Battle of El Alamein.

The Full Monty, however, is also the title of a very successful English film. We all know the story, which takes place in Sheffield, in the north of England, in the early 1990s. It describes the vicissitudes of some former employees of the steel industry—pride of the Midlands—completely dismantled during the 1980s by the neoliberalist policies of Madam Thatcher. Desperate, the six protagonists of the film decide to become strippers and to go all the way, to strip down to nothing on stage.

But for those who lived in the north of England during the Thatcher administration, "to go all the way" recalls the warrior mantra of the Iron Lady: to take a clean-slate approach to state-supported industry. And given that this was to be found in the north, the cradle of the Industrial Revolution, the conservative government's frontal attack on the workers took place precisely in the Midlands.

The longest and most dramatic battle that Thatcher fought was the one against the miners, the praetorian guard of the unions run by Arthur Scargill, last dinosaur of the British Far Left. These were dramatic years in which the government decimated the worker population, and a future was traced out in which there were no more smoking chimneys, industry, naval yards, and pubs bursting with workers, one dominated instead by unemployment and precarious work. All this while in China the exact opposite was happening: the dismantling of state-sponsored industry was accompanied by the birth of private factories and laboratories; furnaces started up and rural migrants transformed into a new working class.

With oil at eighteen dollars a barrel and hundreds of millions of Chinese willing to work for a fraction of the wages in England, industrial production in the Midlands no longer made sense—this was Thatcher's argument. The woman who would pass into history as the Iron Lady precisely for her intransigence in confronting the miners had, in reality, challenged an extremely weak adversary: a working class justly dismayed before the open hostility of the government, which was supposed to be the country's champion against foreign competition; a working class that didn't understand why it was no longer needed, who, without a job, had no idea how to make ends meet. In other words, the British prime minister challenged precisely the people she should have been protecting.

Thatcher's mistake was to ignore a reality peculiar to Great Britain: the working class's reluctance with regard to social mobility. The Iron Lady failed to understand that the miners' resistance to the bitter end had nothing to do with Arthur Scargill's Stalinism, but rather with the miners' strong sense of identity. Working in the mines was the only existence the miners had ever known, and they were willing to fight for it. It is a mistake to tear apart the social fabric of a country; this is why even the few conversion projects were poorly managed and ended up failing. The dismantling of the state produced a defeated proletariat class, relegated to urban ghettoes with rampant unemployment, where petty crime favored the birth of the gangs terrorizing the country today. The signs of the socioeconomic decline of the Midlands are still very visible today; the port of Hull, on the east coast, once among the most important in the UK for fishing and naval industries, is a desert inhabited by wolves and stray dogs. Anyone looking for a harshly realistic image of the legacy of Madam saboteur can find it along the rotting wharves, beside the crumbling sheds, instant allegories of the neoliberal revolution in England and irrefutable testimony of the market's incapacity to replace the state as the principle engine of society.

But the principle economic and political error committed by Thatcher, and by Reagan, was another, and that is to not have foreseen that the delocalization to Asia of a large slice of (by now privatized) production would put an end to the supremacy of the West, and in particular of England, a position gained thanks to the Industrial Revolution. Today, at the beginning of 2011, the UK is struggling to emerge from the recession, with a contraction of GDP in 2009 above 5 percent, a negative growth in 2011 and unemployment still on the rise.[1] Aside from the financial industry, still recovering, the country lacks the industrial muscles to get back on top.

The real revolution should have been another. The answer to increased energy costs, which since 1973–1974 have caused the profits of state-owned industries to evaporate, should have been an energy conversion program that would, in the long term, have increased Western competitiveness. The Iron Lady should have looked ahead, like Deng Xiaoping did. But Margaret Thatcher was short-sighted, and failed to understand that it's not enough to knock down one system to revolutionize a country; you also have to create a new one. And even if energy conversion wouldn't have saved the miners, it would at least have avoided the destruction of the British—and a great deal of the West's—industrial infrastructure.

THE FIGHT AGAINST THE UNIONS

The miner's dismay at Thatcher's frontal attack and the absolute rigidity of Arthur Scargill shouldn't surprise us: England was the birthplace of the workers' movement and it is a sort of poetic justice that it was also its deathbed. The murder weapon, naturally, was privatization. Between 1979 and 1993, the British government sold two thirds of its public industry to the private sector.[2]

Initially the experiment was limited to aviation, only recently nationalized, and the naval industry, but soon it extended to the large state monopolies, including basic services like energy and telecommunications. The policy of privatization enjoyed enormous success because, as we have seen, it accompanied the social revolution of the Loadsamoney generation. In 1984 two million people, equal to 5 percent of the adult population, supported the sale of British Telecom: from one day to the next the number of stockholders doubled.[3] In the space of a decade, the government unloaded the industrial pillars of the nation-state: British Aerospace (1981), Cable and Wireless (1981), Amersham International (1982), Associated British Ports (1983), Enterprise Oil (1984), Jaguar (1984), British Telecom (1984), British Gas (1986), British Airways (1987), Rolls-Royce (1987), British Airports Authority (1987), British Steel (1988), and all the regional water companies (1989).

Privatization, occurring under the gleaming eyes of the supply-siders, will pass into history as the legacy of Madam Thatcher. And historians will tell us that the aim was not only to cut the state down to the bone and use the proceeds to create a new unscrupulous entrepreneurial class, but to definitively block union access to public funds, which had up until that point been one of their sources of income, and to undermine their power.[4] This was done because the conservative party saw in the unions the greatest obstacle to both economic recovery and the triumph of neoliberalism. And why? Because a strong union movement could have thrown a wrench in the works of delocalization.[5]

Let's return to Krugman's question from the previous chapter: how is it possible that people elect someone who clearly looks out for the interests of a small elite? At least in the case of Great Britain, struck particularly hard by the energy crisis, the most common explanation refers to a country paralyzed by wildcat strikes, galloping inflation, and negative growth. The Labour government ended up detested by an electorate with little idea of what was happening, who paid high taxes in exchange for mediocre services. When Thatcher pointed the finger at the unions and at the energy-intensive industries, like steel production, the exasperated electorate was only too happy to believe these really were the culprits.

What the people didn't know was that the exceptional competitiveness of Western postwar industry was an extraordinary phenomenon, connected above all to the extremely low cost of oil, remaining at four dollars a barrel for thirty years. No politician had the courage to reveal to the workers or, above all, the industrialists, that a tacit agreement between the United States and Saudi Arabia was at the root of this anomaly, but that the pact was fraying.

Of course the unions, like the parties, bear a great deal of responsibility for the crisis of the 1970s, and this is the case throughout the West. They too abused the welfare state, continuing to milk a cow with no more milk to give. Nevertheless, the solution to the problem was not direct conflict between capital and labor, nor the pulverization of the unions, one of the principle communication channels between workers and industrialists. But this is exactly what happened.

Whereas in China, when Deng set the first reforms in motion, the occasionally violent debates about how to structure them took place behind closed doors, within the Party, the ideological struggle between Conservatives and Labour, between Republicans and Democrats, between the European Right and the Left burst through the media into people's homes. There was neither mediation nor cooperation between the two sides of the barricade, and this was a shame because this type of propaganda politics isn't only bad for nations but also erodes the institutions of the democratic state—the unions and the parties.

With the assumption that unions were the "enemy," no one in the UK opposed a series of labor legislations that progressively reduced their freedom of action. A 1980 law prohibited pickets outside the work area; a 1982 law, which bore the signature of Norman Tebbit, Thatcher's right-hand man, permitted employers to fire strikers, outlawed sit-ins, and abolished collective agreements; a 1984 law, created by Tom King, at the time secretary of state in Thatcher's government, increased the number of reasons for which it was possible to subpoena a union, imposed secret voting of members, and reduced the use of union funds in electoral activity.[6] And in the 1980s, these legislations became the blueprint for laws across Europe.

Paradoxically, the West's most ferocious criticisms of the Chinese system refer to the government's negligence in introducing and enforcing collective agreements—an interesting position if we consider that in the 1980s, in democratic Great Britain, Madam Thatcher de facto abolished collective bargaining. Behind the neoliberal rhetoric there is in fact a desire to compensate for the increased cost of capital, due to the rise in energy prices, with the reduced cost of labor. But neither Reagan nor Thatcher foresaw that their antiunion policies would lead their economies away from the productive sphere, opening up new areas to future Asian competitors. Why is that?

Studies conducted in the 1980s and '90s by the two major English parties showed that the presence of unions in the West decreased between 1980 and 1990, a period during which collective bargaining was reduced to the point of becoming, as it is today in the private sector, the exception to the rule.[7] Thus disappeared that system of collective relationships that provided capital and labor, by means of union representation, with a system of rules and a common language.[8] So, when the globalization tsunami overwhelmed us, we were unprepared. Our real strength had been the combination of advanced capitalism and the working class, navigated with great experience. Once the dialogue was interrupted, the industry broke up and with it the productive fabric. As the West became a provider of services, smoke billowed from factory chimneys in the East.

Delocalization, however, only offered business a breather, in the long term exposing it to brutal competition from countries like China. Today we know better, but some still deceive themselves that our design and creativity, being superior to that of the Chinese, will save us. This is not the case, and if we don't manage to change our current course, we risk ending up begging our subsistence from the Asian tourists visiting our city-museums.

PARTY, INC.

The British experiment was exported to all of Europe, where a new a class of politicians began to undermine the welfare state and replace it with the market-state. Complicit in this is the fall of the Berlin Wall, which put an end to the contraposition of Right and Left, allowing the market to force its way into the void created by the end of ideology. Democracy was impoverished, as can be seen in the sad stories of the decline of representative democracy throughout the West, as parties of the left and the right resemble one another more and more, as the portion of the electorate that actually votes in elections grows ever smaller, and as the influence of corporations on government grows ever larger.

Born in the process of democratization, the two-party and multiparty systems were the means of communication between the base and the peak of the pyramid. In the postwar period they assumed a key role in the functioning of representative democracy.[9] In fact it's hard to imagine representative democracy without parties, and it's no coincidence that one of the most severe criticisms we make of China is the presence of a single party.

Two-party and multiparty systems have also become synonymous with democracy because this type of system relies on changes in power, encouraging citizens to think that even if the party they support loses an election, it could win the next one. The principle of alternate government comes to be seen as the best defense against political violence and authoritarianism.[10] In Italy, the militant groups of the 1960s and '70s justified the use of violence to resolve political controversies as a rebellion against a blocked democracy, a country always governed by the same party or by coalitions it led.

Now it is precisely the neoliberal revolution of Thatcher and Reagan that began the process of ruining the parties, which little by little lost their popular component and became political machines run by an extremely small elite. The dimensions change, the base gets narrower, top management expands. In the 1980s, as Peter Mair and Ingrid van Biezen explain, these metamorphoses gained ground throughout the West.[11] At this point the "private financiers" entered the scene, rich sponsors who supported the political "cause" of one group rather than another. And not least because ideology was dead, they promoted within their chosen party the vision of the market they found most convenient. Once again it is England, in the form of New Labour, that opens the road to this latest change. In 2004, barely 8 percent of party income came from members, compared to 49 percent in the 1960s.[12] Between 2001 and 2005, the contributions of thirty-seven people, among them the steel magnate Lakshmi Mittal, provided for a quarter of New Labour's funding needs. In 2006 an English parliamentary commission on the funding of political parties warned the country about the changes in progress with these words:

The systems that have kept political parties running over the past century are breaking down. As membership has fallen, political parties have become increasingly dependent on large donations from individuals to fund their election campaigns.[13]

In Italy in 1994, Silvio Berlusconi, among the richest men in the world, founded a party, *Forza Italia*, which he financed entirely with his own money. It was a sensational event, unprecedented in Western history, but it brought to the fore a not very democratic fact: politics is controlled by those with the money to buy in.

Thus, in the West the patronage system spreads throughout the corridors of power. Enron "paid" for a large part of George W. Bush's election campaign so that in exchange the electricity market would be liberalized. But in Europe it's still New Labour that leads the pack. In 2006 the scandal of noble titles in exchange for election financing erupted when it was discovered that a group of rich supporters had "loaned" the party fourteen of the eighteen billion pounds necessary to pay for the 2005 election campaign. The victorious Blair government named many of those sponsors baronets.[14]

The impoverishment of the popular base ends up reducing the parties to skeletal organisms at the service of increasingly rich and charismatic leaders. And many members adapt themselves to the new credo of the neoliberalist revolution, celebrating the marvels of the market. The political machine now functions like a bank or any hedge fund, periodically accounting to the board of directors for the dividends that its every move generates for the majority stakeholders. These individuals, obviously, impose their own conditions, which go well beyond titles of nobility, as the case of Enron reminds us.

In this context, electoral victory is essential in order to satisfy generous financiers, who otherwise would leave; and remaining in power becomes a matter of life or death for the party, which can no longer count on the long-term fidelity associated with the old ideologies and members.

It often happens, as in the case of New Labour and of many European parties emerging from the old Left, that the interests of the sponsors conflict with the interests of the members that constitute the party's base. It thus becomes necessary to reduce the party's internal democratic mechanism—a paradoxical necessity in order to guarantee survival in a democracy. Thus, in Italy during the 2010 local elections the Italian Democratic Party did not hold primaries in some regions and the party secretary negotiated with other parties to select candidates, and this occurred against the will of large parts of the party and of the overwhelming majority of the base.

Political battle in the West is no longer trench warfare; it resembles, rather, the virtual battles of videogames: there is very little ideological distinction between the opponents and victory depends largely on how much money is spent to acquire special weapons that the other guy can't afford. It is the party's avatars that do the fighting, the foundations and research institutes, run and financed by secret admirers. The party secretaries, meanwhile, have become true war machines at the service of the new generation of political leaders, charismatic men and women whose personalities have replaced ideology and often the political program as well. The most powerful weapon, naturally, is spin, the alchemy performed by our very own witch doctors of the news.

CHAPTER 16

MEDIACRACY

We all remember the Watergate scandal: Nixon resigns in order not to face trial. The American president was not accused of having authorized the hotel wiretaps, but of having lied to Congress and to the nation. Years later, the phrase "I never had sex with that woman" would be the downfall of Bill Clinton, who miraculously managed not to resign. More recently, despite sexual scandals capable of shaking the entire European continent, Silvio Berlusconi has remained firmly in power. And in 1997 Tony Blair, despite the Formula 1 scandal, also remained in office. Is it just a matter of the difference between moralist America and permissive old Europe? No, it is a sign of changing times. The two fundamental factors in the metamorphoses are the manipulation of the media and the predominance assumed by the leader with respect to the party.

Consent in modern democracies is manufactured through the manipulation of the mass media, the main way in which today's politicians interact with the electorate. Reagan and Thatcher were among the first to engage the services of media gurus who, like Hollywood directors, created their personalities on the basis of carefully executed opinion surveys.

Since then the image consultants of various politicians have become the éminences grises of Western democracy. The leaders here are naturally the Americans. In 2001 the Italian center-left political coalition known as *L'Ulivo* (The Olive Tree) called on the Clinton strategist Stanley Greenberg, and in 2004 the conservative *Alleanza nazionale* (National Alliance) hired Leo Burnett from Chicago.' But it was Silvio

Berlusconi who in 1994 first set out on an election campaign along US lines.

Let's start, however, with the father of political communication. Once elected, Reagan brought with him to the White House a group of image wizards who told those who wrote his speeches what to write, and him how to deliver them. The man whom Americans saw on their television screen was always and only an actor reciting fictions. But nobody noticed, and so the increase in the federal deficit passed unobserved. All the people saw was that Reagan not only lowered their taxes, but promised to keep doing so, and thus he was reelected.

People have short memories and often lack access to numbers, but the press should be more informed. In a democracy the media represent the people's political memory. The press well knew that between 1980 and 1992, during the two administrations of Reagan and one of the elder Bush, the federal deficit quadrupled—but said nothing about it. Why then do we get so up in arms about Chinese censorship? Because we frame the problem in ideological terms, calling the explicit Chinese version "censorship," with an unambiguous term that indicates a limit to the autonomy of the press and thus of freedom of thought and speech. But how should we define the implicit selection of the news that occurs at home?

A revolution like that of the neoliberals, which rests on an economic theory patched together by journalists, lobbyists, and conservative theoreticians, could not function without an equally radical revolution within the fourth estate. And Reagan, who entered the White House just a few years after the Watergate scandal and had witnessed the press's humiliation of Carter, was well aware of this.

It is a mistake, however, to imagine that the transformation of the media into public relations agencies for the political class was connected to any sort of capitalist conspiracy; if anything, it was a question of the reverse process. Guiding the metamorphosis was the skill of media consultants, talented professionals who devoted years of study to a new science born with the advent of mass media and mass democracy: communications.[2]

Consent, as Noam Chomsky wrote, is manufactured in the belly of the political machine and information is the raw material. Press freedom can also be a label applied to an empty box, but it's something we've grown fond of, that continues to make us feel good about ourselves.

In the 1980s, this mythology was consolidated. The pair neoliberalism + Pinochet is translated, in the speeches of Reagan and Thatcher, into the pair neoliberalism + modern democracy, the only Great Wall built in the West against the global advance of communism. But it was a question of pure data manipulation. It's true that on paper the Chilean economy performed better than the one left behind by Allende before he was summarily executed by Pinochet's junta, but behind these positive numbers and the violence was hidden the impoverishment of an entire segment of the population, a social reality that didn't appear in the sterile statistics of GDP and industrial production.

If Reagan and Thatcher, advised by those constructing their political image, transmitted poisonous information to a public that swallowed it as if they drank from a crystal-clear fountain, it is nevertheless New Labour that in the following decade definitively knocked down the wall separating politics from the media arena.[3] It is at this point that key personalities like Peter Mandelson and Alastair Campbell come on the scene. The former had twice previously been forced to leave public office for having abused it; the latter was a journalist for the *Daily Mirror*, among the least authoritative British dailies.

These were the men responsible for modeling the Blair personality on certain slogans. "The politician who never lies" is perhaps the most paradoxical among their coinages. With the elections won, Blair's management blends the government office with that of the premier's spokesman. This means that Campbell, as the man preselected to fulfill this role, would also weigh in on political struggles within the party. The voice of the government and the voice of the party began to merge,[4] and Tony Blair became the avatar of New Labour.

The press was effectively subjugated to Campbell, a neighborhood ruffian who knew how to manipulate his former colleagues, thanks to the complex and costly machine he built around the prime minister. It had an annual budget of four million pounds and counted seventy-four consultants. What the numbers add up to is a veritable secret ministry within the government. They worked twenty-four hours a day, and had a data bank, Excalibur, that processed all the news in the service of a Rapid Rebuttal Unit, a team of people with the task of immediately denying anything they didn't want to circulate. But the brain of the manipulative operations was the Grid, a dense networked plot of government schedules and announcements, allowing officials to choose the best day and time in which to make news public according to the needs of propaganda. On September 11, 2001, Jo Moore, press agent for the then–Secretary of State for Transport, Local Government and the Regions, Stephen Byers, sent across the Grid the following email: "It's now a very good day to get out anything we want to bury."[5]

If the cynicism of Blair and his spin doctors was appalling, so too was their use of lies. Three months after the successful 1997 elections, Mandelson announced a press conference that illustrated the hundred results obtained by the government in its first hundred days. Few journalists realized that it was only a matter of slogans, with the concrete legislative proposals and decisions actually taken being fewer than ten. Campbell and Mandelson's information war machine had the goal of confusing the "enemy" press. And it succeeded brilliantly.

When it came to "friendly" journalists, information was

passed under the table during business breakfasts or at closed-door press conferences. These were news items constructed to obtain the desired reaction from the public, to which were added pseudoevents created to recycle past news and give the idea of constant and effective activity. The Grid ground up the truth and built a new one that flattered Tony Blair. And the press that no longer slept, forced to spit out news twenty-four hours a day, fell right into the trap.

There is officially freedom of the press in the United Kingdom, but in reality it's no longer professional and independent journalists who run the media. Bernard Ingham, Thatcher's spokesman, wrote in a preface to Nicholas Jones's book, *Sultans of Spin*, that if he had faced even a fraction of the accusations that were leveled at Campbell, he would have been forced to resign within months.[6]

Let's now come back to our initial question: what is the difference between our press and that of the Chinese? The former feeds false information to a reader unable to tell the difference; the latter imposes a form of explicit censorship. Therefore, paradoxically, how can we know if what we are told about China is true? It could be a well-crafted manipulation on the part of our "free press," who have every interest in depicting a repressed nation, full of dissidents dreaming of democracy, who fear that the success of the Chinese model might lead us to reflect on the failures of our own, and maybe even push us to demand change—a word everyone in the establishment still fears.

More often it's simply a question of ignorance, as many well-integrated Westerners living in China attest. Here is once again Maurice Ohana, head of Ohanasia:

> My daughter gave birth in a large hospital where every day 600 babies are born. Outside there's always a crowd of people trying to get inside, but the police keep them back. Western journalists would wonder

why they do so and some would maybe interpret this behavior as repressive. Hospital management explained to me that parents generally stay in the hospital for four to five days following delivery. This means that at any given moment in that hospital there are 3,000 babies with 6,000 parents, in addition to 3,000 employees. Imagine what would happen if the doors were open and 30,000 relatives could pass through them at will.

In China it's also necessary to keep the numbers in mind. Quantity is important. The Western media doesn't understand this, just like they don't understand the one-child policy. Without it there would be four billion people in China today. And who would feed all these people?[7]

Many Western journalists are of the opinion that the difficulty of projecting a more truthful image of China also depends on other factors. Patrick Chovanec explains:

Our press is influenced by two factors, one economic and one political. We fear a Chinese superpower without understanding that there is still a long road to travel. And then we always look at this country through the lens of 1989; it's as if China had remained stuck in the time of Tiananmen.

As a consequence, the objectivity necessary to offer readers a truthful image is lacking. Chovanec continues:

In the West there's a tendency to consider China a prisoner of the dictatorship, with the idea that if the people had the chance they would revolt against those in charge of the government. But that's not the case. In the last twenty years personal freedom in China has increased, and the Chinese look on our democracy with ambivalence. The people want to be free but they also want respect for the law.[8]

China is also, and above all, incapable of selling its image to the world. It has no experience with spin or the science of communications, as we hear from Jeremy Goldkorn, founder of the online magazine Danwei.org:

> The Chinese don't know anything about communications, maybe because most of their leaders graduated in engineering. They lack the capacity to spread good news or project a positive image of their country. They make colossal mistakes when they discuss delicate subjects without attending to the reactions of the foreign press.[9]

It *is* true that our media are not telling us there is more press freedom today in China than there was twenty years ago, when the tanks and the army entered Tiananmen Square. From what we read it seems instead there is always less.

BETWEEN WITCHCRAFT AND DEMOCRACY

While in the West the press falls prey to spin, in China investigative journalism is growing, a tremendously powerfully weapon in the hands of civil society that twenty years ago didn't exist. One of the most distressing stories to be brought to light in recent years can be found in Ivan Franceschini's account of the Shanxi furnaces in his book *Cronache delle fornaci cinesi* (Stories from the Chinese Furnaces):

> Toward the middle of 2007, six parents from Henan turn to a local television journalist, Fu Zhenzhong. They're desperate because their children have been

kidnapped and they think they've ended up in the Shanxi furnaces. This is a mostly underground brick industry that exploits enslaved children. The journalist is incredulous but agrees to follow them into Shanxi. And immediately he has to reconsider; the world his companions show him is a terrifying one.[10]

The journalist, using a hidden camera, came away with a record of indescribable scenes. At a construction site, children younger than ten are forced to work nonstop under the eyes of guards who whip them as soon as they slow down. Skeletal adolescents who can barely manage to stay on their feet slave away in a mine. Fu Zhenzhong broadcast the images and the scandal of the furnaces erupted throughout China.

Every national media outlet picked up the story, but it was on the Internet that civil society mobilized and pushed the government to act. Xin Yanhua, the mother of one of the kidnapped and subsequently freed children, circulated a manifesto titled "400 Crying Parents Ask for Help: Who Will Save Our Children?" that opened a furious debate in which millions of people participated. Young activists left for Shanxi and joined groups of parents and other volunteers in the search for the missing children, scouring the furnaces. The government launched interprovincial police operations, drew up five-year plans to fight human trafficking, and approved labor laws making it easier to press charges. In the preface to Franceschini's book we read:

> The response from civil society was swift and overwhelming, belying the stereotype that says Chinese citizens are passive and beholden to power. . . . The real protagonists of this story are not the corrupt officials, human traffickers, and torturers, but the parents, lawyers, journalists, and regular citizens who every day fight to improve the society they live in.[11]

But did we ever learn anything about this example of civil investigative journalism, worthy of the much-lauded Anglo-Saxon tradition?

Our media doesn't tell us that in the last twenty years civil society in China has grown, becoming one channel through which the base is in dialogue with the Party chiefs. The press plays a key role in this conversation. There are scores of stories like the one from Shanxi: charges of corruption on the part of public officials or of criminal activities brought to the public's attention by the press.

Behind these investigations we find professional journalists risking their lives to make China a better country. Among these is Dou Jiangming, who works for the Chinese edition of the magazine *Esquire*, and who created a very popular blog about the story of the Shanxi furnaces. In an afterword to Franceschini's book he wrote:

> When the furnace scandal broke two years ago, my daughter Xiao'an was just a year and a half old. If you want to know what was always pushing me to do more about the furnaces, I can say it was for her. I don't want her to grow up to live in a world like the one I live in today.[12]

Dou is not a dissident, he doesn't think Chinese communism is at the root of the furnace tragedy, he's just convinced that social mobilization is the right weapon for fighting slavery or any other kind of socioeconomic depravation in his country.

In the West too, civil society tries to make itself heard, but rarely does the press become its platform. The sorry story of the armed intervention in Iraq is only one example of how the conversation between population and politicians is a dialogue of the deaf.

Between November 2002 and March 2003 the entire world

took to the streets to make its leaders understand that it did not agree with the invasion of Iraq. Millions of people marched in the capitals of the rich West and in those of the global South as well. Opposition was also particularly fierce within Western political parties; Barack Obama was one of the few US senators to vote against the preventative attack; Hillary Clinton supported it. In the UK, key New Labour figures like Robin Cook resigned in protest of the unconditional support Blair offered to Bush's war; even Jack Straw, then Secretary of State for Foreign and Commonwealth Affairs, in a letter to Blair made public only in January 2010, declared his opposition to the invasion, laying out prophetically all the damage it would do to the party.[13] All such voices were ignored: the noisy interventionists, among them many of the biggest names in Western journalism, ridiculed these voices and tried to pass them off as the expression of a sorry lack of patriotism, or even as cowardliness.

In Italy, where the pacifist movement covered the peninsula with multicolored banners calling for *Pace* (Peace), the list of television, radio, and print journalists who commented positively on the lies—because this is what they were—spread by the spin doctors of Bush, Blair, and Berlusoni in justification of the war is too long to be reproduced in this book. No one took the trouble to verify what Campbell's Grid and its equivalent in Washington, DC, and doubtless also in Italy, produced daily. And yet a bit of time on the Internet would have been enough to find the precise sentences mentioned in the top-secret documents that circulated through the editorial offices of all the newspapers. Large portions of the famous Iraq dossier, the one presented as irrefutable proof of Saddam's nuclear weapons and his ties to al-Qaeda, came from the Web.

Looking over these and other revelations that emerged from the Chilcot Inquiry in London, which in 2010 investigated the responsibility of the Blair government in the fabrication of the proof that Saddam possessed weapons of mass destruction and was allied with bin Laden, one can't help but wonder where, in those years, was Anglo-Saxon and Western investigative journalism? And in general it is hard not to conclude that the interests of the press in the West are closer to the interests of the politicians than to those of the citizens whom it should be duty-bound to inform.

Not only was the armed intervention in Iraq fueled by lies, the manipulation of information, and scant professionalism on the part of our media, it was also illegal according to the principles of international law. The execution of Saddam Hussein has brought only death and destruction to Iraq, a country that in the 1970s was among the most modernized in the Muslim world, with a literacy rate of 74 percent. The invasion violated both the sovereignty of the country and the human rights of the Iraqis. And all this happened in the name of democracy and with the approval of the free Western press.

On the other hand, the events of Tiananmen traveled around the world on our television screens and in the pages of our newspapers, universally—and rightly—deplored as a bloody act of repression. But without that blood, which produced a painful wake-up call concerning the necessity of change for the Chinese government leaders, today there would not exist journalists like Fu Zhenzhong and Dou Jianming, nor would it be possible to imagine media campaigns like the one for the liberation of the slaves of the Shanxi furnaces or those against the child theft racket. Crucial historical turning points like this one cannot be resolved by propaganda but require the exercise of all our intellectual honesty.

We have to ask ourselves if what we have is the democracy we want or something different. It's time we opened our eyes to the social battles Chinese journalism is fighting, not because their press is better than ours, but in order to understand how much ours has been poisoned by the manufacturers of news, opinions, and social responses. China is not necessarily an example to follow, but we might use it as a touchstone in our efforts to redress media distortion at home.

CHAPTER 17

THE THOUSAND EVITAS OF BERLUSCONI

In a little square in Porto Cervo in Sardinia, a crowd of young women have gathered. Tall and slim, they're wearing light summer dresses allowing glimpses of full-body tans. They are loosely arranged in a semicircle around the entrance to one of countless fashionable bars. A wall of heavyset men, all in blue suits and with regulation earpieces, block their way and urge them to return home. The women don't give up, however, some even jumping in their high heels for a peep at the guests in the bar. Two elegant older women out on a walk, their curiosity piqued by all the commotion, approach the scene. They gesture for one of the guards to come over to them, with the intention of asking what is going on, but the man opens a passage for them through the crowd. A bit hesitantly, the women make their way inside under the eyes of the stunned and jealous throng. And they find themselves in front of Silvio Berlusconi.

The president welcomes them warmly and reveals to them immediately that his bodyguards have mistaken them for relatives of his; in fact, the man who gave the order to let them through believed that one of them was no less than the *Cavaliere*'s own beloved mother, Rosa Berlusconi. In their great excitement, the women cover him with praises and he settles in between them, takes an arm of each, and has a photo taken that a few days later will be delivered to them, fully framed and inscribed. Before seeing them off he places a hand on the shoulder of the friend sitting beside him and encourages the women to say hello to him as well. Only then do the two women realize that it's Vladimir Putin.

No Western politician exerts a pop star–like fascination over what the Italians still call "the weaker sex" equal to that of Silvio Berlusconi. Not only is the *Cavaliere* always accompanied by beautiful women, but often, as in this story from Porto Cervo, it is they who seek him out. Even women of a certain age are subject to his charm; statistics show that grandmothers are among his most faithful voters. And yet Berlusconi makes no mystery of what he thinks of women. "Zapatero will have some trouble, too many women in his administration," he declared during a press conference on April 16, 2008.[1]

THE PERÓN COMPLEX

Women are a minority in politics, but that doesn't mean they don't understand its dynamics. It was, in fact, a woman who was the first to discover the power of personalizing the party: Eva Perón, known as Evita.

In 1945 Evita mounted a giant media campaign around the arrest of her lover, General Perón. Although it was the union movement that mobilized the population that forced the government to release him, in the collective imagination she is the one, with her love for Perón, that drove the masses into the streets. From this moment on, Argentinean political history assumes a rose-colored tinge and often takes on tabloid features, a process that swallows up the unionist and socialist connotations of the political movement born around the figure of Perón. The litmus paper that was the press transformed Evita's charisma into an element catalyzing public enthusiasm, and Perónism was born as a movement celebrating the man she loved and admired.

Immortalized in the famous musical *Evita*, the story of this pair of political animals still inspires awe in the field of communication studies. Evita constructed the public image of the future president as a reflection of herself; it is through her eyes that the people see him. She adorned bland populism with exceedingly well-chosen egalitarian slogans and offered the country a pure and clear image of her relationship with Perón. The emancipation of Argentina started with the electoral victories of Perón, not of the unions or of the Socialist Party, and this was so obvious that the latter also went by the name of "Perónist."

The modern politician, formed in the era of the personalization of politics, suffers from a Perón complex; he would like to make of the party his own personal war machine. This is certainly what is behind politicians like Blair and Berlusconi, obsessed by their public image.

Even Barack Obama and Sarkozy have studied at the school of Evita, using the rhetoric of populism. In Davos in 2010, the French leader launched into an interminable tirade against the banks and their abuses. He asked for the cooperation of his European and American colleagues in reforming the economic system. "What's needed is a new Bretton Woods," he repeatedly declared. More than a year earlier, at the G20 in London, he had gone so far as to threaten to quit the conference if his extremely severe resolution against the banks was not accepted. But in the end he stayed on for the traditional farewell photo.

Since the beginning of the credit crisis, the crusade against the banks has been one of the warhorses of the French president, perhaps because it reminds his fellow citizens of their hatred for the aristocracy that brought them to overthrow the monarchy. But no financial heads have yet rolled on Parisian pavement, and the banks continue to be saved with the rebels' descendants' money. Newspaper headlines, the party machine, and even the French Parliament are careful not to accuse the French president of crude populism. Indeed, they have no better solution to his fine words, and given that this type of verbal attack has worked so far, they keep quiet about it.

Barack Obama, the great champion of change, is also a skilled populist orator. A year after his election, none of the promises made in his election campaign had been realized. Master of rhetoric, he is the incarnation of the tribune of the plebs. Obama also knows how to use words as if they were caresses, how to reassure the listener that everything will be all right. He projects, in other words, the image of the politician who has the good of the nation at heart, of the complete altruist. But these are merely well-tested techniques. As *World Report 2010* from Human Rights Watch reminds us:

> US citizens enjoy a broad range of civil liberties and have recourse to a strong system of independent federal and state courts, but serious human rights concerns remain, particularly in criminal justice, immigration, and counterterrorism law and policy. The Obama administration has said it will address many of these concerns but, at this writing nearly one year into Barack Obama's presidency, it had taken few concrete steps.[2]

On the environmental front as well, the dangers of rhetoric become clear. Prior to his participation in the Copenhagen conference, Obama announced that by 2020 he would have decreased American emissions of carbon dioxide by 17 percent—a worthless claim, since this decision belongs to Congress, which by mid-2011 had not turned its attention to the environment. But the news shot around the world and everyone praised the new president, who, unlike Bush, cared about the planet. Hardly anyone, only the experts, noticed that the reduction would occur with respect to 2005 emissions levels rather than those of 1990, the base used by all the countries that ratified the Kyoto Protocol. If this is the new base, then the 17 percent promised by Obama becomes a very modest 4 percent.

The US president's rhetoric and his Perón-style populism mask real problems and prevent the important issues of our time, like the environment and health care, from being confronted and resolved rationally, in the interests of the multitude. In Washington, DC, the lobbies of the oil and oil-related industries maintain three lobbyists for every member of Congress and pay for large portions of their election campaigns. The environment is in danger of ending up like General Motors, once the largest car company in the world, but now about to go bankrupt because, following advice from Wall Street banks, for years they refused to move toward innovating more energy-saving vehicles. And management won all its battles thanks to the support of Congress. In other words, the lobbyists from GM made sure the country undertook no industrial restructuring that today would have helped the business compete with Japanese manufacturers.

There's a reason government is an entity distinct from industry. This distance should permit the leaders to impose policies that, even if unpopular with industry, in the long term are advantageous for both industry and the country. But, in our democratic West, things often happen differently.

The explanation, as always, is financial. The rhetoric and the populism so fashionable today also have their costs, starting with the astronomical costs of the modern politician's election campaign. Behind Obama's every word as he toured the country was the dollar sign; without the greenbacks all those fine words would never have been heard. The same can be said of the stars of modern politics. As we have seen, the "Super Democracy" reality show is no longer paid for by party members; instead it's the individuals and businesses that, through lobbies and pressure groups, practice the Roman principle of *do ut des,* you give something to me and I give something to you.

In China the situation is different—perhaps not better, but

different. A fat wallet doesn't open all political doors. First it's necessary to pass through the vetting process of the CCP, and the initiation process is long and rigidly meritocratic.

Indeed, it's not easy to become a member. Theoretically, anyone of legal age (eighteen) can apply, as long as they can present letters of recommendation from two Party members. But an applicant is not automatically accepted for training (a probationary period that lasts a year); only 5 percent of applications, in fact, make it to this stage.

As in the West, politics is practiced primarily by men, and, in the past, for every female CCP member there were three men. The ratio has improved, but the masculine presence is still overwhelming. Apart from gender, the most significant criterion for membership is education level: traditionally those with a university degree have a better chance of being accepted into the Party and making a career in the government. The general selection criterion, however, remains meritocratic; even without a degree, having excelled in some field makes it easier to obtain the membership card. As Professor John P. Burns attests: "Considerable evidence indicates that China's officials, in general, are increasigly selected based on performance."[3]

Recently, the number of successful businessmen becoming Party members has increased. The CCP both encourages members to work in the private sector and attracts those in the business world, especially those in heavy industry, to enter.[4] The newspaper *China Daily* has calculated that in 2006 the number of members employed in the private sector was 2.86 million, approximately 15 percent, while 810,000 were private entrepreneurs.[5]

These changes are connected to the adoption of the theory of the "three represents" (*san ge daibiao*) enunciated by former General Secretary Jiang Zemin during the Party's Sixteenth National Congress in 2002, reflecting on the country's experience over the last eighty years:

Our Party should continue to stand in the forefront of the times and lead the people in marching toward victory. In a word, the Party must always represent the requirements of the development of China's advanced productive forces, the orientation of the development of China's advanced culture, and the fundamental interests of the overwhelming majority of the people in China.[6]

At least theoretically, therefore, the Chinese Communist Party intends to represent the most dynamic productive and social forces, including entrepreneurs, the highest cultural expressions of the country, and the interests of the entire population.

However, it would be wrong to believe that to enter the Party means to enter the government. The relationship between these organs has changed with the times: between 1949 and 1977 the possibility of a career in government was seven times greater for members. Between 1987 and 1996 this had gone down to three times, and recent data suggests that today Party membership exerts only a marginal influence.[7] In China it is said there are four types of people who have the possibility of making a career in politics: the so-called *wu-zhi-shao-nü*, or the members of no party (*wu dangpai*), intellectuals (*zhishifenzi*), the representatives of ethnic minorities (*shaoshu minzu*), and women (*nü xing*).

So it's not true that anyone wanting to be a part of the national government has to scale the Party ladder. The selection system for the National People's Congress, the highest state body, whose members serve five-year terms, is not internal to the Party. They are elected by the provinces, the regions and the municipalities, and the army.

To occupy these offices it is no longer necessary to be a card-carrying member of the Party.[8] Even if a government composed entirely of nonmember ministers is still unimaginable, in 2007 the ministers of Science and Technology and Health were not signed up. Over the years the CCP has thus demonstrated its willingness to become more open. And to repeat, access to public office occurs primarily on a meritocratic basis, even for consultancy services. According to Wan Yanhai, director of the Beijing-based NGO Aizhixing, which fights the spread of AIDS in China: "In January 2009 I wrote a public letter about the Uyghur situation. The office concerned with ethnic minorities read it and asked me to collaborate with them."[9]

Wan Yanhai's mission is to promote the Muslim community and make it stronger. This could happen by allowing them to choose their own leaders, to build their own society within Chinese society. This is something far removed from current government policies.

Naturally, corruption and misgovernment exist in China as well. *China Daily* often publishes lists of disgraced politicians. Among them is the former mayor of Shenzhen, Xu Zongheng, and the former governor of the autonomous province of Ningxia Hui. Many of these men could be found at the head of public companies, like the general director of the China National Nuclear Corporation, Kang Rixin, or the vice president of China Mobile, the state-owned telephone company. In 2009 the majority of them were expelled from the Party and tried for having accepted money in exchange for personal favors. This is the most common type of scandal. No one, of course, has ever reached the dimensions of the scandals that occurred in Italy with the megafrauds of Fastweb and Telecom Italia Sparkle, but in China as well, corruption in the Party and in the government is extremely widespread, and this is no secret. Here is Ivan Franceschini on the topic:

A few months ago [2009] a report on the corruption of officials came out, authored by an attorney from Shenzhen. It was the first example of this kind of thing to be produced by civil society, and the news even made it on to a couple of front pages. Beyond the triumphalist declarations of the Party, the basic impression remained that the fight against corruption is useful in the Chinese political environment as a weapon for internal political conflicts. You could, for example, consider in this light the purge of various high officials in Shanghai, a city, as one knows, that is a political stronghold of the former president Jiang Zemin. In other cases the fight against corruption can be an instrument used to gain distinction and rise up in the hierarchy of the Party, and this, for example, seems to be the case with Bo Xilai and his recent campaign against corruption in Chongqing. In both cases, the fight against corruption is nothing other than an instrument with which separate political factions attempt to achieve their own ends.

The Party's scant sincerity in this field is also demonstrated by the fact that notoriously corrupt characters continue to sit in the politburo, like Jia Qinglin, tied to the reviled criminal in exile Lai Changxing, and Li Changchun, Party secretary in Henan at the time of the AIDS scandal.

You can't overlook the fact that the fight against corruption in China inevitably comes up against the *guanxi* networks between various officials: if one person falls, then a domino effect is created that goes all the way to the top.[10]

So the world in the East is not so different from the world west of the Great Wall. But notwithstanding the fact that corruption in China is a serious scourge that extends all the way to the peak of the political pyramid, the issue is widely discussed and investigative journalists often manage to catch men considered untouchable. Such news is much more rare in our democracies, where politicians have subjugated the press and often own it. And in China no one who has been sentenced, who has pending prosecutions, or who has been investigated by the judicial authorities can hold public office, unlike in many Western countries.

BERLUSCONI AND HIS WOMEN

Decades after Evita, there is still no more powerful electoral promotion than that of a charismatic, admired, and respected woman who supports a professional male politician, making herself the vehicle and symbol of his love affair with the electorate. Launching Barack Obama in America was Oprah Winfrey, whom many of the tabloids described as being secretly in love with the current president.

Silvio Berlusconi does not make use of an Evita but of a flock of women, all beautiful, who hang on his every word. The former president and prime minister Francesco Cossiga touched on a sore point when he observed that one of the keys to his success was having transformed the political arena into the most closely followed media spectacle in Italy. And given that the winning television formula is to toss loads of beautiful women, preferably half naked, into any situation, only the most attractive make it on to the ballot. Evita too was one of them, and, without a doubt, if her media campaign had been ugly it wouldn't have worked so well. In this type of political spectacle, just as with a tabloid or reality show, one has to be easy on the eye.

So why should we be surprised if the photograph of the four newly sworn-in female Italian ministers became known all over other world? It could have been torn from the pages of *Vogue*: young, beautiful, and, pantsuits notwithstanding, decidedly sexy. The thousand Evitas of Berlusconi project the image of the leader the country wants. And this was also true for the Peróns. Evita's moralism is the mask that makes him appear to be an everyman with the pride and simplicity of a true Argentine.

The narrative of the politician Berlusconi is instead more similar to the story of an irresistible Don Juan, made in Italy, a different kind of fairy tale in which one could even successfully insert the open conflict with his wife. After all, the figure of Veronica Berlusconi, contrary to Evita, had always kept herself resolutely "apolitical," decidedly distant from the propagandistic zeal of her husband's thousand Evitas.

In Italy, of course, womanizers are forgiven everything, as Federico Fellini masterfully illustrated once and for all in his film *I vitelloni*. Showing through the melodrama of Silvio and Veronica are gender stereotypes that in Italy, women's liberation notwithstanding, are still stuck in the times of our grandmothers. 1968, feminism and the widening of our horizons that came with a unified Europe left intact the clichés of the Italian male, womanizer and predator, and his female counterpart, provocative and prey, whose ideal position is always and only horizontal. And forgiveness—both the family's and society's—is guaranteed because the blame always belongs to the temptress, since the times of Adam and Eve. Veronica's anger and Silvio's apologies, in other words, are parts of a farce that we've been reciting in Italy for centuries, in which the roles have become straightjackets for a society that just can't manage to modernize. What's most worrying is the increasingly exact transposition of this archaism into national political life.

All this would be unthinkable in China. Even if Mao had more than one wife, and the last one indeed tried to don the clothes of an Evita, Chinese leaders seem not to possess a private life. Not only do we never see their wives and families, but these men also project an ostentatiously modest manner. Whatever they may think about women and sex, in public every effort is made to appear virtually asexual.

In Italy the opposite is the case: the sexuality of politicians is a marketable product not only for the tabloids but also in the more serious media, to the point of becoming a selling point. Berlusconi has a weakness for beautiful women, and this defect increases not only the male solidarity he enjoys among the Italian ruling class but absurdly also his popularity among the female electorate.

Whether he has hundreds of lovers or not is irrelevant; what is important is that in the collective imagination this man who incarnates all the stereotypes of success for the average Italian is also, and above all else, a great Latin lover. This way of doing politics is nothing new in Italy. Gian Carlo Fusco, in his recently reprinted *Mussolini e le donne* (Mussolini and Women), tells of how in Milan in 1914, when Mussolini finally finds the money to found the newspaper *Il Popolo d'Italia*, he celebrates the event in the well-known brothel on Via San Pietro all'Orto, where he introduces himself with his *nom d'amant*: "Occhiacci." Benito sees women as prey, as conquests. He has them for rent or gratis, like Leda Rafanelli Polli, "writer, painter, libertarian anarchist, harpist, clairvoyant," but above all—according to the future Duce— author of the "most beautiful *masticazzi* [oral sex] in Milan."[11]

Following the Fascist cult of virility were the more sober postwar years and egalitarian fervors of the 1960s and '70s; it is only in more recent years that the return of ostentatious machismo in Italy has provoked a true revolution in the political arena. For a politician, betraying one's wife has become, paradoxically, a point of honor. Both Pier Ferdinando Casini and Gianfranco Fini, supporters of family values and attentive to the words of the Pope, abandoned their own wives to marry their respective mistresses. To find another such celebration of infidelity one would have to go back to the Duce's cohabitation with his lover Clara Petacci. How can we forget the dictator's famous phrase: "Women must stay home, raise children, and be betrayed"? With the unmarried women, on the other hand, one can just have fun, seeing as how they're all potential whores.

Naturally, in this performance there's no room for anyone different—like the gays who are denied the right to marry, or single, career women—in two words, for real society. There's only room for those capable of wielding the weapon of beauty, the women with whom, to say it with Mussolini, one betrays one's wife. They are the thousand Evitas at the service of Mussolini.

PERÓNISM, INC.

Evita Perón's revolution represents a touchstone for communications studies, demonstrating that it pays to remove the political features from the party and transform it into an association of fans. Thus the new dimension of the party is concerned with elections and government-subsidized celebrations and nothing more. The money coming from the rich sponsors should flow into the premier's foundations and research institutes.

Election campaigns, as we have seen, resemble battles between marketing experts promoting entirely similar products. The techniques employed are typical of the economy of the imaginary: slogans and the creation of artificial needs. Bush and Blair convince us to export democracy to Iraq in order to live in greater security here, employing an industry of fear that is only too happy to cooperate. An absurdity, and yet today there are still people convinced not only that Saddam represented a threat to the West, but that his death made us safer. If you understand the mechanism and logic that regulates the behavior of groups, you can control and subjugate the masses as you wish and without their knowledge, as Edward Bernays explains in his famous essay, *The Engineering of Consent*.[12] Thus everything is possible for the witch doctors of information.

As we have seen, the media gurus reduce election messages to commercial slogans, like Obama's "Yes We Can" or the Berlusconian mantra "Meno male che Silvio c'è" (Thank goodness Silvio's here). These phrases capture the image that the marketers want to transmit of the politician in the same way advertising slogans create a mythology around products: there is no difference between "Yes We Can" and "A Diamond Is Forever". Whose responsibility is it to launch these slogans? The party's, transformed into a marketing firm concentrated on the promotion of the leader rather than a program. In Italy, Berlusconi's *Forza Italia* (Forward Italy) and then *Il Popolo della Libertà* (The People of Freedom) have been at it for years. It's obvious that for this type of politician, presidential democracy is the formula that works best. In 2006, the *L'Ulivo* coalition won the Italian national elections, but Silvio Berlusconi received the majority of preferential votes. If the contestants for the top job had been Prodi and Berlusconi instead of two giant coalitions, the latter would have won. Conversely, in the US midterm election of 2010, reaction against Barack Obama became a galvanizing force for the right, and the Democratic party suffered huge losses because conservative Americans were voting against the person at the top of the party, even though he was not on the ballot.

Thus the general tendency is toward a system of authoritarian control of the party on the part of the leadership and a personalistic presidentialism, à la Perón. Confronted with these transformations, the media become an exceedingly powerful instrument in politics. And whoever controls them can be said to already have one foot in the presidential palace.

According to an April 2003 report produced by Soria Blatmann for Reporters Without Borders:

> Silvio Berlusconi is the prime minister and the richest person in the country. Media companies are the main-

stay of his economic empire. He is the owner of Mondadori, among the country's largest publishing companies, and of Mediaset, which owns three television stations. At the same time he is the head of government and thus in a position to exercise a great influence over RAI [*Radiotelevisione italiana*, the Italian public broadcasting service]. Similar conglomerates control a significant portion of the media companies in other European countries, Bertelsmann and Kirch in Germany, the empire of Rupert Murdoch in the United Kingdom or Vivendi in France. But Berlusconi's media empire–political power pair represents a unique phenomenon in Europe.[13]

We are far, far away from Confucius's image of the prince, from the virtue of setting an example, but at the same time very, very close to what the philosopher wrote about the desire to emulate the prince. In our voyeuristic Western society, where everyone is glued to the "Super Democracy" reality show, the electorate–television viewer doesn't vote for ideological reasons, but for their own advantage or personal satisfaction. Being elected depends also, and above all, on the ease with which one manages to be admired. And no one seems to better incarnate the conflicting and egoistic desires of modern Western society than Silvio Berlusconi.

PART FOUR

IMAGES OF THE FUTURE

CHAPTER 18

SCENES FROM A MARRIAGE

In Guangzhou, one of China's first Special Economic Zones, the best deals are to be found at Canaan Market, the market of the Africans, in the neighborhood known as "Chocolate City." Visiting Canaan is like popping over to Africa, from the smells of the food sold by street vendors to the hairstyles of the women shopping. Here one can find the least expensive "Made in China" goods, sold by Chinese as well as by Africans. Both groups, however, wear African-style clothes, so every stall offers a palette of colors that can't help but strike anyone accustomed to the grayness of this city, polluted by the thousands of factories hidden in its belly.

All the buyers are Africans, naturally, and many of them still have the dust of that land on their shoes. Since November 2009, Kenya Airways has flown nonstop from Nairobi to Guangzhou. The flight is always full, and many travelers come straight to the market from the airport. The emotion is such that they can't resist.

For an African, Canaan is Toyland, brimming with everything: from the plastic sandals that revolutionized an entire continent, erasing for good the image of African children and adults with bare feet, to the counterfeit Prada bags so appreciated in Soweto, to iPods and pirated videos and CDs. The prices are exceptionally low, accessible to anyone with a little money set aside who makes it this far, the industrial heart of southern China. It doesn't take much to get into the "Made in China" business.

As in all true markets, in Canaan you can always find what

265

you're looking for: from old Singer sewing machines to African SIM cards, even prostitutes for those wishing to distract themselves after a tough day of bargaining. Such days are exhausting, because this isn't a shopping mall, it's an arena, a scene of combat, where the final price is the fruit of hours of discussion, offers and counteroffers, threats and promises. Even simply crossing the rows of stalls is a trial, the vendors tug at you from all sides, piling on offer after dizzying offer.

English is the lingua franca, but in the background one hears the melody of hundreds of African dialects. And the music, blending in with the voices of the merchants and customers from one corner of the market to the other, is African rap. Joseph Nwaosu, a Nigerian exporter, sums up for us what's behind a market like this:

> When you go to the United States or Europe, there isn't much opportunity. You are going to get a menial job, with barely enough to send home. But here we don't have jobs. We set ourselves up.[1]

Canaan is one of the true marketplaces of globalization, initiated only recently in the global South, far away from the elegant boardrooms of the international banks and the electronic crawl boards of the exchange floors. Canaan is where the future Rockefellers of developing countries come to make deals, not Paris. Born in 2002, this is indeed a market reserved for products from the Third World and directed at the Third World, to which, as we've seen, China still feels itself to belong. What's for sale here, however, is not traditional goods but the same merchandise we find in our own stores, the accessories of globalized life. At one stall there's a pile of hair extensions all ready to be woven in. They look like those found in any Parisian hair salon, even the colors correspond to those in the photo of three models under the large L'Oréal logo. But the only thing French here is the logo. The hair is from India, the treatment occurs in China, and the final touch comes from the African hairdressers who will weave in the hair according to local fashions.

The West forgot markets like this a long time ago. Adam Smith would go crazy here and David Ricardo wouldn't need to write his theory of comparative advantage; a digital camera would be enough to show him the advantages that commerce reserves for nations. Westerners don't come here, however, not even to peek in. And this is a mistake because the market offers us a precious window—anyone who doesn't understand that on these stalls the future of the planet is being built is either blind or dumb. Canaan has a revolutionary message for us inhabitants of the First and Second Worlds: if you don't wake up, the only nations to make it to the finals of the globalization World Cup will be the Third Worlders.

TIANANMEN AS MATCHMAKER

The African merchants who shuttle between Canaan and their own countries remind us of those Arabs who once traveled the Silk Road. Arriving by jumbo jet rather than a camel, these adventurous businessmen also serve as a bridge between "Made in China" and African poverty. And like the travel companions of Marco Polo, their deals are the principle engine of economic growth for their countries.

The first African merchants to reach Guangzhou arrived via Bangkok and Kuala Lumpur. It was 1997 and the crisis in Asian markets prompted them to continue their migration on into China. They set themselves up and soon began to send back home products that were much less expensive than those from Southwest Asia. But only with the new millennium did the exodus of Africans toward China explode: between 2000 and 2005, the number of those arriving with tourist visas quadrupled,[2] and today it is estimated that at least forty thousand Africans reside in Guangzhou, constituting the city's largest foreign community. The influx is such that China has been forced to establish rigid immigration rules, but being illegal matters little to the Africans; once in the country as tourists they can disappear into the Chocolate City maze.

The backstory of the union between China and Africa is the paradoxical matchmaking event described to us by Ian Taylor, Africanist and lecturer at the Scottish university St. Andrews: "The international political consequences of the events of Tiananmen Square represent the turning point in the relations between China and Africa."[3] Here is a startling statement that's worth analyzing.

As we've seen, the Tiananmen uprisings provoked the indignation of the West. Condemnations rained in and the diplomats of the First and Second Worlds closed ranks. From the suspension of official visits to the canceling of arms sales, China became a pariah. Under the banner of the defense of human rights, the West's interference in the private affairs of China became oppressive: embassies in China offered asylum to dissidents and support to those who chose exile. Amidst the uproar, Beijing received the unexpected diplomatic support of numerous African states. Angola's foreign minister expressed "support for the actions used to quell the revolution" and the Namibian president, Sam Nujoma, sent a telegram congratulating the Chinese army.[4]

Africa is instinctively anti-West. In the 1980s Africa did not look favorably on the interest of the great powers in China and many heads of state were even convinced that this policy was aimed at slowing the country's growth. Thus it was only natural that when its honeymoon with the West was over, Africa would instead close ranks with Beijing. Longstanding victim of the intrigues of former colonial powers and of their often unscrupulous meddling, Africa had little reason to give credit to the incessant Western accusations of human rights violations. Tiananmen, therefore, cemented the alliance against a common enemy: the imperialism and neoimperialism of the wealthy Western countries.

African solidarity struck the Chinese Communist Party as an opportunity to weave a diplomatic web in the global South, in opposition to the one created by Western capitals in the global North. It would be enough to invite the governments opposed to Western intrusion to participate. Thus African reaction to the events of Tiananmen Square convinced Beijing that the continent was the most strategically important future ally for the political and economic development of the country.

The CCP understood that African governments, often autocratic, needed a partner other than the United States, which imposed its own model by means of economic threats from organizations like the IMF or the World Bank. This is exactly what China offered: an alternative, in open competition with the West, and thus not just a source of money and infrastructure, but an entire development model, capitalist but non-Western. This work, begun in the 1990s, is today bearing fruit, as Mark Leonard explains in his book *What Does China Think?*:

> In developing countries—in Africa, the Middle East and Central Asia—elites argue that they should follow the Chinese model of pursuing economic reforms first and political reforms later. And for the first time in a generation, some of their citizens actually believe them. It is no longer axiomatic that liberal democracy is the necessary foundation for development.[5]

Beyond the provision of raw materials that fuel economic growth, it was the legitimization of its own rise in the international community that Beijing aimed at in seeking the diplomatic support of Africa, given that more than a quarter of the votes in the United Nations' General Assembly were at stake. In 1995 Jiang Zemin, CCP General Secretary between 1989 and 2002, reformulated Deng Xiaoping's slogan in launching the latest great Chinese leap: "Leave! Become global actors!"

The next year Jiang undertook a long diplomatic trip that passed through several African capitals. And very soon China "leapt" into Africa.

THE PROMISED LAND

Africa is rich in resources, much of which is still available to whoever wants them and knows how to exploit them. Half of the world's reserves of gold, 98 percent of the chromium, 64 percent of the manganese, a third of the uranium, and 90 percent of the world's cobalt and platinum mines, are to be found on this continent. Not to speak of the forests, a legacy in lumber and precious woods that is unique in the world. And then there are the diamond deposits and the oilfields that far exceed those in North America, and 40 percent of the planet's hydroelectric energy.[6] And there are 1.3 billion Chinese, an army ready to make this wealth grow by dint of work. Far from falling on deaf ears, Jiang Zemin's exhortation encouraged a new generation of farmers to seek their fortune in Africa.

Trade between Africa and China was valued at almost $115 billion in 2010, and is growing at a rate of nearly 44 percent a year, with bilateral trade deals now signed between China and forty-five African countries.[7]

If, for Africans, China is the Promised Land, Serge Michel, coauthor with Michel Beuret of *China Safari*, tells us that for the Chinese, Africa is the final frontier, the place to become rich, a land full of opportunity. And here we can draw a parallel with the Chinese who in the 1980s migrated from the countryside to the Special Economic Zones in search of fortune.

In the West we instead tend to see Africa as a wretched, discouraging continent, to the point where many of us have even given up on trying to pull it out of its poverty and misgovernment. What's the point of pumping millions of dollars into some country, however desperate, in which sooner or later a dictator or a genocide will wipe out all the foreign aid and development and renovation projects? Even if the Western press is careful not to criticize the celebrity-fronted beneficent crusades, the idea that Africa could survive thanks to the charity of Bono, Madonna, and Angelina Jolie only confirms in the eyes of Western entrepreneurs the continent's identity as a place impossible to do business in.

The Chinese are not of the same opinion. They are, in fact, very positive and energetic in their relationship with the African nations. A tour through the capital of the Republic of the Congo, Brazzaville, provides confirmation enough. All the construction companies are Chinese, having arrived in great numbers in 2003, at the end of the Second Congo War, to rebuild the country. No Western company wanted anything to do with it; the Republic of the Congo was considered too risky. The Chinese, on the other hand, opened their wallets and applied their own model of modernization to the country.

It is also, and above all, for its own inhabitants that China is the Promised Land, but until today they have not been in a position to enjoy its fruits. The Western narrative would have us believe that this is owing to Chinese exploitation, and the influence of the media is such that not only our relations with China, but also our relations with Africa, have been influenced by the distortions in this mirror.

A series of academic investigations conducted in Africa confirms the interference of the media in the evaluation of the relations between Africans and Chinese, and these were the results: First, African views are not nearly as negative as Western media make out, but are variegated and complex. Second, the survey results are at variance with the dominant Western media representation that only African ruling elites are positive about these links. Third, we find that the dominant variation in African perspectives is by country, compared with variations such as age, education, and gender. The differences among countries in attitudes toward China are primarily a function of the extent to which national politicians have elected to raise the "Chinese problem" and, secondarily, the extent of Western media influence in African states.[8]

An excellent example is the different perception that the inhabitants of Zambia and of Sudan have of the Chinese presence. Zambia is an exceptionally poor nation in which 80 percent of the population lives below the poverty line. The Movement for Multi-Party Democracy, in power since 1991, is neoliberalist and followed the advice of the IMF and the World Bank, which has not produced the expected results. More recently, however, the country has begun to seek out assistance and cooperation from China. In 2006 Michael Sata, the leader of the opposition Patriotic Front Party, based his election campaign on anti-Chinese messages. Using strongly populist language, he described China as the new colonizers of Africa. This strategy brought him considerable financing from the government of Taiwan, as well as support from neighboring Malawi.[9]

Sata's charges were picked up by the Western press, which painted Zambia as one of Beijing's African victims. Unfortunately, the charges were false. In 2006, Sata made a Taiwan-financed trip to London and Boston where he publicly declared that European colonialism was better than Chinese colonialism. He added that eighty thousand Chinese in Zambia were in possession of work permits, while the central government had produced barely two thousand.[10]

The Western media did not denounce Sata's crude populism, which made some inroads in a population oppressed by incompetent government and corrupt elites. And the Chinese were turned into the object of their anger and frustration, some of it in the form of racist behavior.[11]

The other side of the coin is provided by Sudan, the largest state in Africa. China is far and away the largest investor in this nation: $8 billion in just fourteen energy sectors through 2008! Sudan is happier than Zambia to have China as a commercial partner. This partnership helped the economy grow at a yearly rate of 10 percent. Today China is the single biggest commercial partner of Sudan, and is the largest exporter and importer. It purchases 60 percent of the country's exports and absorbs 71 percent of all Sudanese exports. According to the CIA World Factbook, China accounts for 58.29 percent of Sudanese trade, followed by Japan (14.7 percent), Indonesia (8.83 percent), and India (4.86 percent). China also provided Sudan with military aircraft; the Sudanese Air Force currently includes sixty-six Chinese-made aircraft. Finally, China pledged to invest in the country's water infrastructure, air, and seaports.

The Western press has willfully changed the data concerning cooperation between the two countries in order to make us believe that the Chinese presence has all the signs of modern colonialism. Sudan's $4 billion in exports to China in 2007 included 40 percent of the oil Sudan produced, but contrary to media depictions, China's African oil is not mostly from Sudan. Of the 31 percent of China's 2006 oil imports that came from Africa, Angola's share was 14 percent, Sudan's 5 percent, Congo (Brazzaville)'s 4 percent, and Equatorial Guinea's 3 percent.[12] Then there's the problem of arms deals. We periodically read in all the papers how China is accused of selling arms to Sudan. And yet China represents barely 2 percent of the world arms market, and this percentage is falling. Although it is one of the seven nations who sell arms to Sudan, it isn't the most important: between 2000 and 2007 it represented 7 percent of the value of the arms imported by Sudan, while the West's friend, Putin's Russia, represented 87 percent.[13] Sudan is itself the largest producer of conventional weapons in Africa, whereas China exports nonconventional weapons, those used by the rebels of Darfur. And little does it matter that the United Nations has not imposed an embargo on this type of weaponry in Sudan and that the sales are thus legal: China is presented as the country that supplies the rebels of Darfur with weapons to yield against the government, the United States, and Chad.[14]

It's difficult to understand what is really happening in Africa and in the rest of the world, especially when China's involved, and this is due to the mistaken perception that the world has seen this nation as a monolithic actor because of its communism. Communism doesn't mean that all businesses are run by the state. China's central government has more or less the same control over private companies that Western governments have in their own countries. When a Chinese oil company causes an environmental disaster, the international community complains to the CCP and blames the entire population, even if neither has any control over the running of the company in question. When British Petroleum acts improperly or causes some ecological catastrophe, nobody points the finger at Downing Street, complains to Gordon Brown, or makes racist accusations against the English. The same could be said with regard to the Italian multinational oil and gas company Eni in countries like Nigeria. Paradoxically, then, the behavior of Chinese energy companies is capable of damaging Beijing's diplomacy and foreign policy precisely because these companies are relatively independent and operate in a competitive system.

THE ANTI-CHINESE SPIN

The Chinese presence in Africa has put an end to Western hegemony on the continent, meaning that all development economics textbooks have become obsolete and need to be rewritten. But Beijing with its army of state banks has also eclipsed the roles of the World Bank and the IMF, and the West is finding this humiliation very hard to swallow. The Chinese are accused of the worst atrocities, for example of damaging the African economy because they want to make of Africa not only a source for raw materials, but also the market in which to sell their products. It is an absurd idea: as we will see in the next chapter, serious Africanists are in agreement that China has provided the continent with important leverage vis-à-vis its old Western partners and also given some of the poorest people access to various products. But the West doesn't give up, instead spinning us a different story. And so the international press commented negatively on the exponential growth of manufacturing imports from China (rising between 1996 and 2005 from $895 million to $7.3 billion). This would be like saying that the trade with the Far East in the times of Marco Polo damaged Venice.

The media tell us that the Chinese textile industry is responsible for the destruction of Africa's own traditional textile production. Today in every African village, even the smallest, there is a store selling "Made in China" goods at prices accessible to all, and there is no industry in Africa that can compete with them. But does the fault really lie with China? A glance into the continent's trade statistics gives us an answer.

South African textiles began to lose ground when the country entered the WTO, when the protectionism of apartheid was dismantled. But the fate of South Africa has been shared by other African nations. Between 1975 and 2000, employment in the textile industry in Ghana fell 80 percent and production by 50 percent. In the clothing sector in Zambia, between the 1980s and 2002, fifteen thousand jobs were lost. Similar stories abound; at the source of them all is the low level of African competitiveness caused by certain international dynamics set in motion not by China but by the rich

West—among them the Multifibre Arrangement (MFA).

In 2000 the African Growth and Opportunity Act offered African countries a series of incentives to liberalize their national markets. The less developed nations would be able to acquire and use less expensive materials coming from abroad. On the wings of this concession a large portion of the Western manufacturing industry migrated to Africa in order to outflank the MFA, which established for its signatories, in particular the European Union and the United States, limits on the import of low-cost products, above all from India and China. Thus was created a sort of productive triangle, whereby the Western companies produced in Africa, with Asian material, products they would then sell in the West.

Exports of "Made in Africa" textiles to the United States shot up, increasing between 2000 and 2004 by 130 percent. Everyone applauded the generosity of the rich West for having begun to wear African clothes. The data was artificial, of course, given that this merchandise was for the most part produced using foreign raw materials, by non-African businesses, many of them Western. Naturally, when in 2005 the MFA expired, 87 percent of the American manufacturing industry and 73 percent of its European counterpart returned home, and the African textile industry disappeared; only then did everyone point the finger at China, who had hurried to fill the void created by this collapse. But it certainly isn't China's fault if African textiles are not competitive: Africanists like Serge Michel and Ian Taylor argue that the boom in exports of the first years of the new millennium confused the issue. The only factor that made African products competitive was the preferential treatment on the part of the Western countries, which they offered, for example, to their respective former colonies. Once this element was removed, the success of "Made in Africa" textiles was revealed as the flash in the pan that it was.

THE LESSON OF CHINA

If it is true that Western spin falsely describes China as a parasite, it is also true that China is in Africa to do business, not to bestow charity. The labor relations are then real relations and, given that the Chinese bring capital and know-how and the Africans raw materials and work, it's up to both to establish equitable relationships. This means that the local governments are left the task of fighting battles that workers, unions, and Western politicians, and in part Chinese politicians, have already fought.

An analysis of union struggles in Africa reveals the important influence that competition, the civil society's level of maturity, and the solidarity of the workers' movement exert on the bargaining process. Two examples, one in Zambia and one in Tanzania, offer good illustrations of these factors. In 2007, in the Zambian copper mines run by Chinese companies, after years of strikes and struggle, the miners succeeded in formalizing their labor contracts. In Tanzania, workers in the textile sector failed to do the same. In Zambia, the Chinese compete with foreign multinationals and the miners are organized, and the government is kept under strict surveillance by a hostile civil society that holds it responsible for the poverty in which it is forced to live. In Tanzania the Chinese presence in the textile sector is recent, the profit margins are very low, and there is no political presence that watches over the business.[15]

It's a mistake to consider China in Africa as a monolithic element. Precisely because the script that the two actors read from takes its distance from the tragic tale of colonialism, but reflects the classical relations of production, the interaction will vary from state to state and from industry to industry. It's left to each African country to conquer piece by piece those privileges that all workers' movements have wrested from employers through long and hard union struggles.

It is precisely the differences in wages and treatment of workers that tell us that the new Chinese presence in Africa is one of the keys to interpreting this fascinating new story that is redesigning our planet. China may be communist, but its economy is capitalist. And Africa is, at the same time, the last frontier that this economic system has to conquer and the Promised Land where it will undergo its final transformation.

CHAPTER 19

THE LAST FRONTIER

In 2002 the bloody Angolan Civil War came to an end. Waged over a twenty-seven-year period, it was the longest conflict of the Cold War theater. Trapped between the squabbling US and Soviet hegemons, Angola was afflicted by fratricidal struggles that continued on well past the collapse of the Berlin Wall. The results were appalling: more than half a million dead, the vast majority civilians, and among the survivors hundreds of thousands left mutilated due to the mines strewn all over the country. Over the course of more than a quarter of a century, all infrastructure was destroyed; when peace finally returned, it was necessary to rebuild the nation's socioeconomic foundations from scratch. As was the case with many African countries, Angola instinctively looked to the West for help to rebuild.

The nation's relations with the international financial community, however, were not the best. The immense and rusty bureaucratic machine of international organizations had no desire to interact with the survivors of a war that belonged to the remote past. The local authorities didn't know how to comport themselves, didn't know the golden rules involved in begging for international aid, nor did they have connections with Hollywood or other celebrities, who have made of Africa the little garden of their good actions. Angola, presenting itself on the globalization scene more than ten years late with respect to the other poor countries, hadn't a clue how to navigate the stormy waters of Western economic cooperation.

First to close its purse was the International Monetary

Fund. During the conflict, long periods of hyperinflation alternated with those of stability, and this prevented the IMF from producing an economic résumé for the country, a document vital to economists for the preparation of an intervention plan aimed at repairing and restarting the economy. The World Bank kept its due distance as well, limiting itself to strictly humanitarian operations. Between 2002 and 2003, therefore, the response of the rich West was negative and perfectly foreseeable: the charity assistance of the rich states and the international organizations are always subordinate to economic stability and the absence of debt, and dependent on the participation of the IMF. And since the latter wouldn't have anything to do with Angola, assistance was not forthcoming. It seems absurd, but the same organizations born from the ruins of World War II, at Bretton Woods, to help nations recover from the tragedy of war did not lend a hand fifty years later to the last victim of the Cold War.

Naturally, without the approval of the IMF and the World Bank, Angola was unable to access private financing. The market, that supernatural creature that every morning in the first years of the new millennium added tens or hundreds of points to the Dow Jones and thus made money for anyone gambling on the Stock Exchange, had no desire to venture into a country considered so risky as not to merit the help of the IMF. Not even the scent of the oil that abounded below Angola's surface sufficed to convince the crowd of American oil companies, which in 2002 were busy stalking the White House with lobbyists in the expectation that the preventive war in Iraq would soon start. Indeed, everyone was just waiting to have a go at that cake and thought of nothing else. Even the bankers who at the beginning of the century shuttled between Wall Street and Reykjavik didn't want to hear about Angola. Too risky, one heard them repeat in the glass palaces of high finance, better to divide up Iraqi oil and squeeze the teats of the Icelandic cow till the milk's gone. A few years later, to general bewilderment, all these considerations would prove mistaken.

Between 2004 and 2007, as Iraq plunged into chaos, insurgents blew up oil and gas pipelines, companies like General Electric returned home with tails between their legs, and Iceland teetered on bankruptcy, Angola registered the largest increase in oil extraction growth in the world, overtaking Russia, Azerbaijan, Brazil, and Qaddafi's Libya.[1] In the same period, the West had opened its arms to Libya after twenty years of embargos, a "diplomatic" gesture in exchange for lavish quantities of gas and oil in a time of rising energy costs. But while Qaddafi set up his tent outside Villa Pamphili in Rome and performed his anti-Western show at the 2009 G20 meeting, Angola proceeded to produce nearly as much oil as Nigeria.

What made this miraculous recovery possible was China, which back in 2002 agreed to finance the country's reconstruction in exchange for a supply of energy. And it did so with such determination as to squeeze out the other big contender, India. Thus, while Italian and American companies were courting the dictator Qaddafi, the former financier of terrorism now promising extravagant oil deals, China established a very similar relationship with Angola, a country governed by a less capricious and decidedly more democratic government, but, above all, with energy reserves far richer than those to be found in Libya.

THE NEW DEVELOPMENT PHILOSOPHY

"China needs natural resources and Angola wants development": thus did the latter's president, José Eduardo dos Santos, sum up in 2007 the relationship between the two nations.[2] The universal principal is always the same—*do ut des*—but the Chinese have adapted it to the demands of a planet that, thanks to globalization, is shattering all the power structures of the past. In particular they are going after those of the Industrial Revolution, which are nothing if not the bars of a cage forcing a fixed model of North-South relations on the world. The first bars to be broken are those of the colonial legacy.

Serge Michel argues for five strengths characterizing China's adventure in the African Third World:

> One, China has no colonial past. Two, it has a pan-African approach, unlike Europeans who only worked in their former territories. Three, China sets no political conditions on its cooperation (such as democracy and transparency). The only requirement is that the African country must sever its ties with Taiwan. Fourth, China finances infrastructure, such as dams, roads, and railroads, and it constructs them with its own labor. Fifth, China is the last centralized system and can easily offer package deals.[3]

The model Michel describes can be found throughout Africa in conflict with its traditional Western counterpart. In Guinea the range of projects that the Export-Import Bank of China has financed range from bauxite mines, to the dams for hydroelectric plants that power refineries, to the railroads used to transport the finished product. Its American competitors are only interested in the bauxite; they have never wanted to finance refineries because, they argued, there is not enough electricity in the country to run them, even though at least 122 sites have been identified as ideal for constructing dams and hydroelectric plants. Give us the raw material, we'll take care of the rest—this is the predatory approach of the rich countries; instead the Chinese construct the necessary infrastructure. And we ask why the most attractive contracts go to them.

Whereas Western attitudes have not changed much since the colonial era, Beijing, also because of the still-open wound of its own colonization, is very careful to establish relationships on equal terms. Its economic and military success notwithstanding, China preserves many of the characteristics of a country of the global South, and like Africa its geopolitical perspective comes from the bottom, as was made clear in Mao's Three Worlds Theory, taken up again later by Deng. In the theory's terms, a "great power" (*chaoji daguo*) is defined as such not for the extent of its territory, demographic heft, or economic resources, but according to its motivations and its behavior. A state becomes a superpower when it forces its own initiatives and aggression on other countries, or else pursues hegemony, dominion based on force. It's what the Soviet Union and the United States did at the end of World War II.

During the Cold War, the ambitions of the US and the USSR gave life to an international system composed of three worlds: the first, consisting of the two hegemonic superpowers; the second, consisting of Europe, Japan, and Canada; and the third, which includes China alongside the other Asian countries, Africa, and Latin America.[4] Today the theory still significantly informs Chinese relations with the global South, positioning China among the Third Worlders and binding its fate to developing and oppressed nations such as, precisely, those in Africa:

> The ideological underpinnings of the political relations between Beijing and the African continent can be traced back to relationships consolidated during the period of the wars for African independence between 1950 and the early '60s, between the newly born People's Republic of China, still simmering with revolutionary fervor, and a continent in turmoil after decades of Western colonial domination.[5]

Let's be careful: this is not a matter of Chinese good guys and Western bad guys; our beloved dichotomies don't work here. It's more likely that in China's DNA the business gene replaced the colonization gene. The relationship the Chinese have created with their African partners is simply one of reciprocal advantage. But for the Africans this approach comes as a breath of fresh air, as the first time in history they find themselves treated as equals rather than subordinates.

However, the Chinese are also, even if not in the Maoist sense, a superpower. No other nation has so much money in its state coffers, something on the order of $2 trillion in available reserves. Nor can any other nation with such ease move thousands of workers to Africa and have them adapt to the demands of each host country. The Chinese are, above all, pragmatists, a quality of which Africa stands in desperate need. When a Chinese company won the bid to build a railroad from Mecca to Medina, eight hundred workers converted to Islam in order to obtain work permits.[6]

China always does things on a grand scale, as we know, and in this it is without rival, especially in the East. At the November 2006 Forum on China-Africa Cooperation, forty-eight nations participated, and fifty-one of the fifty-three African nations attended the 2010 Shanghai Expo. In economic terms as well, Africa could not have found a richer partner. At the 2007 Tokyo International Conference on African Development in Yokohama, when the Japanese prime minister announced his country's intention to set aside $6 billion for cooperation with African nations, it made many in the audience smile. The Export-Import Bank of China alone has already spent more than twenty billion in three years on similar projects. The Chinese presence in Africa is overwhelming. In 2008 there were 227 Japanese businesses operating in Africa, as compared to 900 Chinese businesses.[7]

Beijing has by now created a bridge with Africa, revolutionizing the relations of power in the world, to general astonishment. When the Congolese need a new dam, the Chinese—unlike the World Bank, which often imposes impossible conditions—build them one in the blink of an eye and accept their payment in oil. Serge Michel explains:

> The typical response of international organizations to requests for financing from African nations is: no, you have to live in the dark because you have debts and your nations are unstable. The Chinese on the other hand respond: but of course, not only will we finance whatever you want—a dam, a hydroelectric plant—we'll build it ourselves and you can pay us in oil or raw materials. This is the definition of a mutually beneficial arrangement.[8]

China's entry into Africa, therefore, has increased the competitiveness of the African nations on the international market. In the wake of decolonization, the former "bosses" continued to dictate the conditions of cooperation with their former "subjects." Michel continues:

> Now they're forced to come to terms with China, an exceedingly tough and experienced competitor. This is the case with Niger. A former French colony, it possesses immense uranium deposits, overseen from the beginning by the French company Arivas, which enjoys a monopoly. This means that the head of this company has immense power and acts as a de facto vice president of Niger. When the government began to offer concessions for the exploitation of uranium to the Chinese, the French were furious. Ultimately, to maintain their contracts, they were forced to offer better terms than the Chinese. Niger has intelligently used Beijing as leverage against the French to free itself from its postcolonial chains. This truly extraordinary story gives us a good idea of the commercial revolution that the Chinese presence is fueling in

Africa.[9]

THE ANGOLA MODEL

The history of Angola and of so many other African countries is emblematic of China's ability to forge new commercial relationships with the global South that break out of the colonial mold. It is difficult for us in the West to comprehend the nature of this connection because, imprisoned in our preconceptions, we understand only relationships based on force. The West stubbornly insists on seeing the Chinese presence on the continent as the last chapter in a history of commercial domination, which explains why, in our collective imagination, Africa is at the same time both the theater of struggles for control of world resources and the place to make amends for our past colonial crimes.

The image of Hollywood divas and pop singers who elect themselves champions of the African poor is based on this crude dichotomy: China preys on resources while we rich and famous Westerners save the population from hunger with our aid, seeking forgiveness for the massacres of local populations, the slave trade, and the theft of resources. Hollywood's mantra—"now they're the bad guys and we're the good"— blankets the covers of tabloids and glossy magazines. But behind our "goodness" there's a hidden commercial machine that to this day reproduces patterns we know only too well. A Western diplomat summed up the complex variety of subjection still in force:

> When I speak to my friends from Angola I always tell them: the little stroll you're taking with the Chinese does you good, but if you want to get serious, if you want to enter the big leagues, you have to return to us.[10]

But rather than a stroll, the relations between China and Angola represent a large-scale modernization plan. In 2006, the country's GDP growth reached 18.6 percent. The IMF, which can by now refer to a series of positive statistics, published projections for 2007 and 2008 and spoke of growth rates of more than 20 percent. And this is indeed what happened. The GDP grew from $42 billion in 2002 to $113 billion in 2009, nearly tripling.[11] On the inflation front, from 300 percent at the beginning of the century it fell to 12 percent in 2006 and below 10 percent the next year. Even the country's balance of payments is enviable, with oil income producing surpluses in internal revenue and the trade balance.[12]

In 2008 the World Bank was obliged to acknowledge the Angola miracle and praised the development model applied in the country, the so-called Angola Model. Its designer, of course, was China, which between 2002 and the end of 2009 allocated and facilitated loans of approximately $19 billion. But it's not trade that distinguishes the Angola Model from the other modernization models applied in Africa. As we saw with Libya, every commercial relationship between African nations and the West, and especially those concerned with oil, are bilateral trade deals. No, the revolutionary aspect is the mutually beneficial arrangement mentioned by Serge Michel, which Ian Taylor explains:

> Beijing realizes that the Africans don't want to be treated with charity and benevolence, they want to be business partners with whom you can establish economic relationships that are advantageous to their own economy and their own development. This is where the idea of creating a model of economic and commercial relations based on a win-win situation comes in.[13]

The Chinese formula is also a blend of diplomacy and the market. Beijing establishes high-level diplomatic relations, offering African governments the respect that Westerners reserve for their similars, thereby paving the way for its companies. Angola's head of state makes regular visits to China, and the converse is true for the Chinese prime minister. Western diplomacy works in the same way. But Beijing goes a step further than handshakes and official dinners and places its banks, all still state-run, at the disposal of Chinese companies.

In 2004 in Angola, China extended its first credit line of $2 billion, money that was distributed by Chinese lending institutions. The financing naturally went to Chinese firms, which won all bids, and it couldn't be otherwise since, after twenty-seven years of war, the know-how needed for reconstruction no longer existed in Angola. But these companies hired local labor and the bilateral contracts financed large public works projects like the reconstruction of 371 kilometers of highway between Luanda and Uíge, a logistical artery essential for commerce. The population applauded the government for having secured such a rapid and successful reconstruction.

In those countries where cooperation works, Beijing does not skimp on traditional financial assistance either. And Angola, where modernization requires socioeconomic infrastructure, has becomes its biggest beneficiary. This money has built schools, community centers, roads, housing projects, and ports.[14] The development package is complete and, as should be obvious, based on the Chinese economic model.

OIL DIPLOMACY

No one any longer doubts that the Chinese commitment to Africa is serious. The continent absorbs more than 50 percent of China's development assistance funds, capital that provides for both general development and specific, high-prestige projects like public works and stadiums, which no Western financier or international agency would consider. This is precisely what has convinced so many African nations to engage in extensive and enduring cooperation with China. The intermediaries are ad hoc organizations like the Export-Import Bank of China, which extended $12 billion in credit to African countries in 2006, in the process making the World Bank look like a provincial credit union.[15]

But let's let the numbers speak for themselves; in the words of Ian Taylor:

> In 1990, business between Africa and China amounted to $1.67 billion; in 2008 it jumped up to $106.8 billion, with an increase of 44 percent with respect to 2007. What's guiding the commercial cooperation, naturally, is oil. With the exception of South Africa, Beijing's four most important partners are all oil producers: Angola, the Congo, Equatorial Guinea, and Sudan. It seems obvious to me that crude dominates China's investment profile in Africa. This is because China always needs more of it.[16]

Thus when we speak of Chinese investment in Africa, we are referring principally to the supplying of energy. China has been importing oil since 1993 and the need to procure it has substantially influenced its foreign policy. Africa is the right continent to satisfy this growing need, as, once again, Ian Taylor explains:

> At the beginning of the 1990s, Beijing didn't have much choice: the Middle East was a risky investment, and in any case access to the region was regarded as a prerogative of the United States; Central Asia, on the other hand, was under Russian control. Africa, though, was hardly considered and, with the exception of Nigeria and a few other countries, its oil

resources were intact or only marginally exploited. But it was the invasion of Iraq that convinced China to intensify its energy ties with the continent. Beijing was afraid the United States would use oil as a diplomatic weapon.[17]

At the dawn of the new millennium, then, Chinese energy policy reflected both the changing geopolitical situation and Beijing's fears. To put it into action, the Party encouraged national energy companies (NOCs) to step up their purchases of oil in international markets and facilitated the acquisition of oil reserves abroad through bilateral agreements with foreign governments. But according to Taylor, it would be wrong to conceive of this penetration strategy as a monolithic entity completely directed by the Party:

> Beijing did not impose any geographical restrictions on the various NOCs, thus creating a degree of overlap that often results in open competition, particularly between China National Petroleum Corporation, China Petroleum & Chemical Corporation, and China National Offshore Oil Corporation. The first two clashed violently over a project to build an oil pipeline in Sudan. This means that the NOCs compete among themselves not only for oil and gas deposits in Africa, but also for political advantages. The concept is that the more a company succeeds in winning important contracts, the more likely it is to receive the diplomatic and financial backing of Beijing for its subsequent investments.[18]

Beijing's support for the Chinese NOCs in Africa is fundamental because it guarantees access to loans from the state-run commercial banks and this reduces the cost of capital available to them. This model of ruthless competition at the national level makes the companies infinitely more competitive than their Western counterparts, as well as more easily governable. A phenomenon like Enron would be inconceivable in China because the market is competitive, not elitist, and between politics and the business world there seem to be strong firewalls, in contrast to what we see in the West, where governments often kowtow to the dictates of corporations—whereas in China, while the state supports corporate interests, it is nonetheless the state that is firmly in charge.

As we have seen, Beijing's support tends to be dynamic and decisive: when a Chinese business is drawing up an important contract, the government intervenes, organizing official visits, guaranteeing new lines of credit, and diplomatically supporting the autonomy of the state on the international stage, as happened in 2009 in Sudan. But this is because the state is obtaining clear and specific policy objectives, not merely drumming up business. Today Chinese NOC imports from Africa fulfill 31 percent of Chinese oil requirements, while their American counterparts account for only 18 percent of US needs. It is clear that Africa is strategically much more important for China than it is for the US.

CHAPTER 20

GLOBALIZATION AND CRIME

In China cigarettes are a bit like flowers. Packets of particularly treasured brands are brought as gifts for those who invite us to dinner in their home, or are offered on official occasions. Under the Christmas tree or at weddings, expensive varieties are typical gifts, and even in tombs, beside the deceased, a few good-quality cigarettes are always left. The cigarette culture in China is complex, ancient, and has its own language: it is said there is a packet for every occasion and social position. The famous and very expensive Panda brand cigarettes (eighteen dollars per packet), Deng Xiaoping's favorite, are offered only to members of the government. Workers smoke Hongtashan or Yun Yan instead, which cost very little and can be found everywhere. Golden-Pack Shanghai cigarettes are an excellent calling card during high-level business meetings; if they are offered it means there is great willingness to negotiate. When low-level entrepreneurs are about to close a deal, they instead exchange the blue packets of Baisha.[1]

China is the greatest producer of tobacco in the world—unsurprisingly, given the symbology associated with it. But precisely because there exists in the country a culture of smoking and an industry that supports it, international organized crime has chosen it as the global epicenter of cigarette counterfeiting. China is currently the source of 99 percent of the counterfeit cigarettes consumed in the United States. And the illicit industry rolls only Western cigarettes, which up until a few years ago were principally smoked beyond the country's borders.

The international market is immense. Every year the Chinese consume 2.2 trillion cigarettes. The companies that produce them are all controlled by the state and in 2007 sales amounted to 8 percent of China's budget. Thus the government has a strong interest in combating the counterfeiting, but also in protecting the industry: "Until this April, officials in the central Chinese province of Hubei were required to smoke a collective 230,000 packs of regional brands a year."[2]

It's not easy for the Chinese government to root out the counterfeiting weeds in the tobacco industry garden, precisely because it is so flourishing. In Yunxiao, in the southwest of Fujian province, in the last twenty years the economy has grown to the point that the region's millionaires are famous all over China. The industry that made them rich, on the other hand, is not to be seen, hidden in the countryside, "carved deeply into caves, high into the hills, and even buried beneath the earth"[3]—all factories producing counterfeit cigarettes, of course. As soon as the authorities close one, the owners open up another close by. Yunxiao covers twice the area of New York City and lives exclusively by cigarette counterfeiting. The sector is a very young one, and still growing.

Global demand has been sharply increasing since 1997, and in just over ten years Chinese production has ramped up to the point that today it makes nearly 500 billion fake cigarettes a year. At approximately 250 billion, half of national production, Yunxiao is the center of the counterfeiting industry. And the quality is excellent.

Paradoxically, at the origin of this exponential growth are the antismoking campaigns in Western countries, with their heavy taxes on tobacco that make counterfeiting a good business. The flourishing market is for the moment controlled by Western organized crime working through Chinese intermediaries, with dizzying profits: a packet of fake Marlboros produced in China costs around twenty cents and can be sold in the United States for twenty times as much. It's a business almost as profitable as drug trafficking, especially if you consider how much smaller the possible penalties are: a substantial fine or a few years in jail rather than the life imprisonment or death penalty that awaits drug traffickers in many countries, China included.

The worst of the damages goes well beyond the loss of internal revenue, approximately $40 billion a year worldwide. It is in the smokers' health where the greatest effects are felt, since counterfeit cigarettes are even more dangerous than authentic ones. The producers use chemical elements that are less expensive but more damaging to the well-being of the consumer, who is unlikely to notice the counterfeiting, as the Chinese have reached exceedingly high levels of sophistication. "In 2001, Chinese manufacturers were producing eight different varieties of counterfeit Marlboros. As of last year, though, Chinese counterfeiters were manufacturing separate versions of Marlboro tailored for some 60 countries," writes Te-Ping Chen.[4] Every packet is adapted to the specific regulations and details imposed in the various countries: health warnings, tax and state-monopoly stamps, all carefully reproduced. "The Italian state-monopoly wrappers on Chinese counterfeit cigarettes are excellent," confirms Aldo Ingangi, deputy state prosecutor attached to the Naples court, adding that counterfeiters in Italy exploit the connections that local criminals have within the State Mint and State Printing House.[5]

In the first chapter we discussed how the opening of the Chinese market in the 1980s attracted entrepreneurs from the Chinese diaspora to the Special Economic Zones. These men spoke the language and were acquainted with Western tastes, an explosive combination for the nascent "Made in China" capitalism. They found themselves in the ideal position for exploiting the cheap labor on offer and producing at knockdown prices the goods in demand in the richest markets. Our own entrepreneurs arrived later, when the work of the pioneers from Hong Kong and Taiwan had already paved the way and investment in China was less risky.

In the 1990s, organized crime completed an entirely analogous journey. Bridging the gap between China and the West's illicit vices during this decade were the triads, criminal organizations that developed principally within the Chinese diaspora, along the way establishing strategic ties to their more sophisticated but, above all, more globalized Western counterparts. And the structure of the triads greatly resembles that of the Calabrian criminal organization the 'Ndrangheta. According to Giampiero Rossi and Simone Spina in their reporting on the Chinese mafia in Italy:

> The Chinese mafia's strength lies in its fragmentation, in the myriad cells constantly in contact with each other. . . . More than an octopus [*piovra*, also a term for the mafia], the Chinese mafia might be compared to a multi-headed dragon. There is no worldwide management structure or even a top boss in a position to influence the choices of the various clans. Instead there are independent gangs, connected by an invisible net extending around the world.[6]

The cells of the triads are the Chinese version of the basic organizational unit of the 'Ndrangheta, the 'Ndrine, and their range of activity is just as great. From the slave trade up to the counterfeiting of cigarettes, the triads have carved out their place in the global underworld. Of course, they have learned some techniques from their more sophisticated Western brethren, but it would be a mistake to consider them fledgling organizations, born from the liberalization of the Chinese economy and therefore less dangerous. On the contrary, the triads represent a serious threat to the future precisely on account of their resemblance to our mafias. They certainly have already built up a frightening résumé.

Legend has it that in 1674 the Manchurian army of the future Qing dynasty set fire to the Buddhist temple in Fujian. All but five of the monks died in the blaze. Experts in bladed weapons, enough to win the nickname "Tigers of Shaolin," these monks fled to the south of China. In Guangdong they founded the first of a series of secret societies. The Chinese call them *Tien-ti-jen*, the Society of Heaven and Earth, and their symbol is an equilateral triangle, which is why in the nineteenth century the English renamed them triads.[7]

According to many historians, however, the motivations behind the birth of the triads were economic. The triad came to light in 1760 in Fujian and was a mutual aid association for merchants and immigrants, inspired by *guanxi*. However it started, "the power of the triads grew to the point that the leaders of the secret societies established important ties with the political authorities and became hidden architects of the country's fates."[8]

The triads participated in the great revolts that rocked China beginning in the middle of the nineteenth century, including the 1900 Boxer Rebellion. They failed, however, to insert themselves into the country's reconstruction process after the fall of the Qing Dynasty in 1911. It is at this point that they entered the criminal world. While maintaining their centuries-old traditions, especially initiation rites, the triads changed their goals and became an expression of the power of the large family groups that controlled them—exactly like what happened in Italy with the transformation of the mafia from a secret organization against the Piedmontese monarch into a criminal society.

Like the mafia in the first years of the twentieth century, in the 1980s the triads went international. A study by the Canadian Security Intelligence Service that came to light in 2000 estimated that the largest triad, Sun Yee On, consisted of between forty-seven thousand and sixty thousand active members throughout the world; the second largest, the 14K triad, was reported to have approximately twenty thousand members and to be very active in Europe.[9]

Today there are four "Dragon Cities," the poles of the Chinese crime compass: Manchester, Perth, San Francisco, and Vancouver. This is where the big Asian criminal groups are concentrated and from where they stretch out the tentacles of their international cooperation. They are the outposts of Chinese criminality that has its bases in Macao, Taiwan, and of course in Hong Kong, where the triads regrouped following the Maoist victory. Operating on all continents, today these organizations run 80 percent of the heroin trade in Australia, control a large share of the human trafficking from the East, are active in the slave trade, and launder money in the financial centers of Asia, South America, Africa, and Europe. But it is in Italy that they attended the university of crime, graduating with top marks.

THE *BEL PAESE* SCHOOL OF CRIME

Just a few figures will suffice to explain the importance of the Italian mafia's role in the ascent of the triads to the Olympus of the illicit. The principal points of entry for counterfeit goods sold in Europe are ports, and Italian ports are among the most highly utilized: from Genoa to Gioia Tauro, from Trieste to Palermo, and of course to the busiest, Naples.[10] It's enough simply to approach the port of Naples to understand: the wharves are crowded with ships carrying containers with the label of COSCO, the China Ocean Shipping Company, which recently joined with the Swiss company MSC to run the port's most important terminal. Naples is the principle European point of entry for Chinese fakes, with 70 percent of all the goods destined for Italy arriving here in a large portion of the 250,000 containers cleared through customs here annually. Estimates refer to €400 million in taxes evaded every year, a figure owing much to the growing and increasingly solid alliance between the Camorra and Chinese organized crime.[11]

The phenomenon of the triads in Italy is a recent one, however, exploding roughly a decade ago; the driving sector is counterfeit consumer goods. According to Fausto Zuccarelli, District Attorney in the Public Prosecutor's office in Naples and Deputy Director of the National Antimafia Office:

> Initially Chinese criminals brought in low-quality products destined, necessarily, for the black market, and so the consumer knew he was buying a shoddy product. Their strength in those first years was the capacity to offer goods at very low prices. Today, however, the Chinese are also producing quality products and inserting themselves accordingly into a different black market, the market for counterfeits you don't notice as such, where the fakes are no longer on tables outside but in the stores selling the so-called original product.[12]

It is the interaction with the Italian criminal organizations, like the Camorra in Naples and the surrounding areas, that helped the Chinese knockoff industry to adapt to the needs of the society that is its destination market, and over the years perfect it to the point that it competes with the real industry. Until a few years ago the basic production took place in China, and then the semiprocessed material arrived in Italy, where it received the finishing touches, done primarily in the city of Nola, near Naples, and in the Tuscan province of Prato. For the past five years or so, however, the counterfeiting process has moved entirely to China; there's no longer any need for the local Italian touch. The finished product reaches Europe clandestinely or via the technique of underinvoicing. The jump in quality took place thanks to the cooperation of the triads with the Camorra, which in the past maintained quality control in Italy. The Chinese learned from them not only how and what to produce, but also how to apply these controls.

Today the Camorra has taken on other roles, such as that of a simple investor providing capital, or a broker. This is the case with the designer knockoff industry, where the triads are entrusted with contracts to do much of the counterfeiting once run by the Camorra. The latter, however, because it maintains control of the territory, continues to have the task of mixing the counterfeit product in with the originals.

> The Camorra constrains retailers to sell the counterfeit products beside the originals on the same shelves. The consumer doesn't notice, and if he has any problems with the product he'll complain to the company that makes the originals, which hardly ever has a way of checking if the product is a fake.[13]

Law enforcement agencies know well that when a counterfeit product reaches the retailer, especially in the department stores and the outlets, the owners are aware that it's a fake, but they don't bother themselves about it. This is the market and the society of today. Again Zuccarelli explains:

> The big brands also know they are being counterfeited, and they know very well that the businesses they subcontract the manufacturing out to, for any product, a bag, a belt, a wallet, they in turn subcontract to illegal Chinese businesses that do the work at even lower prices. And they know this because they impose production costs that are too low, that can only be obtained through exploitative labor and completely ignoring health and safety rules. The designer brands don't want to saddle themselves with "ele-

vated" costs, they want higher and higher profits. For a bag that sells for 800 euro, they very often pay around thirty. And even if they're aware of the counterfeiting of their products, they don't publicly fight it because it's all publicity, it's a way to circulate their own products in the streets.[14]

The Western consumer is therefore an accomplice of the counterfeiters of our time. But are we aware of this?

THE CULTURE OF FAKES

At the root of the spread of fakes we find the relationship with copyright. On one side the developing countries fight it, as fruit of the Western hegemonic culture; on the other side, the West defends it with all its might, while nevertheless continuing to buy counterfeit goods that cost less. Thus we could affirm that the emerging countries, in opposing the concept of intellectual property on philosophical as well as economic grounds, demonstrate greater honesty. They ask for shorter-term licenses and for measures making the legislation less rigid, in order to have the opportunity to "copy" when this process becomes necessary for their economic growth.

And here the technological and pharmaceutical patents of Western multinational corporations are extremely important. No one can deny that current legislation is designed to protect the monopolies and oligopolies of the rich countries' biggest businesses. And all the others, for whom the costs are prohibitive, are cut out of important scientific and commercial developments. Recourse to fakes is for them an instrument for escaping this disadvantage. Actually, development in the global South is to be counted among the prosperous North's socioeconomic objectives from the moment we wish for a planet without profound differences, for practical as much as for political reasons. But whereas the

South continues to consider intellectual, scientific, and technological property a public good, the rich North sees it as a way to maintain its economic supremacy over the markets.[15]

For this reason, one of the most widespread criticisms of the Chinese economic miracle is precisely the absence of creativity, regarded as a virtually exclusive prerogative of the West. This common stereotype does not correspond to the truth, but above all it is completely obsolete in a world characterized by cultural contamination. All popular models are regularly exported, or copied: from politicians to pop singers to television formats, originality has a short life span. Cultural recycling is the order of the day and China, a country that has synthesized the communist and capitalist models into capicommunism, is one of the best when it comes to reinventing modernity.

In the past, physical barriers to the spread of information and objects encouraged the persistence of local cultures with markedly original characteristics. Today everyone wants the same product in real time, another reason behind the spread of fakes. *Harry Potter*, *The Da Vinci Code*, and a love story between an adolescent with clear socialization issues and a vampire are all mass cultural phenomena overwhelming North and South. What is the element that causes these stories to go global? Certainly not originality.

Today fashions are often born from plagiarism or, better, from the reworking of already existing concepts. The cultural fabric is, therefore, a mix of the new and the not new. In the solitude of the global village, cultural copies offer consolation. And this, together with technical reproducibility, is the fundamental aspect of the modern concept of cultural identity that is being born, destined to shatter copyright as we know it. A best-selling book in Germany was written by a seventeen year old, Helene Hegemann, and recounts the adventures of an adolescent in the Berlin drug world. Beyond the thematic echoes of the best seller by Christine F., the author has copied entire passages from another similar book, *Strobo*, and from the blog of its author, Airen. Helene Hegemann has defended herself from accusations of plagiarism by declaring that originality no longer exists, only authenticity. In the literary fabric woven by Hegemann, the words of Airen assume a different position than in the original. And what is relevant is the positive judgment of the jurors for the Leipzig Book Fair prize, who included her book, *Axolotl Roadkill*, on the list of finalists. A glance at the German Amazon site shows that Hegemann's success has increased sales for *Strobo*, and the two books can even be purchased together at a large discount.

Young people are tuned into this new way of conceiving creativity. This has been made clear in Sweden where a new political reality has been born, the Pirate Party, whose primary proposal is to knock down obstacles to culture, from fees on listening to music to authors' royalties, and its popularity is obviously thanks to the Internet. Initially derided and considered "not serious," the Pirate Party has rapidly—if temporarily, according to membership numbers and opinion polls—become the third-largest party in Sweden, with two representatives in the European Parliament. However, by the time of the national elections in 2010, it did not reach the 4 percent of votes requirement to get into parliament. Meanwhile, analogous parties have cropped up in at least twenty other nations, all of them with higher percentages of young members than in other currently existing parties. So, while the sea change from old to new party affiliations hasn't yet occurred, the potential is there for that to happen at any time.

Young people and emerging economies are in other words united in the battle against the commercialization of culture by Western monopolies and oligopolies. Seven giant companies, the majors, control the worldwide market for music and films, a situation that until the advent of the Internet permitted them to "dictate" conditions of access. The culture of fakes is thus, in some ways, a consequence of the capitalist system's innate avidity. An example of this new way of seeing the spread of cinematic and musical copies is provided by a group of students from the University of Leeds in England:

> We almost never go to the movies, all the films we're interested in we download off the Internet and watch them on the computer. For us students, going to the movies is too expensive. We download music too and trade it with each other using file sharing. Don't the major labels know we're broke? That we have to get into debt to go to university while our parents didn't pay anything and everyone had a scholarship to live on? What are we supposed to do, not eat so we can buy CDs or pay for a movie ticket?[16]

These are protests we are in part ready to share, even if we might object that it is precisely among young people that the culture of designer labels is so widespread, to the extent that they are ready to shell out dizzying amounts to have a certain bit of writing, and not others, across the waistband of their underwear. In any case, it is good to always keep in mind the two aspects of the problem: the philosophical judgment concerning the end of originality is one thing; support for organized crime is another. In China they know this well.

BEIJING'S BUSINESSMEN TURN A DEAF EAR

Chinese criminal organizations have a strong interest in continuing to cooperate with the Camorra and other Western mafias because, in addition to guaranteeing capital (which the triads are however starting to accumulate), they provide the market outlets and contacts with the local community.[17] Thus the criminal world is reproducing the same dynamics we saw develop in the economic sphere in the 1980s and '90s. China becomes the world's cut-rate factory and Western manufacturers relocate their production there, then sell the products to the rich West. The Chinese have learned their trade from the Westerners so well that they have surpassed them, setting up factories producing fakes and copying designer labels, but they need Western partners in order to commercialize their products.

As was the case with our own industrialists, sooner or later the Chinese criminal organizations won't have any more need for their Italian counterparts to serve as intermediaries. What will be the tipping point? Will the triads contest the territory of the Camorra and the others? Will Italy be the first theater in this conflict? It's possible. Chinese organized crime in Italy is growing at a steady rate, as just a glance at a 2007 report from the National Antimafia Office shows. Preventive seizures carried out in the first half of 2007 against Asian criminal organizations amounted to €20 million, a fortune if we consider that the same type of seizures against the 'Ndrangheta were barely €6.3 million; against the Camorra, €12.5 million. In the same year only the seizures against the Cosa Nostra registered such a high figure.

The Chinese government is perfectly aware that China has become the world's leading source for counterfeit goods. And when this activity provokes public indignation, it takes certain measures. In 2007, following a series of food scandals, China tried and executed its former top food and drug regulator on corruption charges.[18] When fakes set sail for foreign shores, however, Beijing loses interest: now the problem belongs to the governments of the destination countries.

For the time being, turning a deaf ear has worked in this market. But it is inevitable that the exponential growth of the worldwide illicit market and the astronomical profits for the participants will end up also threatening China. With 1.3 billion inhabitants, when this market has reached the maturity of the West's, China will represent the last great frontier for the illicit.

According to this reasoning, counterfeiting in China is another product of its interaction with the West: the other, darker side of the coin of economic growth launched by Deng in that distant 1978. The severity with which Beijing punishes those who engage in criminal activities in its own country has thus far contained the growth of organized crime, which limits itself to using China as a provider of illicit products to sell in the West. But in the long term it will be difficult to keep the triads and their partners in foreign business from the great Chinese metropolises. The shadowy threat that has hung over Beijing from the moment it decided to participate in the global village is neither democracy nor the Revolution, but crime. And there is no Great Wall mighty enough to keep it at bay.

CHAPTER 21

ROUSSEAU IN CHINESE CHARACTERS

In 2010, the Library of Congress in Washington, DC, exhibited side by side two extremely rare maps of the world. The 1507 Waldseemüller map was the first to represent the new continent, America; the other was the astonishing map created by the Jesuit missionary Matteo Ricci, commissioned by the Chinese imperial court in 1602, which places China at the center. These old pieces of parchment describe two different worlds that coexist on the same planet, and are the expression of the geopolitical vision of those who created them just under a century apart. And even as we have thus far been more tied to Waldseemüller's vision, which appears to revolve around the American continent, it is likely that in the future the vision of Matteo Ricci, the first Westerner admitted to the imperial court and inside the Forbidden City, will be our polestar.

The message that the Jesuit brother passed on through his detailed account of the world to the east and to the west of the Great Wall is one of reciprocal respect. The map celebrates the greatness of the Middle Kingdom, as the Chinese call their land. The Jesuit knew well both this land and the one from which he hailed, the West, which he described to the emperor by means of the map. And like all great civilizations, the two had many, many points in common.

Matteo Ricci would be an exceedingly valuable presence in the diplomatic chaos in which we find ourselves today; he could help us to cast light amid into the gloomy news landscape to which the spin of politicians has banished us and to rationalize relations between East and West, but above all to exchange information vital for the future of the world. The map, in fact, served to present to the Chinese Empire the great conquests of Western civilization in order that it would evaluate and make them its own.

The Jesuit's message was religious, naturally, but it was also accompanied by notions of astronomy that owed much to Galileo. The map shows that the sun is larger than the moon and a table includes the distances between the planets of the solar system and Earth. This is the universe of the Catholic god, and it contains both the great civilizations known to the Jesuit. Ricci seemed to say to the Chinese, look upon the wonders you have built, the Great Wall, this empire that has survived for more than four thousand years—all this belongs to the Creator, and we want to share this wonderful discovery with you. The Chinese were grateful, not offended; on the contrary, it was an honor for them to reflect on these foreign truths. This is confirmed by the fact that the Jesuit has become part of the cultural background of every Chinese. His tomb was not desecrated during the Revolution and still today it is often visited; in fact it was moved and can now be found at CCP headquarters. The Chinese don't know who Marco Polo is, but everyone, truly everyone, knows the story of Matteo Ricci.

Let us try to borrow from this Italian the instrument of the map and ask China today to draw a similar one for us, which relates the story of their democracy and ours. This doesn't mean that we must "convert" to the Chinese model, just as the Chinese didn't convert to Catholicism, but the moment has arrived to stand before this nation, which still represents an enigma, with the humility of one who wants to understand above all and not to judge.

THE CHINESE SOCIAL CONTRACT

A question that many are asking themselves is: who governs China? The media wants to make us think that it's a small group of people, the equivalent of the Soviet politburo, in other words an elite; and there's still some who think there's a single individual pulling the strings, like in the democratic Russia of Vladimir Putin. This, however, is not the case. The Chinese government elite includes the entire public administration of the country, a veritable army: in 1998 this consisted of half a million people, of which 900 belonged to the national Party machine and 2,500 to the provincial, another 39,000 who worked in the prefectures, and finally 466,000 in the counties and municipalities. The majority, roughly 95 percent, were Party members,[1] but, as we have already seen, even at very high levels of the hierarchy one comes across men and women without a Party membership card in their pocket. And these have arrived at such heights thanks to an exceedingly severe meritocratic selection process.

These days, the base of the governmental pyramid consists of an army of forty million officials, of which a minority, approximately 38 percent, belong to the Chinese Communist Party. These represent the country's future governmental cadres. During Maoism the situation was decidedly different, and the entire base was a member of the Party. We can thus suppose that with the passing of time the percentage of members atop the pyramid will be progressively less.[2]

The CCP currently has seventy-six million members, a small percentage of the population. And yet it would be a mistake to regard them as an elite like the Soviet Communist Party[3]—more pertinent would be a parallel with the former Italian Communist Party. Only 25 percent of CCP members are part of the state machinery. The remaining 75 percent occupy local positions, especially in China's eight hundred thousand villages or in industry. So, the overwhelming majority of members do not participate in the running of the state.[4]

Belonging to the Party is a choice, not an obligation, and does not bring special privileges. The CCP is interested in the real support of the society, not the number of cards the people carry. What's more, unlike the Russian Revolution and others in the West, the Chinese Revolution was a mass movement, not an exercise in the political arts. In this respect, for the Chinese, it was a democratic revolution because it was literally guided by the people. And given the dimensions of the country, it could not have been otherwise.

The legitimacy of the Chinese dictatorship of the proletariat had its roots in the popular quality of the Revolution, which expressed the general will of the public. And this is as true today as it was fifty years ago. When, during the last CCP congress, Hu Jintao mentioned the word "democracy" sixty times, he was referring to this type of legitimization, not to our sense of the term.[5]

It is tremendously difficult for us in the West to understand all this because we continue to see China through the lens of the spin of the anticommunist crusade of the 1980s. But if instead we put on the eyeglasses of Matteo Ricci, then everything changes. We become aware that for the CCP, as for the population, the Party represents the people, at least as long as the social contract underlying this system is not torn asunder by a revolution—of which there is no indication for the present. And if we reflect for a moment on this point we realize that our own system as well, despite its age and rotten state, still stands for the same reasons: no one has burned our social contract in the public square.

Unlike in the West, in China revolution belongs to the political process more than the polls, thus it is spoken about openly and feared by both the government and the governed. When Professor Yang Fengchun states that all the other parties—including the Kuomintang Revolutionary Committee, Chinese Democratic League, National Democratic Construction Association, the Chinese Association for the Promotion of Democracy, the Democratic Party of Farmers and Workers, the Chinese Zhi Gong Party, the September 3 Society, and the Democratic League of Taiwanese Self-Government—are all subordinate to the CCP because the CCP "won state power," he is referring to the absence of revolutionary uprisings since 1949.[6] The political power of the Revolution is even sanctioned by its Constitution, where one reads:

> The Communist Party of China (CPC) is the vanguard of the Chinese working class, the faithful representative of the interests of the Chinese people of all ethnic groups, and the core of leadership of the Chinese socialist cause . . . After its establishment, the CPC led Chinese people in unfolding the New-Democratic Revolution against imperialism, feudalism and bureaucrat-capitalism . . . the CPC finally achieved a victory in 1949 and established the People's Republic of China, which, under the leadership of the working class and based on the workers-peasants alliance, upholds the people's democratic dictatorship.[7]

It's clear that the meanings Chinese and Asians attribute to the words "democracy," "dictatorship," "capitalism," and "imperialism" are different from our own. The overwhelming majority of those who live in Asia do not perceive China as a communist dictatorship, but as a democratic country. This is confirmed by an investigation conducted by the Asian Barometer Study: on the question of how democratic the Asian nations are on a scale of 1 to 10, China scored a 7.22, coming in third on the continent and ahead of Japan, the Philippines, and South Korea.[8]

If we then venture through our own country's history and revisit the European tradition from which was born the concept of the modern democracy, we realize that at bottom there are many points of contact between the fathers of the Western nation-state and communist China. And these points are the pillars upon which both built the economy of well-being.

DEMOCRACY MADE IN CHINA

Everyone knows *The Social Contract* by Jean Jacques Rousseau, the manifesto of participatory democracy. But few are aware of another such manifesto written by James Mill, the father of liberal democracy, considerably more loved by Madam Thatcher and President Reagan.[9] Rousseau was the father of the nation-state, which would bring prosperity to the nations of Europe up until the energy crisis; Mill instead influenced the first American presidents and overbearingly returned to the stage with the advent of neoliberalism. To the question "What is democracy?" both would respond without hesitation the will of the people, but they would mean two different things. In the first case the will of the people is the popular will; in the second, the interests of various groups that make up the people. Rousseau understood the collective as a single entity, whereas for Mill there were differences that ought to be respected.

A good example of the expression of the popular will is the way modern society manages the problem of traffic during rush hour. In a liberal democracy, it is up to the individual to decide whether to take the car or public transportation. In Rousseauean western democracies, the population uses public transportation and often walks to reach it. Anyone who's found him or herself stuck in a Shanghai traffic bottleneck at rush hour well knows that this is not the model applied in China, where in any case urban development is exploding and difficult to manage. However, at the opening of Expo 2010 there were twelve metro lines and 420 kilometers of tracks, making it the longest network in the world, and another seventeen will be introduced by 2020.[10] Extremely modern, clean, and efficient, the Shanghai subway is already enormous and serves much of the city.

In a Western liberal democracy, the problem of traffic is not resolved by strengthening public services, but by charging vehicles to access the central zones of the city. This is the principal of Ken Livingstone's "congestion charge" in London, subsequently adopted in many other cities. The practical result: the rich can drive; everyone else is obliged to get around on often inefficient public transportation. At least public coffers are enriched in the process, but this is still a solution that is weakened by the fact that it affects people very differently depending on their social class, fails to strengthen public services, and undermines public transportation systems rather than strengthening them.

And yet, the Chinese model of democracy very much recalls that of Rousseau; at its core it is a social contract signed by all parties. The revolutionary victory sanctions it, and the CCP becomes the interpreter of the popular will. Perhaps for the Chinese it is easy to accept this principle because for five thousand years they have been governed by dynasties that are overturned and substituted by revolutions from below when they no longer function.[11] We have had rather fewer revolutions. And why should China today have to abandon this tradition and embrace the model of Western liberal democracy,[12] especially considering the disasters caused by the Western model in the last twenty years, in the former communist bloc and in the rest of the world?

Let us take another look at Matteo Ricci's map, and how other frightening lands appear. In the north of Russia, he explained, live dwarf populations forced to take refuge in caves for fear of being devoured by giant cranes. In South America, the mountains are inhabited by cruel assassins who, to pass the time, take turns killing each other. These images are products of their time, and Ricci uses them to show the Chinese the superiority of European civilization and that of the Middle Kingdom, China, but an imaginary contemporary Chinese cartographer could also draw some unsettling panoramas—Iraq and Afghanistan, for example.

For the Chinese, the world that the American superpower has presided over for the past twenty years has been neither peaceful nor "civilized." Liberal democracy is an instrument in the hands of an arrogant and reckless elite that wants to dominate the planet, the offspring of Dick Cheney, George W. Bush, and their neoconservative friends. Let's put ourselves for a moment in the shoes of that Chinese cartographer and gaze upon our own world with his eyes. Yes, the Chinese occupied Tibet. But in the name of US democracy the indigenous populations of America were exterminated, a genocide that occurred in modern times under the cynical motto "The only good Indian is a dead Indian." America actively participated in the slave trade, becoming rich on it, and for generations was openly racist. And if we must speak of dissidents, liberally employed by Western media in condemning the Chinese dictatorship, we'll also have to recall the American witch hunts of the McCarthy period. And going further, to take pity on Chinese farmers and workers means remembering that in America, and also in Europe, there exist great economic inequalities; it's easy enough to come across a homeless person on any street corner, digging in the trash for food. In our countries, organized crime controls entire territories and productive sectors, and lynchings and political assassinations are certainly not unknown. And let's not forget the worst of the excesses of Western democracy, its wars, including those currently raging in Afghanistan and Iraq. Such wars are America's legacy, inseparable from America's very identity as a superpower, and there are no such stains on China's record.

But there's more. If the meritocratic fundamentals of China can be traced back to the teachings of Confucius, in the DNA of Western civilization we find the theory formulated by the father of conservatism, the Englishman Edmund Burke. In the seventeenth century Burke spoke of a "natural aristocracy," "the rare few, who have the ability, the experience, and the inclination to govern wisely in the interest of the whole society."[13]

And where can such people be found if not among the rich? After having touched with his own hand the corruption that raged during revolutionary France, Burke became convinced that the class of rich landowners was destined for command because it, more than any other, had the management of the state at heart. This same certainty ensures that in the twenty-first century Wall Street provides the American government with the cadres that oversee finance: the regulators come from the same cohort as the regulated.

The syllogism economic power = politics is a constant in American history. Upon nomination to the Eisenhower cabinet, Charles Erwin Wilson, for years the head of General Motors, responded to a journalist's question about potential conflicts of interest with the statement that "what's good for General Motors is good for America," a phrase that Obama implicitly made his own when in 2009 he used taxpayer money to save General Motors from bankruptcy.

In modern China it's not the moneyed elites who run the show. Preventing the newly rich from taking over the running of the state is not only the Communist Party—where you don't get in because you're rich, nor get rich because you got in—but also Confucian meritocracy. In Burke's time it was inconceivable for a Westerner that an ordinary farmer could scale the administrative hierarchy if he managed to pass the imperial examinations. In China this opportunity was open to all. In Burke's time, meritocracy didn't exist in Europe, as Shakespeare reminds us:

> O, that estates, degrees and offices
> Were not derived corruptly, and that clear

> honour
> Were purchased by the merit of the wearer!
> How many then should cover that stand
>   bare!
> How many be commanded that command!
> How much low peasantry would then be
>   glean'd
> From the true seed of honour! and how
>   much honour
> Pick'd from the chaff and ruin of the times
> To be new-varnish'd![15]

And perhaps still today in our society, the idea that the best get ahead is only an illusion.

HUMAN RIGHTS

In China there is meritocracy, but here there is freedom. And the confirmation of this commonest of convictions comes from China itself, a country where human rights are not respected. In the West the situation is entirely different. This is our instinctive response to the imaginary Chinese cartographer. But are we really so sure? China has ratified six of the thirteen human rights treaties produced by the United Nations Commission on Human Rights and is a signatory on another two. The United States has ratified five and is a signatory on another three; Japan has ratified eight. Both the United States and Japan have ratified or signed the same treaties as China.[16]

In the matter of human rights it is necessary to also interpret the Chinese ideograms, and that's not easy: there is a danger of the meaning of the words being lost in the translation. The global South, in general, accuses the West of cultural imperialism when it imposes the same human rights in all countries. The gist of the relativist vision of the less privileged is this: to someone without enough to eat, freedom of speech has little importance; first he has win the right to survive. And it is hypocritical, as well as ideological, to pretend that human rights are not also subject to a scale of priorities that depends on the context in which each country finds itself, as also happens in the West.[17]

The Chinese cartographer explains to us that the rich countries have remained stuck in the first generation of human rights, the generation born with the French Revolution and inspired by the individualism of modern Western culture. And we are talking specifically about civil and political rights. The second generation of human rights was born from the socialist movements at the beginning of the last century, from the workers' movements. The third and last generation fights for the right to economic and cultural development and is the fruit of the anticolonial revolutions that broke out after World War II and led to the independence of the former colonies in the 1960s.[18]

China, emerging economies like India and Brazil, and the entire global South belong to the second and third generations of human rights; and we to the first. Our NGOs are also the product of Western culture and thus give a great deal of attention to civil and political rights while neglecting to promote the social, economic, and cultural rights that the world's poor still lack.

The Chinese cartographer reveals to us that China and the other countries that are only now approaching our levels of well-being are not in a position to guarantee human rights as we understand them, those rights that we today consider indispensable after having in our own time long ignored them. Even as the Chinese are free to say what they want in private, they cannot launch campaigns or publicize their political opinions as we do without risking censorship. The Internet is monitored and some sites are blocked, but there are quite a few gaps in China's Great Firewall. In any case, the country has more compelling problems than the possibility of roaming free in cyberspace: a large portion of the population is still waiting for its turn on the carousel of economic prosperity, and for them the freedom from want counts for more than any digital freedom.

The anti-Chinese campaign conducted by the West under the banner of human rights also appears to be fought according to the well-known principle of "two weights and two measures," one to the east and one to the west of the Great Wall. Although the United Nations did not support the preventive attack on Iraq, for example, the Americans and their allies went to war all the same. They violated the national sovereignty of a country based on information that today we know was false. Did anyone stop to think about the human rights of the Iraqis killed by the bombardments or during the civil war? And why didn't the United Nations react to this illegal attack? These are questions the Chinese legitimately ask, well-informed about Western indifference with respect to the atrocities they cause. During the 2008 American elections so much was said about Joe the plumber and nothing about Ahmed the carpenter, the one who lived with his family in Falluja before the city was razed to the ground. And yet America is a country at war. Paradoxically, the Western press is more interested in the execution of a Western drug trafficker than in the death and mutilation inflicted on the Iraqis by the American army.

What should we call the atrocities of Abu Ghraib? Aren't these human rights abuses? And the Geneva Conventions? Has someone checked to see if they still exist? And that is to say nothing about the use of torture and extraordinary renditions. These unsettling discoveries not only failed to unleash a revolution against the officials responsible, but they didn't even prevent George W. Bush in 2004 and Tony Blair in 2005 from being reelected. And what can we say about the racism spreading across our civilized Europe? Anti-immigrant patrols in the cradle of the Renaissance, Italy? The war in Bosnia and

Kosovo? It is obviously much easier to be a champion of human rights somewhere else.

The Chinese cartographer has drawn these events in red, the color of the victims' blood, and seems to say to us: your "freedom," your respect for human rights, are only ideological categories masking oppression, abuse, and contempt for your fellow men in excess of what you condemn in others. And this illusion has grown immensely with the passing of the years: the nations emerging from the ruins of World War II were much freer than today's versions. The most disquieting aspect is the ease with which we forget the appalling events committed in our name and allow ourselves to be deceived by Western media propaganda.

CLASH OF THE TITANS

In February 2010, the United States sold arms to Taiwan to defend itself from a possible Chinese attack. It did so in order to punish Beijing, which had not wanted anything to do with imposing economic sanctions or applying political pressure on Iran. The contract, worth more than $6 billion, provoked the anger of the Chinese government. The response was severe, as it was a few years earlier when the Bush administration did the same thing. On that occasion Beijing froze military relations with the US, blocking all defense-related commercial contracts. The situation was eventually resolved when Hillary Clinton visited China in February 2009. Perhaps the same kind of resolution will happen again this time.

Immediately after the news of the arms sale to Taiwan, China froze all its military contracts. And this time it threatened to go further and punish all the companies involved in the contract, among them Boeing, Lockheed Martin, Sikorsky, and Raytheon. In particular, China could have canceled or delayed certain purchases, ceased technological cooperation, or limited American commercial space by decreasing, if not outright forbidding, access to the Chinese market. China seemed to be saying to Washington that this type of diplomacy can only make the global economic crisis worse. More than ever, America and the world need China.

The United States is the biggest arms producer in the world and sells them to whomever it wants. According to Pentagon statistics, this comes to 174 countries, among them Mexico, where 90 percent of the arms used by drug traffickers have the "Made in USA" label, and brings the country $32 billion in arms sales. And yet Americans openly condemn this type of trade when other countries take part in it. The United States behaves like a superpower and respects only the rules that suit it. Thus the US ignores the October 2009 UN resolution that compelled it to end its embargo on Cuba. And no one has the courage to condemn this behavior; instead, everyone prefers to renew their praises for the Western country that elected its first president of color. But things are changing.

On our Chinese cartographer's new map, at the level of international diplomacy, China is lifting its head. And it appears particularly absorbed by the topic of human rights. In 2004, a guarantee of civil rights was inserted into the constitution; since then the defense of human rights has become a public priority and the government has produced a detailed annual report on the situation in America, using official information from the US.

Naturally, Beijing is concentrating on what are termed third-dimension human rights. Thus in the government's 2009 report, one reads that US Census Bureau statistics show that in 2007, 12.5 percent of the population, that is 37.3 million Americans, live in poverty, an increase of roughly a million from 2006. With regard to racial discrimination as well, the Chinese cite some interesting statistics. The first comes from the State of Black America study commissioned by the National Urban League, according to which approximately a quarter of all families of color live below the poverty line, three times the number of whites. As reported by the Department of Labor, in the third quarter of 2008, the unemployment rate among blacks came to 10.6 percent, while that among whites was half as high.[19]

The battle between the titans of the globalized world is also being fought with the weapon of human rights. And while out of fear of terrorism we ignore the Geneva Conventions and suspend habeas corpus, China is bounding ahead. This is the case with the death penalty, which is still applied in the US.

At the beginning of 2007, China's Supreme Court regained the power to approve death sentences, which in the 1980s had been entrusted to superior courts at the provincial level, as part of anticrime campaigns. And the number of executions dropped, with the Chinese Supreme Court rejecting 15 percent of all the death sentences decided by inferior-level courts, adducing lack of proof and irregular judicial procedures.[20]

Even the Americans admit that China is improving in terms of human rights. The Congressional-Executive Commission on China, an organ of the American Congress, wrote in 2009:

The first-ever National Human Rights Action Plan, which the government released in April, contains policy commitments, which, if implemented effectively, could lead to improvements in fair trial rights and detainee rights. Also in April, the Supreme People's Procuratorate launched a five-month campaign to ensure "proper management" of detention centers in the aftermath of a spate of unnatural deaths of detainees at Ministry of Public Security–run detention centers during the first few months of 2009. In August, the Supreme People's Procuratorate announced that confessions obtained through torture would no longer be admissible as evidence in death penalty cases. The revised PRC Lawyers Law, which has been in effect for over a year, reportedly has led to some improved access by lawyers to their detained clients in certain jurisdictions; however, serious implementation challenges remain.[21]

However, we are far from the ideal. One example is the incarceration of Liu Xiaobo, a noted intellectual and literary critic and one of the authors of the Charter 08 (the manifesto signed by three hundred Chinese intellectuals and human rights activists calling for democracy in China), who was sentenced to eleven years in prison on Christmas Day, 2009. Awarded the Nobel Peace Prize in 2010, the Chinese government refused to allow him to receive it. Then there's Hu Jia, environmentalist and activist in the battle against AIDS, who was sentenced to three and a half years in prison in March 2008 after the court found him guilty of "instigating others to subvert the state's political power and socialist system,"[39] on the basis of some interviews given to foreign media and some articles with political content published on the Internet. Hu has suffered from liver trouble for some time; his condition has worsened in prison.

The road thus remains long and steep, but the Chinese are making good progress along it; we instead truly seem to have lost our way.

CHINA HANDS

China is a complex universe, difficult to understand, and certainly impossible to sum up in a book, a documentary, or a newspaper article. But this is true of all countries. At the same time, China is nevertheless still a nation like all the others, even if one of exceptional geographic and demographic dimensions. It is, therefore, possible to study some of its aspects in depth and, on the basis of this information and with great humility, venture some projections into the future. It is what, in the last one hundred and fifty years, has been attempted by certain individuals devoted to an unusual activity: sociocultural espionage. They are spies, China Hands.

China Hands is the name the Japanese gave at the end of the nineteenth century to a group of merchants and adventurers who, attracted by China's riches, had relocated there. Their long stay allowed them to penetrate the culture and then explain it to their compatriots. The goal was not altruistic; indeed, the first international spies were set on promoting the supremacy of Japan in Southwest Asia in a moment full of opportunity for the nation.

At the end of the nineteenth century, in this part of the world, Japan was the only country to survive the hordes of Western colonizers. And given that it was also the only industrialized country, it seemed logical for it to assume leadership of the region. But how to go about obtaining this wasn't clear to Tokyo: was it more advantageous to promote cooperation and trade with its neighbors, or to invade them and force economic development following the model of the European colonizers? This was the dilemma that the spies, having become the eyes and ears of the empire, were determined to resolve. Around 1870, Kishida Ginko, considered their founder, became convinced that what made nations like England, France, and the United States great was international trade. And Japan could emulate this greatness by promoting trade with China rather than subjugating it by force of arms.

A few years later, in 1888, the Japanese consul in Hankow, he too a spy in Chinese territory, explained in a report that Chinese merchants were more astute in every field, including the exportation and the imitation of new Japanese products. Thus he suggested educating Japanese in the Chinese way of doing business through a cultural exchange that facilitated penetration of the market. Notwithstanding these suggestions, in 1894 Japan invaded China and the war lasted some years.

The espionage work picked up again immediately after the war ended. At the beginning of the last century, Tokyo sent groups of Japanese students to live in the Chinese hinterlands for long periods. Everyone had a specific task: study the agricultural system, transport system, the geography, and so forth, to produce a detailed map of the Chinese lifestyle. The image of the country that emerged was completely different from the one Tokyo had made of the nation. But nobody acted.

These students had some very interesting comments on the Chinese political situation, years before Mao's victory. Ide Saburo, a student from the Toa Dobu Shoin school, founded in Shanghai by the son of Kishida, wrote: "Though uniquely knowledgeable about China at a time when China was uniquely important to Japan, Shoin graduates were not destined for the top, even in China."[1]

The Japanese spies suggested colonizing China with the weapons of trade and economics, using Chiang Kai-shek as leverage. Only later, after some had lived for many years in Manchuria and had a chance to become acquainted with the background of the communist revolt, did attitudes change.

But the times changed as well, World War II was around the corner and in Tokyo an interventionist wind blew: the strongest voice belonged to the warmongers who wanted to invade China. Up until the eve of the invasion of Shanghai, the spies sought to convince the emperor to open a dialogue with the communist league and in so doing avoid a war they feared they would lose. But the emperor's response was categorical: do your duty as Japanese subjects and become interpreters for the invading army. The spies were absorbed into the war machine and their voices snuffed out forever.

AMERICAN SPIES

Japan's entry into World War II created a series of logistical problems for the Allied Powers, first among them the United States. China became a strategic country, and, for the duration of the conflict, generals and admirals looked at the map and assessed the possibility of a Japanese invasion from the north of China.

Washington, of course, was close to the nationalists, whom it had been helping with shipments of arms and supplies and courses in military preparedness. The communists had already been dismissed from consideration by the White House, which considered them a ragtag army. And it is true they lacked the necessary arms and munitions; all they had was what they had managed to steal from the nationalists.

During the war, however, the American general Joseph Stillwell came away discouraged by the followers of Chiang Kai-shek, and positively impressed by the communists, who displayed extraordinary patriotism and enviable cohesion. Washington decided to act on the basis of this and other analogous reports only toward the end of the war, when it sent a group of "observers" to Yenan. Thus was born Operation Dixie, led by Colonel David Barrett, whose participants included American spies of the highest caliber such as John

Service, who had been born in China and spoke perfect Mandarin, and John Davies. Operation Dixie lasted from July 1944 to March 1947, and the unanimous opinion was that the communists would win the civil war.

On December 24, 1945, Doctor Melvin Casberg returned from China to Washington, DC, arriving at the General Headquarters of the Office of Strategic Services, the future CIA, and made three statements.

> He told his audience that civil war between the Communists and the Nationalists was unavoidable, and he predicted that the Communists would win. He also predicted that after the Communists took over, China would not maintain close ties with the Soviet Union. Third he offered the opinion that in the long term Chou En-lai and those who wore his mantle would have the greatest influence on China.[2]

Although history would prove him right, those listening to him on that distant Christmas Eve burst out laughing. Casberg was only a doctor and knew precious little about military and political strategy, and so his report was dismissed.[3] But he was not the only one to make such predictions. Colonel Barrett wrote in one of his own reports:

> One reason a good many people, including myself, had a generally favorable impression of the Communist regime in Yenan was that the overall look of things there was one which most Americans were inclined to regard with favor. In Chungking [Chongqing] we were accustomed to seeing police and sentries everywhere. In Yenan there was not even a sentry, as far as I could see, posted at Headquarters 18th Group Army. If there was anyone on guard at Mao Tse-tung's unpretentious place of residence, he

was not in evidence to a casual passerby.

When Chairman Mao appeared in public, as he frequently did, he traveled on foot, or in the one battered truck, with enclosed cab, which as far as I ever knew, constituted the Communists' sole motor transport. There was no parade of long black cars, often moving at high speed, which one saw in Chungking when the Generalissimo traversed the streets, and no cordon of guards and secret service operatives such as always surrounded him in public.[4]

• • •

One thing about the Communists was difficult to regard as a staged show, and that was the condition of their troops, who appeared tough and well nourished, with uniforms well suited to the season of the year, except for footgear which was mostly rubber-soled cloth shoes, not much better than the straw sandals worn by most National Government soldiers.[5]

• • •

At the time the Dixie Mission was in Yenan, a common sight in National Government territory was that of men roped together being taken to recruit centers. Once while traveling in Kiangsi Province in 1942 I noted that the jailhouse in a certain city was so crowded with what I assumed was either criminals or suspects, many of whom were peering through the bars of the prison windows as I passed. When I asked the Garrison Commander why there were so many people in jail at that particular time, he said they were not ordinary jailbirds, but men pressed into military service who had been locked up for the night so they could not run away. If

men were ever delivered tied up for army duty in the
Communist areas, I never saw it.[6]

The American spies also revealed that the communists
would have liked to establish relations with the Americans,
whom they felt close to as a people born from a revolution
against a colonial power.

As in Japan, in America too the precious counsel of the
spies went unheeded. In 1949, when Mao came to control a
large part of the country, the world had already fallen into the
Cold War, and in the United States Senator McCarthy raged.
The spies became enemies of the state and ended up being
hunted down like common criminals. The charge was to have
contributed to the communist victory in China. McCarthy
used their work behind combat lines in China in constructing
the foundations of his communist witch hunt.

MODERN SPIES

What characterizes the story of the international spies is the
diffidence, often becoming open hostility, which their visions
of China generated in their governments. And even though in
the course of more than a century all their predictions have
come true, none of their counsel has been taken up; on the
contrary, the governments that commissioned them often did
the exact opposite. Today, faced with the power of the Chinese dragon, we risk making the same mistakes. The modern
spies whose voices we have listened to in these pages describe
a country that is shattering so many of the stereotypes we
hold most dear. And although in the course of this book we
have confronted and contested a great number of them, it is
good to mention yet another: that concerning the poverty in
which the communist government forces its population to
live. In March 2009, in the World Bank report on poverty,
one reads:

China's progress in poverty reduction over the last 25 years is enviable. . . . But for China there would have been no decline in the numbers of poor in the developing world over the last two decades of the 20th century.[7]

Thus, even the World Bank can be counted among the modern spies.

Let's ask ourselves why erroneous stereotypes systematically prevail over the professionalism of these informers, why we prefer to take refuge in narrow-minded preconceptions rather than open our minds to new truths, as suggested by those whose knowledge of the matter is greater than ours. Is it perhaps the fear of seeing, mirrored in Chinese innovation, the faults in our own system?

This is essentially what this book has tried to do: to present through the Chinese perspective a critical vision of our capitalism and our democracies. When the spies placed Tokyo and Washington, DC, before the same mirror, the reflected image was not what their employers were hoping for. The Japanese empire could not accept the commercial supremacy of a colonized people, decimated by foreign invasion, nor could Washington believe in the power of patriotism incarnated by a ragtag army carrying stolen rifles. And yet three hundred years ago, so many of the American colonists who followed Washington and Jefferson had nothing more in their hands than pitchforks. It's easy to forget the humble origins from which all our democracies are born, as it is easy to ignore the innumerable lessons of history, from the heroism of the Huns who overcame the Roman superpower to the Italian wars of independence.

The international spies remind us that if we are to save our democracy we must look to the East, to those still fighting to attain it, and not to those at home who have reduced democracy to a mere instrument of personal power.

ACKNOWLEDGMENTS

The idea to analyze the problems of Western capitalism through the Chinese perspective was born on a flight from London to Shanghai with Claudia Segre. She was the first to suggest to me the theme of *Maonomics* during a long conversation about the credit crisis and the 2010 Shanghai Expo. It is, therefore, only right that she be the first to be thanked.

As always, my agents Luigi and Daniela Bernabò have done excellent work. During a wonderful dinner at their house I had the opportunity to lay out my ideas to Carlo Alberto Brioschi and Michela Gallio, and from that conversation emerged the traces of the book we initially called *Marx Won*. After months of failed attempts it was Carlo Alberto who came across the right title: *Maonomics*. But it was Michela Gallio who always stayed close during the long months of writing. Over the course of many, many years spent writing essays, I have had occasion to work with many editors and I must admit that no one demonstrated as much passion for my work as Michela, and with no one else did I establish such a wonderful rapport. And so to Michela goes all my most sincere gratitude.

A special thank you goes also to Federico Bastiani, my assistant, who never ceases to resemble a guardian angel even more closely, eternally ready to come to my aid and look after me as I travel the world. Since he began to work for me my life has decidedly changed for the better. Thanks as well to my husband's assistant, the refined, intelligent, amiable, and ironic Christina Masazza, for always being available to give me a hand; and thanks to my agent Diana Finch, a tireless reader and editor of my writing and valuable colleague. Thanks to Per Axelson at Leopard, my Swedish editor, for the unstinting support and for sharing with me some of his memories of Maoist China. Thanks too to Antonio Zoppetti, who with great professionalism manages my blog and innumerable Facebook pages.

Thanks to my tremendously valuable researchers, without whom this book would not exist: to Bjorn Axelson, whose vast knowledge of Chinese Marxism is truly impressive, who spent six weeks in China conducting fascinating interviews for me; to Matteo Ballero, who unveiled a great many mysteries of Chinese organized crime and conducted research on the relations between China and Africa; to Annabelle Grossman, who worked on the market for fakes and on the concept of copyright; to Marco Masulli, who acted as my translator in the United Arab Emirates; to Eleonora Pierro, who worked on the philosophy of Confucius; to Giovanni Valsecchi, who helped me to organize Chinese history; to Claudio Vescovo, who explained to me Chinese policy in the field of renewable energy; to Tian Xu, who worked on the conditions of Chinese workers in Europe and was my guide in China; and to Shawn Wathen, who worked on the parallels between Osama bin Laden and Attila the Hun. A special acknowledgment goes to Ivan Franceschini, who organized all my travels in China, checked page after page of what I wrote, and introduced me to the world of Chinese labor, teaching me to love China. Without his help this book never would have gotten off the ground.

Thank you as well to all my Chinese sources, starting with the Italian Institute of Culture in Beijing, directed by the marvelous Sinologist Barbara Alighiero and her colleagues, Patrizia Liberati and Claudio Poeta, who supported me in my research by organizing meetings with Beijing's Italian community; with their assistance I began to understand a nation so different from my own. Thanks too to Saro Capozzi, who introduced me to Shanghai; to Liu Kaiming, who explained to me the evolutionary path of the Special Economic Zones; and to Rosario di Maggio, who described the world of Chinese labor to me so well. Heartfelt thanks to my missionary friends: to Gerolamo Fazzni of *Mondo and Missione* (World and Mission), who introduced me to Mario Marazzi, a truly historic character, who has lived in Canton for the last forty years, with whom I spent two unforgettable days; and to Gianni Criveller, also an expert on China and a scholar of Matteo Ricci, who introduced me to the trade unionists of Hong Kong. Thanks to Meng Wei Na, who offered me a window on the world of Chinese human solidarity, and thanks to all the countless other Chinese sources, a full list of which would be too long to include here.

Thanks to my friends Terry and Andy Feury, who hosted me in Hong Kong, and to Loretta dal Pozzo, who hosted me in Singapore and organized so many interviews for me.

As always, my friends have stayed close, often helping me to clarify complex concepts and to revisit Marx, so thanks to Giovanna Amato, Edith Champagne, Cecilia Guastadisegni, Johannes Kiezer, Roberto Giuliani, Sabina de Luca, to the priceless Silvia Marazza, to Simona Marazza, Isabella and Libero Maesano, Valerio Nobili, and Grant Woods. Thanks to my friends scattered around the world and always interested in my research, with whom I often discussed the chapters as I was writing them and at times even clashed: Clare and Rex Chalmers, Eleonor and Stephen Creaturo, Vivian and David Ereira, Nick and Deb Follows, Mary Jo and Greg Hennen, Amanda and Jimmy Hobson, Lesley and George Magnus, Barbra and Bruce MacEvoy, Angelica and Vittorio Pignatti. thanks to all my colleagues from VB who always stood by me. To my cousins who helped me during the illness of my mother as I wrote the first chapters of this book, Marina and Fabrizio Napoleoni and Davide Tamburano; and thanks to the countless friends of my mother for having helped me to manage the hospital stay, and to my Aunt Giovanna, who even at a distance was always so close to me.

This book is dedicated to my youngest son, Julian, because not long ago he reminded me that he has always shared my dedications with his older siblings, and that he wanted one all to himself. But, as always, without the understanding and affection of my children and my husband I could not continue to write. And so to them, Alexander, Andrew, Leigh, and Ron, go all my affection and gratitude.

NOTES

INTRODUCTION

1. The labor reforms began prior to the crisis. Some go so far as to maintain that the crisis, along with the wave of bankruptcies in China that preceded it due to the enforcement of the new law concerning employment contracts, represented a step backward in the application of these reforms.
2. Michael Forythe, "Helping China Spell Democracy," *International Herald Tribune*, September 30, 2009.
3. Philip Pan, *Out of Mao's Shadow: The Struggle for the Soul of a New China* (London: Picador, 2008), 275.

PROLOGUE: DEPRESSIONS IN PROGRESS

1. Irving Kirsch, Brett J. Deacon, Tania B. Huedo-Medina, Alan Scoboria, Thomas J. Moore, and Blair T. Johnson, "Initial Severity and Antidepressant Benefits: A Meta-Analysis of Data Submitted to the Food and Drug Administration," *PLoS Medicine* 5, no. 2, http://www.plosmedicine.org/article/info:doi/10.1371/journal.pmed.005 0045.
2. Francis Fukuyama, *The End of History and the Last Man* (New York: Free Press, 1992).

CHAPTER 1: EXPLOITATION FACTORIES

1. Anita Chan, *China's Workers under Assault: The Exploitation of Labor in a Globalizing Economy* (Armonk, NY: East Gate Books, 2001), 106–112.
2. Ibid., 121–126.
3. Martin Jacques, *When China Rules the World* (London: Allen Lane, 2009), 98.
4. Lijia Zhang, *Socialism is Great* (New York: Anchor Books, 2009), 7.
5. Zhao Ziyang, *Prisoner of the State* (London: Simon & Schuster, 2009), 247.

6. Stephen Roach, *How Global Labor Arbitrage Will Shape the World Economy* (Global Agenda, 2005).
7. Interview with Liu Kaiming, May 2009.
8. Interviews with Maurice Ohana, December 2009 and January 2010.
9. Jacques, *When China Rules the World*, 98.
10. Sang Ye, *China Candid: The People on the People's Republic* (Berkeley: University of California Press, 2006), 38.
11. Ibid., 39.
12. Interview with Patrick Chovanec, December 2009.
13. Leslie T. Chang, *Factory Girls* (New York: Picador, 2009), 12.
14. Pun Ngai has changed the name of the factory in order to not put the workers at risk.
15. Pun Ngai, *Made in China* (Hong Kong: Duke, 2005), 23–24.
16. Chan, *China's Workers under Assault*, 117.
17. Chang, *Factory Girls*, 5.
18. Children's Employment Commission, *Appendix to the Second Report of the Commissioners, Trades and Manufactures, Part II: Reports and Evidence from Sub-Commissioners* (London: William Clowes and Sons, 1842), http://www.origins.net/BritishOrigins/gallery-employment/index.aspx.
19. Chan, *China's Workers under Assault*, 56–59.
20. Ibid., 58.
21. Ibid., 133–134.

CHAPTER 2: THE RACE TO THE BOTTOM

1. *Workers' Magazine*, All-China Federation of Trade Unions, 1993.
2. Economist Intelligence Unit report on China, August 21, 2006.
3. Joseph Kahn, "China's Leaders Manage Class Conflict Carefully," *New York Times*, January 25, 2004.
4. Stephen Roach, "Globalization's New Underclass," Morgan Stanley, March 3, 2006, http://www.morganstanley.com/views/gef/archive/2006/20060303-Fri.html.
5. Interview with Wang Tao, UBS economist in Beijing, May 2009.
6. Interview with three Chinese workers from the Hong Kong Confederation of Trade Unions, Hong Kong, May 2009.
7. Roach, "Globalization's New Underclass."
8. Loretta Napoleoni, *Rogue Economics: Capitalism's New Reality* (New York: Seven Stories, 2008), ch. 2.
9. P. L. Josephine Smart, "Land Rents and the Rise of a Petty Bourgeoisie in Contemporary China," *Anthropology of Work Review* 14, no. 2 (1993): 3–6.
10. Phyllis Andors, *The Unfinished Liberation of Chinese Women, 1949–1980* (Bloomington: Indiana University Press, 1983).
11. Denise Chong, *The Concubine's Children* (New York: Penguin, 1994).

12. Interview with Fausto Zuccarelli, June 2009.
13. Massimo Pisa, "L'albergo in un tombino per i cinesi clandestini" (Manhole Hotel for Illegal Chinese Workers), *La Repubblica*, March 25, 2009.
14. Interview with Arthur Kroeber, December 2009.
15. International Labour Organization, "Chinese Immigrants Victims of Labour Exploitation in Paris," June 21, 2006.
16. A version of this essay can be found at http://mises.org/daily/2443.
17. "*Diario di un clandestino*, Parts 1 and 2," *Polonews.info: la Cina raccontata dai cinesi ai cinesi*, accessed June 15, 2010, http://www.polonews .info/articolo.php?id=118; http://www.polonews.info/articolo.php?id=119.

CHAPTER 3: CHINESE NOUVELLE CUISINE

1. Napoleoni, *Rogue Economics*, ch. 4.
2. Bret Swanson, "Entrepreneurship and Innovation in China 1978–2008," *Progress on Point* 15, (13 September 2008), 9–10.
3. Interview with Arthur Kroeber, December 2009.
4. Ibid., 10.
5. Zhao, *Prisoner of the State*.
6. Jasper Becker, *Hungry Ghosts* (New York: Henry Holt and Company, 1998).
7. Zhao, *Prisoner of the State*, 98.
8. Interview with Yu Keping, November 2009.
9. Interview with a university professor in Beijing who wishes to remain anonymous, November 2009.
10. Mark Leonard, *What Does China Think?* (London: Fourth Estate, 2008), 51.
11. Interview with Patrick Chovanec, December 2009.
12. Ibid., 61.
13. Ibid., 65.
14. John Watkins, "Beijing's Path Forward," *International Herald Tribune*, November 11, 2009.
15. David E. Sanger and Michael Wines, "China Leader's Limits Come Into Focus as U.S. Visit Nears," *New York Times*, http://www.nytimes.com/2011/01/17/world/asia/17china.html.
16. Interview with Wang Dong, November 2009.
17. Franco Mazzei and Vittorio Volpi, *Asia al centro* (Asia at the Center) (Milan: Egea-Università Bocconi Editore, 2006), 155.
18. Manuel Castells, *End of Millennium*, 2nd ed. (Oxford: Blackwell Publishers, 2000), 270–271. See also Martin Jacques, *When China Rules the World* (London: Allen Lane, 2009).
19. Zhao, *Prisoner of the State*, 119.
20. Joseph Fewsmith, *China Since Tiananmen: The Politics of Transition* (New York: Cambridge University Press, 2008), ch. 2.

21. Napoleoni, *Rogue Economics*, ch. 3.

CHAPTER 4: BEYOND THE GREAT WALL

1. Gavin Menzies, *1421: The Year China Discovered the World* (London: Bantam Press, 2002).
2. China.org.cn, "One Country, Two Systems," China Facts & Figures, http://www.china.org.cn/english/features/china/203730.htm.
3. By the "Left" of the party one generally refers to the faction that continues to draw inspiration from Mao and his policies; by the "Right," the faction that is more open and favorable to reforms. See Willy Lam, "Power Struggle Behind Revival of Maoism," *Asia Times*, November 24, 2009, http://www.atimes.com/atimes/China/KK24Ad01.html.
4. Fewsmith, *China Since Tiananmen*, ch. 2.
5. Leonard, *What Does China Think?*.
6. Sang Ye, *China Candid* (Turin: Einaudi, 2006), 19.
7. Ibid., 19.
8. Interview with Liu Kaiming, November 2009.
9. Fewsmith, *China Since Tiananmen*, 4–5.
10. Nan Lin, "Local Market Socialism: Local Corporatism in Action in Rural China," *Theory and Society* (June 1995); Flemming Christiansen and Junzuo Zhang, *Village Inc.: Chinese Rural Society in the 1990s* (Honolulu: University of Hawaii Press, 1998).
11. Jean C. Oi, "The Role of the Local State in China's Transitional Economy," *The China Quarterly*, 1995; Jean C. Oi, *Rural China Takes Off: Institutional Foundations of Economic Reform* (Berkeley: University of California Press, 1999).
12. Napoleoni, *Rogue Economics*, ch. 1.
13. Brahma Chellaney, "Europe Got Freedom, Asia Got Rich," *International Herald Tribune*, November 4, 2009.

CHAPTER 5: THE NEOLIBERAL DREAM OF MODERNIZATION

1. Interview with Mao Yushi, January 2010.
2. Milton Freidman, "Chicago Boys and Pinochet," *Commanding Heights*, PBS video interview, 8:16, http://www.pbs.org/wgbh/commandingheights/shared/video/qt/mini_po 2_07_300.html.
3. Ibid.
4. Ibid.
5. Ibid.
6. Michael Lewis, "Wall Street on the Tundra," *Vanity Fair*, April 2009.
7. Andri Snaer Magnason, *Dreamland: A Self-Help Manual for a Frightened Nation* (London: Citizen Press, 2008), 156.
8. Ibid., 173.

9. Ibid., 215.

10. The Black–Scholes formula is used in the pricing of European-style options and is based on the Black-Merton-Scholes model.

11. Philipp Bagus and David Howden, "Iceland's Banking Crisis: The Meltdown of an Interventionist Financial System," *Mises Daily*, Ludwig von Mises Institute, June 9, 2009, http://mises.org/daily/3499.

CHAPTER 6: THE WORLD IS FLAT

1. J. P. Morgan, "JPMorgan Chase Reports Fourth-quarter 2010 Earnings," January 14, 2011, http://www.jpmorgan.com/cm/cs?pagename=JPM_redesign/JPM_Content_C/Generic_Detail_Page_Template&cid=1294354943312&c=JPM_Content_C.

2. Colin Barr, "Jamie Dimon, Bonus King," CNN Money, February 18, 2011, http://finance.fortune.cnn.com/2011/02/18/jamie-dimon-bonus-king/.

3. Gallup, "Gallup Daily: U.S. Employment," March 14, 2011, http://www.gallup.com/poll/125639/Gallup-Daily-Workforce.aspx.

4. Office for National Statisitics, "Inflation," February 15 2011, http://www.statistics.gov.uk/cci/nugget.asp?id=19.

5. Interview with Patrick Chovanec, December 2009.

6. Interview with an Italian trader, October 2009.

7. City Spy, "Lehman, Credit Suisse and the Rumour Mill," *Evening Standard*, August 22, 2008, http://www.thisislondon.co.uk/standard-business/article-23542966-lehman-credit-suisse-and-the-rumour-mill.do.

8. Paul Krugman, "The Big Squander," *New York Times*, November 19, 2009.

9. BBC, *The Last Days of Lehman Brothers*, September 29, 2009.

10. Matt Taibbi, "The Great American Bubble Machine," *Rolling Stone*, June 13, 2009.

11. John Authers, "Goldman's Success Is a Double-edged Sword," *Financial Times*, October 17, 2009.

12. John Gapper, "Goldman Should Be Allowed to Fail," *Financial Times*, October 22, 2009, http://www.ft.com/cms/s/0/3bc2f674-bea2-11de-b4ab-00144feab49a.html.

13. Karl Marx, *Il capitalismo e la crisi*, ed. Vladimiro Giacché (Rome: Derive approdi, 2009), 24–26.

14. Richard Freeman, "The Great Doubling: The Challenge of the New Global Labor Market," Federal Reserve Bank of Boston, August 2006.

15. Ravi Jagannathan, Mudit Kapoor, and Ernst Schaumburg, "Why Are We in a Recession? The Financial Crisis Is the Symptom not the Disease!," Working Paper No. 15404, National Bureau of Economic

Research, Cambridge, MA, October 2009, http://www.nber.org/papers/w15404.

16. Freeman, "The Great Doubling."

CHAPTER 7: FINANCIAL NEOLIBERALISM AS PREDATOR

1. *Wall Street Journal*, "For John Meriwether, Will Third Time Be a Charm?" http://blogs.wsj.com/deals/2010/10/04/for-john-meriwether-will-third-time-be-a-charm/.

2. Jagannathan et al., "Why Are We in a Recession?"

3. Walter E. Williams, "Government Deception," Creators Syndicate, Inc., April 8, 2009, http://www.dgda.org/newsletters/April2009Newsletter.pdf.

4. *Wall Street Journal*, "Systemic Risk and Fannie Mae: *The Education of Joe Stiglitz and Peter Orszag*," December 1, 2009, http://online.wsj.com/article/SB10001424052748704204304574543503520372002.html.

5. Interview with Paolo Tosi, January 2010.

6. Alan Greenspan, Adam Smith Memorial Lecture, Kirkcaldy, Scotland, February 6, 2005, http://www.federalreserve.gov/boarddocs/speeches/2005/20050206/default.htm.

7. Karl Polanyi, *The Great Transformation: The Political and Economic Origins of Our Time* (Boston: Beacon Press, 2001), 135.

8. Ibid.

9. Roosevelt spoke these famous words in his State of Union address on January 11, 1944, as he presented Congress with the second "bill of rights," later known as the "Economic Bill of Rights." The phrase originates from the 1762 English property law case *Vernon v. Bethell* and credited to the Lord Chancellor of England.

CHAPTER 8: IN UNION THERE IS STRENGTH

1. Kate Hutchings and David Weir, "Guanxi and Wasta: A Comparison," *Thunderbird International Business Review* 48, no. 1 (January 2006): 141–156.

2. Samuel P. Huntington, "The Clash of Civilizations?." *Foreign Affairs* 72, no. 3 (Summer 1993): 22–49.

3. Napoleoni, *Rogue Economics*, 233.

4. Ibid., ch. 12.

5. Patricia Yollin, "Microcredit Movement Tackling Poverty One Tiny Loan at a Time," *San Francisco Chronicle*, September 30, 2007, http://www.sfgate.com/cgi-bin/article.cgi?f=/c/a/2007/09/30/MN7QRSUKA.DTL.

6. Interview with Mao Yushi, January 2010.

7. IslamWeb, The Prophet Muhammad's Modesty and Humbleness, http://www.islamweb.net/emainpage/index.php?page=articles&id=1344 55.
8. Interview with Edham Yaqoobi, November 2008.
9. Raffaele Oriani and Riccardo Stagliano, *Miss Little China* (Milan: Chiarelettere, 2009), 35.

CHAPTER 9: FROM MUHAMMAD TO CONFUCIUS

1. Anthony Reid and Zheng Yangwen, *Negotiating Asymmetry: China's Place in Asia* (Singapore: Singapore University Press, 2009), 13.
2. Xu Shen, *Shuowen Jiezi* (Explanation of Simple and Compound Characters), early second-century Chinese dictionary presented to Emperor An of the Han Dynasty.
3. Franco Mazzei, "Capire la Cina. Dalla geopolitica alla geocultura," in *Campania e Cina*, eds. Massimo Galluppi and Franco Mazzei (Naples: Esi, 2005).
4. Interview with Li Juan, January 2010.
5. In point of fact the question of human nature's positivity was affirmed not by Confucius but by a later philosopher, Mencius, who maintained that in the human heart there are four beginnings (or sprouts) of virtue. By contrast, another Confucian philosopher, Xun Zi, argued that human nature is fundamentally wicked and that only study and social conventions are capable of curbing it.
6. Daniel A. Bell, "From Marx to Confucius: Changing Discourses on China's Political Future," *Dissent* (Spring 2007), http://www.dissentmagazine.org/article/?article=767.
7. Ibid.
8. Interview with Arthur Kroeber, December 2009.
9. Interview with Wang Dong, January 2010.
10. *Southern Weekly,* "The Harmonious Society," October 12, 2006.
11. A more widespread interpretation holds that the Cultural Revolution was launched by Mao in order to regain power in a party that was gradually distancing itself from his positions.
12. Lucian W. Pye, *The Spirit of Chinese Politics* (Cambridge, MA: Harvard University Press, 1992), 15.
13. Raffaele Oriani and Riccardo Stagliano, *I cinesi non muoiono mai* (Milan: Chiarelettere, 2008), 25–27.
14. Ibid.
15. Ibid.

CHAPTER 10: THE GREAT WALL OF RENEWABLE ENERGY

1. Jonathan Watts, "China's New Faith in Solar Energy Projects is Hailed by Environmentalists as a Milestone," *Guardian*, May 26, 2009.

2. Zhang Qi, "China Hikes 2011 Solar Power Target," *China Daily*, http://www.chinadaily.com.cn/bizchina/2009-07/03/content_8350947.htm.

3. Zhang Qi, "Himin Sees More Shine in Dezhou's Solar Valley," *China Daily*, February 9, 2009, http://www.chinadaily.com.cn/bizchina/2009-02/09/content_7456117.htm.

4. The impossibility of accumulation, rather than price, is the problem: there is as yet no way to store electricity, so long as hydrogen cells are not utilized or another technology is not invented. The construction of an intercontinental electrical grid is not worth considering (at least given the current state of technology), as the rates of dispersion and the infrastructural costs would be too high.

5. See the environment360 website of Yale University, at http://e360.yale.edu/.

6. Lecture delivered at the Fundación Ideas, Madrid, Spain, July 20, 2009.

7. Interview with Claudio Vescovo, November 2009.

8. Daniel K. Gardner, "Meet China's Green Crusader," *New York Times*, November 1, 2009.

9. Napoleoni, *Rogue Economics*, ch. 4.

10. Gardner, "Meet China's Green Crusader."

11. United Nations Environment Programme, *Global Green New Deal: An Update for the G20 Pittsburgh Summit*, September 2009.

12. David Cui, Andy Zhao, Tracy Tian, CFA, et al., "A Primer on China's Seven Strategic Industries," Bank of America-Merrill Lynch, January 17, 2011.

13. Interview with Claudio Vescovo, November 2009.

14. International Energy Agency, "China Overtakes the United States to Become World's Largest Energy Consumer," July 20, 2010, http://www.iea.org/index_info.asp?id=1479.

15. Italy, on the contrary, is tragically behind. According to the European target, 20 percent of energy consumption must derive from renewable sources by 2020. Whereas countries like Spain and Germany have made it clear that they will surpass their own targets, Italy—which currently produces roughly 6 percent from renewable sources—has announced that such a goal will not be met, and that to make up for this deficit green energy will be imported from neighboring countries such as Albania, Serbia, Montenegro, and Tunisia.

16. Interview with Claudio Vescovo, Novevmber 2009.

17. Claudio Vescovo, *New Energy Finance* (Fall 2009).

18. Testimony of Senator James Inhofe before the United States Senate Committee on Banking, Housing, and Urban Affairs, during a hearing on the "State of the Nation's Housing Market," October 20, 2009.

CHAPTER 11: LOOKING AT WASHINGTON AND BEIJING THROUGH CHINESE EYES

1. Austin Ramzy, "Will Obama and Hu Jintao Find Middle Ground?," January 18, 2011, http://www.time.com/time/world/article/0,8599,2042941,00.html.
2. Kenneth G. Lieberthal, "Recalibrating U.S.-China Relations," January 17, 2011, http://www.brookings.edu/opinions/2011/0117_us_china_relations_lieberthal.aspx.
3. Interview with Li Chan, January 2010.
4. Floyd Norris, "China Cuts its Holdings of U.S. Debt," *International Herald Tribune*, January 23, 2010.
5. Ramzy, "Will Obama and Hu Jintao Find Middle Ground?"
6. Interview with Li Chan, November 2009.
7. Interview with Patrick Chovanec, December 2009.
8. Interview with Arthur Kroeber, December 2009.
9. Ibid.
10. Paul Gilbert, *Terrorism, Security, and Nationality: An Introductory Study in Applied Political Philosophy* (London: Routledge, 1994).
11. He has not been executed because only after 1993 did the United States introduce the death penalty for acts of terrorism.
12. William S. Lind, Keith Nightengale, John F. Schmitt, Joseph W. Sutton, and Gary I. Wilson, "The Changing Face of War: Into the Fourth Generation," *Marine Corps Gazette* (October 1989).
13. Stephen E. Ambrose and Douglas G. Brinkley, *Rise to Globalism: American Foreign Policy Since 1938* (New York: Penguin, 1998), 82.

CHAPTER 12: LATE IMPERIAL SPIN

1. Michael Grant, *The Fall of the Roman Empire* (New York: Scribner, 1997), 60.
2. Salviano di Marsiglia in Jacques Migne, *Cursus Patrologiae* 53, 1855.
3. Kevin Phillips, *Wealth and Democracy: A Political History of the American Rich* (Portland, OR: Broadway, 2003), 111.
4. Myron Magnet, *The Dream and the Nightmare: The Sixties' Legacy to the Underclass* (San Francisco: Encounter Books, 1993).
5. Hugh Kennedy, *Mongols, Huns & Vikings* (London: Cassell, 2002), 20–21, 27.
6. Grant, *The Fall of the Roman Empire*.
7. Kennedy, *Mongols, Huns & Vikings*.
8. United Nations Office on Drugs and Crime, "Afghanistan Opium Survey 2008," November 2008, http://www.unodc.org/documents/crop-monitoring/Afghanistan_Opium_Survey_2008.pdf.

9. Ehsan Ahrari, Vanda Felbab-Brown, Louise I. Shelley and Nazia Hussain, "Narco-Jihad: Drug Trafficking and Security in Afghanistan and Pakistan," NBR Reports, December 2009, http://www.nbr.org/publications/issue.aspx?id=192.
10. United Nations Office on Drugs and Crime, Addiction, *Crime and Insurgency: The Transnational Threat of Afghan Opium*, Vienna: United Nations Office on Drugs and Crime, 2009), http://www.unodc.org/documents/data-and-analysis/Afghanistan/Afghan_Opium_Trade_2009_web.pdf.
11. Grant, *The Fall of the Roman Empire*, 97–100.

CHAPTER 13: SABATEURS OF THE NATION-STATE

1. Interview with Yu Fangqiang, December 2009.
2. Interview with Wan Yanhai, director of the Aizhixing Institute of Health Education in Beijing, January 2010.
3. Interview with Li Juan, January 2010.
4. Geoffrey Smith, *Reagan and Thatcher* (London: The Bodley Head, 1990), 1–11.
5. Ibid.,
6. Andrew Adonis and Tim Hames, "Introduction: History, Perspectives," in *A Conservative Revolution?*, eds. Andrew Adonis and Tim Hames (Manchester: Manchester University Press, 1994), 1–16.
7. Ibid.
8. Ibid.
9. Ibid.
10. Ibid.

CHAPTER 14: SUPPLY-SIDE ECONOMICS

1. Paul Krugman, *Peddling Prosperity: Economic Sense and Nonsense in an Age of Diminished Expectations* (New York: W. W. Norton & Co., 1995).
2. Ibid.
3. Ibid.
4. Interview with Maurice Ohana, December 2009 and January 2010.
5. Interview with Mao Yushi, January 2010.
6. Interview with Patrick Chovanec, December 2009.
7. John Hills, *Thatcherism, New Labour and the Welfare State* (London: London School of Economics, 1998).
8. Terry O'Shaughnessy, "Economic Policy," in *A Conservative Revolution?*, 94.

CHAPTER 15: THE FULL MONTY

1. Office for National Statistics, "GDP Growth Contracts by 0.6% in Q4 2010," February 25, 2011, http://www.statistics.gov.uk/cci/nugget.asp?id=192.
2. Peter Riddel, "Ideology in Government," in *A Conservative Revolution?*
3. Geoffrey K. Fry, *The Politics of the Thatcher Revolution: An Interpretation of British Politics, 1979–1990* (Hampshire: Palgrave Macmillan, 2008).
4. Ibid.
5. Ibid.
6. Ibid.
7. Ibid.
8. Ibid.
9. Ingrid van Biezen, "Political Parties as Public Utilities," *Party Politics* 10, no. 6 (2004): 701–722.
10. Paul Whiteley, "Where Have All the Members Gone? The Dynamics of Party Membership in Britain," *Parliamentary Affairs* 62, no. 2 (2009): 242–257.
11. Peter Mair and Ingrid van Biezen, "Party Membership in Twenty European Democracies, 1980–2000," *Party Politics* 7, no. 1 (2001): 5–21.
12. Richard Heffernan and Paul Webb, "The British Prime Minister: Much More Than First Among Equals," in *The Presidentialization of Politics: A Comparative Study of Modern Democracies*, eds. Thomas Poguntke and Paul Webb (Oxford: Oxford University Press, 2005), 150–160.
13. House of Commons Constitutional Affairs Committee "Party Funding," 2006, http://www.publications.parliament.uk/pa/cm200607/cmselect/cmconst/163/16305.htm.
14. Heffernan and Webb, "The British Prime Minister," 158–160.

CHAPTER 16: MEDIACRACY

1. Barbara Jerkov, "E Fini per la sfida elettorale si affida ai guru di Chicago," *La Repubblica*, February 2, 2004; see also Marcello Foa, *Gli stregoni della notizia* (Milan: Guerini Associati, 2008), 222.
2. Foa, *Gli stregoni della notizia.*
3. Nicholas Jones, *Sultans of Spin* (London: Orion, 1999).
4. Foa, *Gli stregoni della notizia*, ch. 4.
5. Ibid., 153.
6. Jones, *Sultans of Spin*, 24–25; see also Foa, *Gli stregoni della notizia*, 152.
7. Interview with Maurice Ohana, December 2009 and January 2010.
8. Interview with Patrick Chovanec, December 2009.
9. Interview with Jeremy Goldkorn, December 2009.

10. Ivan Franceschini, *Cronache delle fornaci cinesi* (Venice: Cafoscarina, 2009).
11. Ibid.
12. Franceschini, *Cronache delle fornaci cinesi* (Venice: Cafoscarina, 2009).
13. Michael Smith, "Revealed: Straw's Secret Warning to Blair on Iraq," *Sunday Times*, January 17, 2010.

CHAPTER 17: THE THOUSAND EVITAS OF BERLUSCONI

1. http://ilbuoncaffe.blogspot.com/2008/04/berlusconeider.html.
2. Human Rights Watch, *World Report 2010* (New York: Seven Stories Press, 2010) http://www.hrw.org/world-report-2010.
3. John P. Burns, "The CCP's Nomenklatura System as a Leadership Selection System: An Evaluation," in *The Chinese Communist Party in Reform*, eds. Kjeld Erik Brodsgaard and Zheng Yongnian (London: Routledge, 2006), 39.
4. Bruce J. Dickson, "Integrating Wealth and Power in China: The Communist Party's Embrace of the Private Sector," *The China Quarterly*, no. 192 (2007): 138.
5. Wu Jiao, "Party Membership Up in Private Firms," *China Daily*, July 17, 2007.
6. Wikipedia, "Three Represents," http://en.wikipedia.org/wiki/Three_Represents.
7. Andrew G. Walder, "The Party Elite and China's Trajectory of Change," in *The Chinese Communist Party in Reform*.
8. China.org.cn, "White Paper on China's Political Party System," http://www.china.org.cn/english/news/231852.htm.
9. Interview with Wan Yanhai, January 2010.
10. Franceschini, *Cronache delle fornaci cinesi*.
11. Gian Carlo Fusco, *Mussolini e le donne*, (Palermo, Italy: Sellerio 2006).
12. Edward Bernays, "The Engineering of Consent," *Annals of the American Academy of Political and Social Science* (March 1947).
13. Soria Blatmann, *Conflitto d'interessi nei mezzi di comunicazione: l'anomalia italiana*, Reporters sans frontières, (April 2003), http://www.didaweb.net/fuoriregistro/documenti/19401rapp.pdf.

CHAPTER 18: SCENES FROM A MARRIAGE

1. Evan Osnos, "The Promised Land (Guangzhou's Canaan Market)," *The New Yorker*, February 9, 2009.
2. Ibid.
3. Interview with Ian Taylor, June 2009.
4. Ian Taylor, "China's Foreign Policy towards Africa in the 1990s," *Journal of Modern African Studies* 36, no. 3 (1998).
5. Leonard, *What Does China Think?*, 96.

6. Richard Behar, "China Saps Mozambique of Timber Resources," *Fast-Company.com*, July 1, 2008.

7. Malcolm Moore, "China in Africa at a Glance," *Telegraph*, February 10, 2010, http://www.telegraph.co.uk/news/worldnews/africaandindianocean/zimbabwe/8315107/China-in-Africa-at-a-glance.html.

8. Barry Sautman and Yan Hairong, "African Perspectives on China-Africa Links," *The China Quarterly*, no. 199 (2009): 728–759.

9. Ibid., 749.

10. Ibid.

11. Ibid.

12. Ibid.

13. Ibid.

14. Ibid.

15. John Lungu, "Copper Mining Agreements in Zambia: Renegotiation or Law Reform?," *Review of African Political Economy*, no. 117 (2008): 41–53.

CHAPTER 19: THE LAST FRONTIER

1. Alex Vines, Lillian Wong, Markus Weimer, and Indira Campos, "Thirst for African Oil: Asian National Oil Companies in Nigeria and Angola," Chatham House Report, August 2009.

2. Ibid.

3. Interview with Serge Michel, *Foreign Policy*, May 30, 2008, http://www.foreignpolicy.com/articles/2008/05/29/ask_the_author_serge_michel.

4. Marie-Claire Bergère, *La Cina dal 1949 ai giorni nostri* (Bologna: il Mulino, 2000).

5. Stefano Gardelli, *L'Africa cinese: gli interessi asiatici nel continente nero* (Milan: Egea-Università Bocconi Editore, 2009), x–xi.

6. Chiara Paolin, "Ferrovia per la Mecca, appalto cinese e i suoi operai diventano islamici," *La Repubblica*, September 12, 2009.

7. Interview with Serge Michel, *Foreign Policy*.

8. Interview with Serge Michel, *Konflikt*, Swedish Public Radio, September 13, 2008.

9. Ibid.

10. Ibid.

11. International Monetary Fund, World Economic Outlook Database, April 2009, Angola, http://www.imf.org/external/pubs/ft/weo/2009/01/weodata/weorept.aspx?pr.x=88&pr.y=8&sy=2002&ey=2010&scsm=1&ssd=1&sort=country&ds=.&br=1&c=614&s=PPPGDP,PPPPC&grp=0&a=#download.

12. Indira Campos and Alex Vines, "Angola and China: A Pragmatic Partnership," working paper, presented during the CSIS Conference,

"Prospects for Improving U.S.-China-Africa Cooperation" (December 5, 2007), CSIS, March 2008.

13. Interview with Ian Taylor, June 2009

14. Wenran Jiang, "Fuelling the Dragon: China's Rise and Its Energy and Resources Extraction," *The China Quarterly*, no. 199 (2009): 585–609.

15. Chris Alden, "China in Africa," *Cape Argus*, October 30, 2007, http://www.saiia.org.za/china-in-africa-project-opinion/china-in-africa.html.

16. Interview with Ian Taylor, June 2009.

17. Ibid.

18. Ibid.

CHAPTER 20: GLOBALIZATION AND CRIME

1. *Wallpaper*, no. 123 (June 2009): 84–85.

2. Te-Ping Chen, "China's Marlboro Country: The Strange, Underground World of Counterfeit Cigarettes," *Slate Magazine*, June 29, 2009.

3. Ibid.

4. Ibid.

5. Interview with Aldo Ingangi, June 2009.

6. Giampiero Rossi and Simone Spina, *I Boss di Chinatown: la mafia cinese in Italia* (Milan: Melampo Editore, 2009), 137–138.

7. Ibid., 124–125.

8. Ibid., 125.

9. Canadian Security Intelligence Service, Report 2000/07, "Transnational Criminal Activity: A Global Context," http://www.csis.gc.ca/pblctns/prspctvs/200007-eng.asp.

10. Rossi and Spina, *I Boss di Chinatown*, 184.

11. Ibid., 185.

12. Interview with Fausto Zuccarelli, June 2009.

13. Ibid.

14. Ibid.

15. Ibid.

16. Group interview with students from the University of Leeds in England, January 2010.

17. Interview with Fausto Zuccarelli, June 2009.

18. Joseph Kahn, "China Executes the Former Head of its Food and Drug Agency," *New York Times*, July 10, 2007, http://www.nytimes.com/2007/07/10/world/asia/10iht-china.1.6587520.html.

CHAPTER 21: ROUSSEAU IN CHINESE CHARACTERS

1. Walder, "The Party Elite and China's Trajectory of Change," in *The Chinese Communist Party in Reform*.

2. Ibid.
3. Dickson, "Integrating Wealth and Power in China," 837.
4. Walder, "The Party Elite and China's Trajectory of Change," in *The Chinese Communist Party in Reform.*
5. Tania Branigan, "Young, Gifted and Red: The Communist Party's Quiet Revolution," *Guardian*, May 20, 2009.
6. Yang Fengchun, *Chinese Government* (Beijing: Foreign Language Press, 2004), 67.
7. Constitution of the Chinese Communist Party, emended and adopted during the Seventeenth National Congress of the Chinese Communist Party "General Program."
8. Branigan, "Young, Gifted and Red."
9. John Street, "Rousseau and James Mill on Democracy," in *A Textual Introduction to Social and Political Theory*, eds. Richard Bellamy and Angus Ross (Manchester: Manchester University Press, 1996).
10. David Barboza, "Expo Offers Shanghai a Turn in the Spotlight," *New York Times*, April 29, 2010, http://www.nytimes.com/2010/04/30/world/asia/30shanghai.html.
11. In a certain sense this is a cruder government of the people, less sophisticated than the modern model of conflict resolution that is Western democracy, but not for that any less democratic. In the end it is the people who, if they so desire, and when they no longer agree with something, overturn and revolutionize.
12. Liberal democracy derives from a utilitarian culture centered on the individual, light years away from the Chinese concept of family and community. This attitude is evident in politics, in economics, and, as we will demonstrate below in this chapter, in human rights. Thus it is not only the damages caused by the democracy-neoliberalism model that do not convince the Chinese; it is an inescapable cultural difference.
13. Edmund Burke, *Reflections on the Revolution in France*, reprinted in John Greenaway, "Burke and de Tocqueville on Conservatism," in *A Textual Introduction to Social and Political Theory.*
14. William Shakespeare, *The Merchant of Venice*, edited by John Russell Brown, Arden Shakespeare, 2nd ser. London: Thompson Learning, 1964.
15. Wan Ming, "Human Rights Lawmaking in China: Domestic Politics, International Law, and International Politics," *Human Rights Quarterly* 29 (2007): 727–728.
16. Chih Chieh Chou, "Bridging the Global and the Local: China's Effort at Linking Human Rights Discourse and Neo-Confucianism," *China Report* 44, no. 2 (2008): 140.
17. The Raoul Wallenberg Institute divides human rights into three categories: education, housing, and "rights connected to the loss of liberty" (see *A Study on Methods and Tools for Analysis in the Work on Human Rights* [RWI, 2005],

http://www.rwi.lu.se/publications/reports/indicatorreport.pdf). The sub-division of human rights into three generations was first proposed in 1979 by the Czech French jurist Karel Vašák at the International Institute of Human Rights in Strasbourg. This subdivision takes up again the three great watchwords of the French Revolution: Liberty, Equality, and Fraternity. The three generations can also be found in some of the articles of the Charter of Fundamental Rights of the European Union.

18. Fu Shuangqi and Wu Xiaojun, "China Hits Back with a Report on U.S. Human Rights Record," *China View*, February 26, 2009, http://news.xinhuanet.com/english/2009-02/26/content_10904794.htm. For the complete version, see also *China View*, "Full Text of Human Rights Record of United States in 2008," February 26, 2009, http://news.xinhuanet.com/english/2009-02/26/content_10904741.htm.

19. Antoaneta Bezlova, "China Mulls Death Penalty Reform," *Asia Times*, June 18, 2008, http://www.atimes.com/atimes/China/JF18Ad01.html.

20. Congressional-Executive Commission on China, *2009 Annual Report*, One Hundred Eleventh Congress, First Session, October 10, 2009, 88–89.

21. "Hu Jia Sentenced to 3.5 Years in Jail," *China Daily*, April 3, 2008, http://www.chinadaily.com.cn/china/2008-04/03/content_6590051.htm.

EPILOGUE: CHINA HANDS

1. Douglas R. Reynolds, "Chinese Area Studies in Prewar China: Japan's Toa Dobun Shoin in Shanghai, 1900–1945," in *Journal of Asian Studies* 45, no. 5 (1986): 949.

2. Carolle J. Carter, *Mission to Yenan: American Liaison with the Chinese Communists 1944–1947* (Lexington: The University Press of Kentucky, 1997), 207.

3. Barbara Tuchman, "If Mao had Come to Washington," *Foreign Affairs* (October 1972): 51–52.

4. David D. Barrett, *Dixie Mission: The United States Army Observer Group in Yenan, 1944* (Berkeley: Center for Chinese Studies, University of California, 1970), 82.

5. Ibid., 85.

6. Ibid., 86.

7. World Bank, *From Poor Areas to Poor People: China's Evolving Poverty Reduction Agenda; An Assessment of Poverty and Inequality in China*, March 2009, iii.

GLOSSARY

14K: Hong Kong–based triad or organized crime society of approximately 20,000 current members, originating in Canton. The 14K triad is active throughout the world, particularly in Western Europe but also in Australia, Canada, Russia, Southeast Asia, and the United States. [See also Sun Yee On]

Bretton Woods System: Agreements signed by delegates from all forty-four Allied nations in 1944 in the eponymous New Hampshire town where they met for a 3-week conference that established the rules and regulations governing the international monetary system. The negotiations pitted two distinct projects against each other: the English plan, proposed by the economist John Maynard Keynes, which called for the creation of a global currency to be known as Bancor; and the American plan, presented by Harry Dexter White. White's prevailing proposal imposed a system of fixed exchange between the world's currencies and the US dollar, which became the only currency convertible to gold at a fixed price of 35 dollars per ounce. The Agreements also created the International Monetary Fund, charged with monitoring the stability of the new system, and the International Bank for Reconstruction and Development. In 1971 President Nixon unilaterally cancelled the direct convertibility of the US dollar to gold, thus putting an end to the Bretton Woods system and giving birth to today's dollar standard.

Charter 08: Manifesto initially signed by 303 Chinese intellectuals and human rights activists to promote political reforms and a democratization of the Chinese political system. The Charter first appeared on the Internet on December 10, 2008, asking the government to implement nineteen reforms aimed at considerably improving respect for human rights within the People's Republic of

351

China. Inspired by the Czechoslovak dissidents' Charter 77, Charter 08 has to date garnered over 8,000 signatures.

Formula 1 Scandal: 1997 scandal involving the British Labour Party and, in particular, then prime minister Tony Blair, who nevertheless remained in power until 2007. Blair intervened to allow Formula 1 racing to accept tobacco industry sponsorship, prohibited under British law. The scandal erupted in October 1997 when it emerged that Bernie Ecclestone, one of the most powerful men in Formula 1, had secretly donated £1 million to the Labour Party. At the time, Blair denied the existence of any relation between the donation and the exemption to the tobacco regulations introduced by the Party. In 2008, however, documents made public under the Freedom of Information Act demonstrated that Blair had met with Ecclestone on October 16, 1997, and immediately afterward requested the change to the regulation.

Gang of Four: Name given to a group of four Chinese Communist Party officials. The Gang, whose members included the fourth and last wife of Mao Tse-tung, was accused of responsibility for the escalation of violence associated with the Cultural Revolution (1966–1976). The Gang of Four was openly opposed to the policies of Zhou Enlai, premier in those years and leader of a faction that included Deng Xiaoping and Hua Guofeng; the latter became, thanks to a series of events, Mao's successor as leader of the CCP. Hardly a month after the death of Mao Tse-tung on September 9, 1976, the Gang of Four was accused of orchestrating a coup d'état; its members were arrested and found guilty of the persecution of 750,000 people, 34,000 of whom died during the Cultural Revolution. Chinese popular opinion celebrated their arrest and sentencing, which signaled the end of the Revolution and of the social violence that characterized its final years.

Glass-Steagall Act: Law passed in 1933 by the American Congress creating the Federal Deposit Insurance Corporation and introducing banking reforms aimed at controlling excess speculation. The law allowed the Federal Reserve to regulate interest rates in savings accounts and prohibited banks from owning other financial companies. Both provisions were repealed, the first in 1980 and the second, along with the Act itself, in 1999.

Livingstone, Ken: English Labour Party politician who was mayor of London between 2000 and 2008. While in office he introduced a system to confront the problem of traffic congestion in the English capital, according to which access to the central area of the city is restricted to those paying a "congestion charge." The system has led to an appreciable reduction in traffic and has been adopted or is being considered in a number of other major world cities.

Mandelson, Peter: English politician who served in a number of Cabinet positions under both Tony Blair and Gordon Brown. Together with these two men he was responsible for the rebranding of the British Labour Party as "New Labour." Under Blair he was obliged to resign on two occasions. The first time was for a failure to declare having received a home loan from a millionaire Labour supporter under investigation by Mandelson's own office. Media pressure forced him to resign on December 23, 1998. The following year he was designated Secretary of State for Northern Ireland, but in 2001 he was once again obliged to resign, this time for having used his influence to facilitate passport application procedures for an Indian entrepreneur under investigation in his native country. In this case the independent commission led by Sir Anthony Hammond found Mandelson not guilty.

Milk Scandal: Scandal that came to light on July 16, 2008, in China, when it was discovered that a number of milk-producing companies were increasing their milk's protein content by using melamine, a highly nitrogenous chemical compound responsible for the death of approximately 300,000 people. The scandal provoked a lengthy major investigation into health standards and corruption in inland China, leading to several arrests and convictions. Many governments blocked the importation of dairy products from China including the European Union, which imposed stricter controls on all food products coming from the People's Republic.

Parties in China: In addition to the Communist Party, there are in China eight minor parties permitted to exist, the so-called "democratic parties." Born for the most part during the war against Japan and the civil war that followed from 1945-1949, they do not currently play the role of an opposition. While marginal, the parties do participate in the political life of the country, to the extent that several of their members occupy prominent positions in various branches of government.

Quantitative Easing: An extreme form of monetary policy that allows for the stimulation of the economy through the printing of paper currency. The new paper currency is introduced into the economic system through the banks. This policy was employed by the Federal Reserve in 2008 and by the Bank of England in 2009 in order to eliminate toxic assets from the balance sheets of American and English banks and to introduce liquidity into the market.

Rio Tinto Group: Anglo-Australian multinational mining company. Founded in 1873, in 2009 it was the world's fourth-largest mining company to be listed on the stock market, with a capitalization of roughly 34 billion dollars. On July 5, 2009, four of the company's employees, three Chinese and one Australian, were arrested in Shanghai on charges of espionage and corruption. It is speculated that the arrests had their origin in a response to the company's refusal to sell part of its assets to Chinalco, a Chinese state-sponsored company that already owned 9.3% of Rio Tinto. The matter quickly became a political issue between Beijing and Canberra. In March 2010, all four were found guilty and sentenced to prison terms ranging from seven to fourteen years.

Sichuan Earthquake: Earthquake measuring 7.9 on the Richter scale that struck the Sichuan province in central China on May 12, 2008, leaving more than 69,000 people dead and approximately five million homeless. The earthquake razed many structures to the ground including several schools, demonstrating the scarce attention to safety standards paid by local government during the construction of these buildings. The government announced plans to spend 150 billion dollars in three years to rebuild the area hit by the earthquake.

Stagflation: Condition in which inflation coincides with economic downturn. The two were once thought mutually exclusive, but worldwide stagflation occurred during the 1970s amid restricted oil supplies and significant levels of unemployment.

Sun Yee On: By far the largest of the Chinese triads, with an estimated 56,000 worldwide members. Like it's rival triad 14K, it is based in Hong Kong. Its activities have a decided influence on the illegal market in the US, with highly active groups in Los Angeles, Miami, New York, and San Francisco. It constitutes one of the largest criminal organizations in Canada, but also operates in Russia, Australia, Japan, and Thailand. It concerns itself with anything that might generate profit on the illegal market.

Volcker Plan: Program proposed by US President Barack Obama and the chair of his Economic Recovery Advisory Board, Paul Volcker, to stave off a new financial crisis and prevent the emergence of financial institutions that are "too big to fail." The plan called for rules that would prevent a commercial bank from owning or investing in hedge funds and private equity funds.

FURTHER READING

Adonis, Andrew and Tim Hames, eds. *A Conservative Revolution?* Manchester: Manchester University Press, 1994.

Allern, Elin H. and Karina Pedersen. "The Impact of Party Organisational Changes on Democracy," *West European Politics* 30, no. 1 (2007).

Aylott, Nicholas. "President Persson—How Did Sweden Get Him?" In *The Presidentialization of Politics: A Comparative Study of Modern Democracies*, edited by Thomas Poguntke and Paul Webb. Oxford: Oxford University Press, 2005.

Bardi, Luciano and Leonardo Morlino. "Italy: Tracing the Roots of the Great Transformation." In *How Parties Organize*, edited by Richard S. Katz and Peter Mair. London: Sage, 1994.

Barnouin, Barbara and Yu Changgen. *Zhou Enlai: A Political Life.* Hong Kong: The Chinese University in Hong Kong, 2006.

Barrett, David D. *Dixie Mission: The United States Army Observer Group in Yenan, 1944.* Berkeley: Center for Chinese Studies, University of California, 1970.

Bellamy, Richard and Angus Ross, eds. *A Textual Introduction to Social and Political Theory.* Manchester: Manchester University Press, 1996.

Box, Richard C., Gary S. Marshall, B. J. Reed, and Christine M. Reed. "New Public Management and Substantive Democracy." *Public Administration Review* 61, no. 5 (2001).

Branigan, Tania. "Young, Gifted and Red: The Communist Party's Quiet Revolution." *The Guardian*, May 20, 2009.

Brodsgaard, Kjeld Erik and Zheng Yongnian, eds. *The Chinese Communist Party in Reform.* London: Routledge, 2006.

Brooks, Barbara J. "China Experts in the Galmusho, 1895–1937." In *The Japanese Informal Empire in China, 1895–1937*, edited by

Peter Duus, H. Ramon Myers, and R. Mark Peattie. Princeton: Princeton University Press, 1989.

Burke, Edmund. *Reflections on the Revolution in France*. Reprinted in "Burke and de Tocqueville on Conservatism," by John Greenaway. In *A Textual Introduction to Social and Political Theory*, edited by Richard Bellamy and Angus Ross. Manchester: Manchester University Press, 1996.

Burns, John P. "The CCP's Nomenklatura System as a Leadership Selection System: An Evaluation." In *The Chinese Communist Party in Reform*, edited by Kjeld Erik Brodsgaard and Zheng Yongnian. London: Routledge, 2006.

Calise, Mauro. "Presidentialization, Italian Style." In *The Presidentialization of Politics: A Comparative Study of Modern Democracies*, edited by Thomas Poguntke and Paul Webb. Oxford: Oxford University Press, 2005.

Carter, Carolle J. *Mission to Yenan: American Liaison with the Chinese Communists 1944–1947*. Lexington: The University Press of Kentucky, 1997.

Chih Chieh Chou. "Bridging the Global and the Local: China's Effort at Linking Human Rights Discourse and Neo-Confucianism." *China Report* 44, no. 2 (2008).

Cooney, Sean. "China's Labour Law, Compliance and Flaws in Implementing Institutions." *Journal of Industrial Relations* 49, no. 5 (2007).

Dickson, Bruce J. "Integrating Wealth and Power in China: The Communist Party's Embrace of the Private Sector." *The China Quarterly*, no. 192 (2007).

Doig, Alan and John Wilson. "What Price New Public Management?" *The Political Quarterly* 69, no. 3 (1998).

Duus, Peter, H. Ramon Myers, and R. Mark Peattie, eds. *The Japanese Informal Empire in China, 1895–1937*. Princeton: Princeton University Press, 1989.

Esherick, Joseph W., ed. *Lost Chance in China: The World War II Dispatches of John S. Service*. New York: Random House, 1974.

Friedman, Thomas. *The World Is Flat: A Brief History of the Twenty-first Century*. New York: Farrar, Straus and Giroux, 2005.

Fry, Geoffrey K. *The Politics of the Thatcher Revolution: An Inter-pretation of British Politics, 1979–1990*. Hampshire: Palgrave Macmillan, 2008.

Han Suyin. *Eldest Son: Zhou Enlai and the Making of Modern China, 1898–1976*. London: Jonathan Cape, 1994.

Heffernan, Richard and Paul Webb. *The British Prime Minister: Much More Than First Among Equals*. In *The Presidentializa-tion of Politics: A Comparative Study of Modern Democracies*, edited by Thomas Poguntke and Paul Webb. Oxford: Oxford University Press, 2005.

Hills, John. *Thatcherism, New Labour and the Welfare State*. London: London School of Economics, 1998.

Hood, Christopher. "A Public Management For All Seasons." *Public Administration* 69 (Spring 1991).

———. "'The New Public Management' in the 1980s: Variations on a Theme." *Accounting, Organizations and Society* 20, no. 2/3 (1995).

Hood, Christopher and Guy Peters. "The Middle Aging of New Public Management: Into the Age of Paradox?" *Journal of Public Administration Research and Theory* 14, no. 3 (2004).

House of Commons Constitutional Affairs Committee. "Party Funding." 2006.

Hua Shiping, *Chinese Utopianism: A Comparative Study of Reformist Thought with Japan and Russia 1898–1997*. Stanford: Stanford University Press, 2009.

Human Rights Watch. *World Report 2010*. New York: Seven Stories Press, 2010.

Johnson, Carole and Colin Talbot. "The UK Parliament and Per-formance: Challenging or Challenged?" *International Review of Administrative Sciences* 73, no. 1 (2007).

Kahn, Jr., Ely Jacques. *The China Hands: America's Foreign Service Officers and What Befell Them*. New York: Viking Press, 1975.

Kampf, David. "China's Rise and the Implications for International Human Rights." *China Rights Forum*, no. 1 (2007).

Katz, Richard S. "The Problem of Candidate Selection and Models of Party Democracy." *Party Politics* 7, no. 3 (2001).

Katz, Richard S. and Peter Mair, eds. *How Parties Organize*. London: Sage, 1994.

Kirby, William C., ed. *Realms of Freedom in Modern China.* Stanford: Stanford University Press, 2004.

Kitaoka Shin'ichi. "China Experts in the Army." In *The Japanese Informal Empire in China, 1895–1937,* edited by Peter Duus, H. Ramon Myers, and R. Mark Peattie. Princeton: Princeton University Press, 1989.

Krugman, Paul. *Peddling Prosperity: Economic Sense and Nonsense in an Age of Diminished Expectations.* New York: W. W. Norton & Co., 1995.

———. "Inequality and Redistribution." in *The Washington Consensus Reconsidered,* edited by Narcis Serra and Joseph E. Stiglitz. Oxford: Oxford University Press, 2008.

Labour Commission. "Renewal a Two-Way Process for the 21st Century." Save the Labour Party, London 2007.

Lilleker, Darren G. "The Impact of Political Marketing on Internal Party Democracy." *Parliamentary Affairs* 58, no. 3 (2005).

Liu Xiaobo. "Beijing's Human Rights Exhibition." *China Rights Forum,* no. 1 (2007).

Mair, Peter and Ingrid van Biezen. "Party Membership in Twenty European Democracies, 1980–2000." *Party Politics* 7, no. 1 (2001).

Marsh, David, Jim Buller, Colin Hay, Jim Johnston, Peter Kerr, Stuart McAnulla, and Matthew Watson. *Postwar British Politics in Perspective.* Cambridge: Polity Press, 1999.

Morlino, Leonardo. "Crisis of Parties and Change of Party System in Italy." *Party Politics* 2, no. 1 (1996).

Oi, Jean C. "Realms of Freedom in Post-Mao China." In *Realms of Freedom in Modern China,* edited by William C. Kirby. Stanford: Stanford University Press, 2004.

O'Shaughnessy, Terry. "Economic Policy." In *A Conservative Revolution?,* edited by Andrew Adonis and Tim Hames. Manchester: Manchester University Press, 1994.

Poguntke, Thomas and Paul Webb, eds. *The Presidentialization of Politics: A Comparative Study of Modern Democracies.* Oxford: Oxford University Press, 2005.

Pollitt, Christopher, Sandra van Thiel, and Vincent Homburg. "New Public Management in Europe." *Management Online Review* (October 2007).

Premfors, Rune and Göran Sundström. *Regeringskansliet*. Malmö: Liber, 2006.

Pressman, Jeffrey L. and Aaron Wildavsky. *Implementation: How Great Expectations in Washington Are Dashed in Oakland: Or, Why It's Amazing That Federal Programs Work At All, This Being a Saga of the Economic Development Administration as Told by Two Sympathetic Observers Who Seek to Build Morals on a Foundation of Ruined Hopes*. Berkeley: University of California, 1984.

Rahe, Paul A. *Soft Despotism, Democracy's Drift: Montesquieu, Rousseau, Tocqueville, and the Modern Prospect*. New Haven, CT: Yale University Press, 2009.

Reynolds, Douglas R. "Chinese Area Studies in Prewar China: Japan's Toa Dobun Shoin in Shanghai, 1900–1945." *Journal of Asian Studies* 45, no. 5 (1986).

———. "Training Young China Hands: Toa Dobun Shoin and its Precursors, 1886–1945." In *The Japanese Informal Empire in China, 1895–1937*, edited by Peter Duus, H. Ramon Myers, and R. Mark Peattie. Princeton: Princeton University Press, 1989.

Riddel, Peter. "Ideology in Government." In *A Conservative Revolution?*, edited by Andrew Adonis and Tim Hames. Manchester: Manchester University Press, 1994.

Russell, Meg. *Building New Labour London*. Hampshire: Palgrave Macmillan, 2005.

Scarrow, Susan. "Political Parties and Democracy in Theoretical and Practical Perspectives: Implementing Intra-Party Democracy." The National Democratic Institute for International Affairs, Washington, DC, 2005.

Serra, Narcis and Joseph E. Stiglitz, eds. *The Washington Consensus Reconsidered*. Oxford: Oxford University Press, 2008.

Smith, Geoffrey. *Reagan and Thatcher*. London: The Bodley Head, 1990.

Snow, Edgar. *Red China Today: The Other Side of the River*. London: Victor Gollancz, 1963.

Stiglitz, Joseph E. "Is There A Post-Washington Consensus?" In *The Washington Consensus Reconsidered*, edited by Narcis Serra and Joseph E. Stiglitz. Oxford: Oxford University Press, 2008.

Street, John. "Rousseau and James Mill on Democracy." In *A Textual Introduction to Social and Political Theory*, edited by Richard Bellamy and Angus Ross. Manchester: Manchester University Press, 1996.

Sundström, Göran. *Stat på villovägar*. Stockholm: Stockholm University, 2003.

Tuchman, Barbara. *Joseph Stilwell and the American Experience in China*. New York: MacMillan, 1970.

———. "If Mao Had Come to Washington." *Foreign Affairs* (October 1972).

United Nations. *Report of the Committee Against Torture*. 2009.

van Biezen, Ingrid. "Political Parties as Public Utilities." *Party Politics* 10, no. 6 (2004).

Walder, Andrew G. "The Party Elite and China's Trajectory of Change." In *The Chinese Communist Party in Reform*, edited by Kjeld Erik Brodsgaard and Zheng Yongnian. London: Routledge, 2006.

Wang Ming. "Human Rights Lawmaking in China: Domestic Politics, International Law, and International Politics." *Human Rights Quarterly* 29 (2007).

Wheen, Francis. *How Mumbo Jumbo Conquered the World*. London: Harper Perennial, 2004.

Whiteley, Paul. "Where Have All the Members Gone? The Dynamics of Party Membership in Britain." *Parliamentary Affairs* 62, no. 2 (2009).

Williams, John. "A Short History of the Washington Consensus." In *The Washington Consensus Reconsidered*, edited by Narcis Serra and Joseph E. Stiglitz. Oxford: Oxford University Press, 2008.

World Bank. *From Poor Areas to Poor People: China's Evolving Poverty Reduction Agenda; An Assessment of Poverty and Inequality in China*. 2009.

Wu Jiao. "Party Membership Up in Private Firms." *China Daily*, July 17, 2007.

Yang Fengchun. *Chinese Government*. Beijing: Foreign Language Press, 2004.

INDEX

New Deal and, 1, 185–88
renewable energy and, 164–67, 170,
   172–75
Chinese paradox, 168–70
Chinese Revolution, 8, 310
Chomsky, Noam, 237
Chovanec, Patrick, 32, 56, 104–5, 185,
   222–23, 240–41
Churchill, Winston, 10
CIA World Factbook, 273
cigarettes, counterfeit, 293–95
I cinesi non muoiono mai (The Chinese
   Never Die) (Oriani and Staglianò),
   155–56
civilization-state, 145, 151–54
clash of civilizations, 135
class consciousness, 40–43
classless society, 12, 74, 75–76
class struggle, 61, 62, 65, 72
Clinton, Bill, 179, 182–83, 235
Clinton, Hillary, 244, 319
coal, 161–62, 164, 169
Cold War, 45, 283
   end of, 1, 3
   Soviet Union during, 73–74
   winner of, 3–4, 5, 13, 19, 113
collective bargaining, 230
collective farms, 30
   dismantling and abolishing of,
      53–54, 71
   as rural brigade, 77
colonialism and colonization, 48, 71,
   81–82
   Africa and, 272–73, 277, 282–83
communism. *See also* capitalist-communism; Chinese Communist Party
   capitalism and, 55, 64–65, 78–80,
      131
   lack of incentives with, 30
   principles of, 150
   Western-style democracy compared
      to, 6, 9
comparative advantage, theory of, 54,
   267
Confucius, 76, 145–51, 261, 314. *See
   also ren*
   on concept of state, 152–54
   on politics, compared to Western-
      style democracy, 153
congestion charge (London), 313, 353
consent, 235, 237
consumerism, 16–19
Cook, Robin, 244
coordination and consensus, 65
copyright, 301, 302
corruption. *See* scandals and corruption
Cossiga, Francesco, 256

cotton, 29, 53–54
counterfeit goods, 293–95, 298–306
credit
   default swaps, 123–24
   Iceland and, 81, 83, 91, 94–95
   microcredit, 138–43
   multiplier, 111
   rating agencies, 105
   recession and, ix, 1, 13, 17, 46, 182
Credit Suisse, 106–7
crime
   globalization and, 293–306
   Internet and, 303–4
   in Italy, 295, 296, 298–300, 304–5
   triads, 296–300, 305–6, 351, 355
Cronache delle fornaci cinesi (Stories
   from the Chinese Furnaces)
   (Franceschini), 241–43
Cuba, embargo on, 320
cultural identity, 135, 302
Cultural Revolution
   impacts of, 33, 58
   Mao Tse-tung and, 51, 150, 153,
      154, 352
   violence of, 51, 352
culture
   Chinese, 134–35, 145, 151–53,
      154–55
   of fakes, 301–4
   Muslim, 134–35, 145, 155
currency
   Bancor (global currency), 351
   Chinese, international monetary
      system pegged to, 1
   stimulation of economy through
      printing paper, 354
   U.S. dollar convertibility to gold,
      351

dagonzei (women), 43
Das Capital (Marx), 11–12, 27, 114
Davies, John, 326
death penalty, 321
De Castro, Sergio, 87
Declaration of Human Rights, 7
deflation, 19, 127, 136
deliberative democracy, 60
delocalization
   factories and, 28–29, 35, 37, 41–42,
      113–14
   impacts of, 116–17, 121, 231
democracy. *See also* Chinese democracy; Western-style democracy
   in Afghanistan, 4, 57, 115, 190
   Athenian, 9–10
   capitalism and, viii–ix, 9, 12–13, 329
   deliberative, 60

Islamic, 137–42
politics and, 122–23, 128
financial bubbles, 92, 94, 115, 120,
127–28, 136, 137
financial crises
of 1929, 128, 130
of 2008, 94, 104, 107, 113, 127–28
Asian, 121, 122, 135–37, 184
financial oligarchy, 112, 121
Financial Times, 111–12
Fini, Gianfranco, 258
First Opium War, 43
First Solar, 163
foreign investment
factories and, 27–29, 32–34, 37, 39,
41
in Iceland, 90–94
Macao island licensed to Portugal, 70
Formula 1 Scandal, 235, 352
Forum on China-Africa Cooperation,
284
Forza Italia (Forward Italy), 233, 260
14K (Chinese triad), 298, 351
1421 (Menzies), 68
Foxconn factory, 39
Franceschini, Ivan, 241–43, 254–55
Freddie Mac, 109, 123–24, 125
Freeman, Richard, 116–17
free market, 54, 63, 73, 88
free systems, 89
free trade, 10
Freud, Sigmund, 18, 20
Friedman, Milton, 86–89, 94, 210,
216–17
Friedman, Thomas, 113, 115, 116
Fukuyama, Francis, 19
Fuld, Dick, 108–9
full monty, 225
The Full Monty (film), 225
Fusco, Gian Carlo, 258
Fu Zhenzhong, 241–42, 245

G8, 110
G20, 110, 125, 249, 281
Gaddafi, Muammar, viii, ix
Gang of Four, 64, 71, 352
GDP. *See* gross domestic product
Geithner, Timothy, 45–46
General Electric, 163, 281
General Motors, 112, 251, 315
The General Theory of Employment,
Interest, and Money (Keynes), 20
Geneva Conventions, 7, 318, 321
Gilbert, Paul, 188
Glass-Steagall Act, 214, 352
global capitalism, 11, 12, 35
globalization

alternative, 134–35
crime and, 293–306
neoliberalism and, 3, 11, 19, 79
responses to, 1, 11, 15–16, 21
Westernization and, 113, 134
globalized economy, 11, 12–13, 125
global labor arbitrage, 41
global labor pool, 116–17
global manufacturing system, 29–30
global warming, 169, 171, 213
gold, U.S. dollar convertibility to, 351
Goldkorn, Jeremy, 241
Goldman Sachs, 103, 108–9, 111–12,
123
gold standard, 129–30
government of law, 147
government of man, 147
Graham, Bob, 140
Great Depression, 130, 215
Great Leap Forward, 82
Great Wall, 193
of renewable energy, 159–75
as state of mind, 68–69
Greenberg, Stanley, 235
Greenspan, Alan, 126–27, 136
the Grid, 238–39, 244
gross domestic product (GDP)
drop in, 114, 136
growth and, 1, 6, 28, 78, 170, 287
Guantánamo Bay detention camp, 7
guanxi banking system, 155–57
guilt, 156

happiness, 15
Hard Times (Dickens), 48
Hassa, Hussein Hamid, 139
Hegemann, Helene, 302–3
heroin, 198–99, 298
Hobbes, Thomas, 126
Hofstede, Geert, 134
homeland, 145
Hong Kong, 61, 69. *See also* Asian
Tigers
honor, 156
Hua Guofeng, 352
Hubbert, M. King, 172
Hubbert peak theory, 172
Hu Jia, 322
Hu Jintao, 60, 149, 179, 181, 310
human rights
in China, 1, 179, 316–19, 320,
321–22, 351–52
treaties, 316
violations of, 7, 268, 318–21
human trafficking, 242, 298
humiliation
century of, 30, 43, 71

public, 35, 154
Hungary, 79
Huns, 193–98, 200
Huntington, Samuel, 135
Hussein, Saddam, 149, 190, 244–45
Hutt, W. H., 48

Iceland, 161, 209
    China and, 81–86, 91, 96–97
    credit and, 81, 83, 91, 94–95
    foreign investment in, 90–94
Ide Saburo, 324
IMF. *See* International Monetary Fund
immigrants, 2–3
"Implications of the New Fannie Mae
    and Freddie Mac Risk-based Cap-
    ital Standard" (Stiglitz, Orszag, J.
    and Orszag, P.), 124
Inclosure Acts, 29, 31
incremental democracy, 52–56
individual, relational quality of,
    146–48
individualism, 130, 139, 317
Indonesia, 135
industrialization, 48, 164–65, 171. *See
    also* factories
Industrial Revolution, 19, 27
    Chinese, second phase of, 166–68,
        175
    mythology of, 47–49
    oil and, 204
    spinning jenny and, 29
inflation, 87–88, 215
Ingangi, Aldo, 295
Ingham, Bernard, 239
intellectual property, 301–2
International Bank for Reconstruction
    and Development, 351
International Herald Tribune, 60
international justice, 7
International Monetary Fund (IMF)
    Angola and, 279–80, 287
    bailouts and, 136–37
    creation of, 63, 351
    financial collapse of 2008 and, 94
    oil crisis and, 63–64
    report by, 47
international monetary system, 1
Internet
    censorship of, 317
    crime and, 303–4
"In union there is strength" motto, 135
Iran
    Islamic finance and, 137
    Revolution, 203
    sanctions on, 319
Iraq

democracy in, 4, 10, 58, 115, 190,
    259
oil in, 280–81
war in, 7, 154, 184, 189, 190, 197,
    198, 243–45, 314, 318
Islam, 145, 155. *See also* Muslims
Islamic Development Bank, 137
Islamic finance, 137–42
isolationism, 68, 81
Italy
    crime in, 295, 296, 298–300, 304–5
    economy of, 114–15
    media in, 244
    politics in, 232, 233, 234, 256–58
    scandals in, 254
    workers in, 44–45, 48–49

J. P. Morgan, 103, 108, 112
Japan, 284, 323–25, 329
    invasion of China, 43, 68, 324–25
Jefferson, Thomas, 195
jewel industry, 41–42
Jiang Qing, 153
Jiang Zemin, 252–53, 255, 270
Jia Qinglin, 255
Jing Huang, 60
job security, 40–41
Jones, Nicholas, 239
*Journal of the Public Library of
    Science*, 17
Jung, Carl Gustav, 18, 20
JWM Partners, 119

Kang Rixin, 254
Karzai, Hamid, 57
Keynes, John Maynard, 130
    Bretton Woods Agreements and, 20,
        351
    *The General Theory of Employ-
        ment, Interest, and Money*, 20
Keynesian theory, 131, 215
King, Tom, 230
Kirsch, Irving, 17
Kishida Ginko, 324
Kroeber, Arthur, 45, 52, 151–52,
    186–87
Krugman, Paul, 215–16, 218, 228
Kyoto Protocol, 250

Laffer, Arthur, 216
Lai Changxing, 255
laissez faire, 39, 129, 131
Lehman Brothers, 105–11, 136
Lenin, Nikolai, 74
Leninism. *See* Marxism-Leninism
Leo I (pope), 194
Leonard, Mark, 72, 269

neoliberal dream of, 81–99
Mohamad, Mahathir bin, 137
monetarism, 215–18. *See also* supply-
   side economics
Montgomery, General, 225
Moore, Jo, 238
Mubarak, Hosni, ix
Muhammad, Prophet, 141, 145
mujahideen, 197
Multifibre Arrangement (MFA), 276
Mundell, Robert, 216
murabaha (Islamic financing structure),
   138–39
Muslims, 133–35, 145, 155, 189–90.
   See also Islamic finance
Mussolini, Benito, 258–59

Nanking, Treaty of, 43
national energy companies (NOCs),
   290–91
national identity, 51, 61, 81
nation-state, 89, 145, 152, 218
   market-state replacing, 203–4, 213
natural aristocracy, 315
'Ndrangheta (criminal organization),
   296, 305
'Ndrine (criminal organization), 296
neoconservatives, 189, 191–92,
   194–95, 314
neoliberalism, 6, 218
   globalization and, 3, 11, 19, 79
   Marxism and, 62
   neoliberal dream of modernization,
      81–99
New Deal, Chinese, 1, 185–88
New Energy Finance magazine, 173
New Labour, 220, 232–34, 237, 353
New Left, 59
New York Times, 41, 164, 211
NGOs. *See* nongovernmental organiza-
   tions
9/11, 137, 183, 188–91, 238
Nixon, Richard
   China and, 179
   U.S. dollar, gold and, 351
   Watergate scandal and, 235
NOCs. *See* national energy companies
nongovernmental organizations
   (NGOs), 7, 205–7, 317
nuclear power and weapons, 161, 244
Nujoma, Sam, 268
Nwaosu, Joseph, 266

Obama, Barack
   China and, 179–82, 187
   election campaign of, 256, 260
   on Iraq war, 244

Perón complex and, 249–51
   policies of, 194–95, 315
   Volcker Plan and, 355
Oddsson, Davíð, 94
Ohana, Maurice, 30, 221, 239–40
oil diplomacy, 288–91
oil industry, 161
   in Africa, 273–74, 280–81, 285,
      287, 289–91
   crisis (1973-1974), 63–64, 87, 203
   embargo (1973), 171–72, 203
   environmental degradation and, 274
   Industrial Revolution and, 204
   in Iraq, 280–81
   in Libya, 281, 287
Omar, Mullah, 198
O'Neill, Paul, 93
open door policy, 26, 28, 32, 49, 52
Operation Dixie, 325–28
opium, 43, 198–99
Oriani, Raffaele, 143, 155–56
Orszag, Johnathan, 124
Orszag, Peter, 124
Out of Mao's Shadow (Pu Ziquiang), 9

Pan Yue, 164–65
participatory democracy, 2, 54, 312
parties, 231–34. *See also specific parties*
   in China, 310–11, 353–54
   two- and multiparty systems,
      231–32
Patriot Act, 137
Paulson, Henry "Hank," 108–9, 123
Peddling Prosperity (Krugman), 218
People's Republic of China, sixtieth anniversary celebrations for, 85
Perestroika, 58
Perón, Eva (Evita), 248–49, 256, 259
Perón complex, 248–56
Petacci, Clara, 258
Pinochet, Augusto, 86, 87–89, 210,
   216, 237
Pirate Party, 303
plagiarism, 302–3
Plato, 11
politics. *See also* parties
   in Britain, 209–14, 232–34
   in China, 251–56, 257
   Confucian, Western-style democ-
      racy compared to, 153
   finance and, 122–23, 128
   in Italy, 232, 233, 234, 256–58
   media and, 235–39, 248–51, 254,
      256–61
   mythology around supply-side eco-
      nomics, 88–89

ABOUT THE AUTHOR

Loretta Napoleoni is the author of the bestselling book *Rogue Economics: Capitalism's New Reality* (a *Publishers Weekly* Best Book 2008) and *Terror Incorporated: Tracing the Money Behind Global Terrorism*, both translated into fifteen languages. One of the world's leading experts on money laundering and terror financing, Napoleoni has worked as a correspondent and columnist for *La Stampa*, *La Repubblica*, *El Pais*, and *Le Monde*, and she has presented on the economics of terrorism for Google UK and TEDTalks. She teaches economics at the Judge Business School in Cambridge.

ABOUT SEVEN STORIES PRESS

Seven Stories Press is an independent book publisher based in New York City. We publish works of the imagination by such writers as Nelson Algren, Russell Banks, Octavia E. Butler, Ani DiFranco, Assia Djebar, Ariel Dorfman, Coco Fusco, Barry Gifford, Hwang Sok-yong, Lee Stringer, and Kurt Vonnegut, to name a few, together with political titles by voices of conscience, including the Boston Women's Health Collective, Noam Chomsky, Angela Y. Davis, Human Rights Watch, Derrick Jensen, Ralph Nader, Loretta Napoleoni, Gary Null, Project Censored, Barbara Seaman, Alice Walker, Gary Webb, and Howard Zinn, among many others. Seven Stories Press believes publishers have a special responsibility to defend free speech and human rights, and to celebrate the gifts of the human imagination, wherever we can. For additional information, visit www.sevenstories.com.